THE

EVERYTHING® GUIDE TO CURRENCY TRADING

Dear Reader,

As you read this book, I hope you get a feel for the excitement, profit, and worldview that others have received from trading the world's currencies. FX trading can give you the ultimate macro, wide-angle view of the world. Looking at the world with a big vision can allow the trained observer of the FX markets feel a kinship with other countries and the people who inhabit them. Whether the news comes from Australia, Greece, or Japan, it is my hope that you gain a macro view that includes the world's economies. While we may live in our homes in our hometowns, currency trading can open you up to the biggest market picture of all: one that is much, much larger than the U.S. stock market alone. While trading in the currency markets can be volatile and risky if not done correctly, currency trading can be set up to minimize risk while maximizing the chance of very significant gains.

It is my hope that you profit from the book, profit from your research, and of course, profit from the macro world of currency trading.

David Borman

Welcome to the EVERYTHING® Series!

These handy, accessible books give you all you need to tackle a difficult project, gain a new hobby, comprehend a fascinating topic, prepare for an exam, or even brush up on something you learned back in school but have since forgotten.

You can choose to read an Everything® book from cover to cover or just pick out the information you want from our four useful boxes: e-questions, e-facts, e-alerts, and e-ssentials.

We give you everything you need to know on the subject, but throw in a lot of fun stuff along the way, too.

We now have more than 400 Everything® books in print, spanning such wide-ranging categories as weddings, pregnancy, cooking, music instruction, foreign language, crafts, pets, New Age, and so much more. When you're done reading them all, you can finally say you know Everything®!

QUESTION

Answers to common questions

FACT

Important snippets of information

ALERT

Urgent warnings

ESSENTIAL

Quick handy tips

PUBLISHER Karen Cooper

DIRECTOR OF ACQUISITIONS AND INNOVATION Paula Munier

MANAGING EDITOR, EVERYTHING® SERIES Lisa Laing

COPY CHIEF Casey Ebert

ASSISTANT PRODUCTION EDITOR Melanie Cordova

ACQUISITIONS EDITOR Ross Weisman

ASSOCIATE DEVELOPMENT EDITOR Hillary Thompson

EDITORIAL ASSISTANT Matthew Kane

EVERYTHING® SERIES COVER DESIGNER Erin Alexander

LAYOUT DESIGNERS Erin Dawson, Michelle Roy Kelly, Elisabeth Lariviere, Denise Wallace

THE EVERYTHING® GUIDE TO CURRENCY TRADING

All the tools, training, and techniques you need to succeed in trading currency

David Borman
Author of *The Everything® Guide to Day Trading*

adamsmedia
Avon, Massachusetts

An Everything® Series Book.

Published by Adams Media, a division of F+W Media, Inc.
57 Littlefield Street, Avon, MA 02322 U.S.A.
www.adamsmedia.com

Contains material adapted and abridged from *The Everything® Investing Book, 3rd Edition*
by Michele Cagan, copyright © 2009 by F+W Media, Inc.,
ISBN 10: 1-59869-829-X, ISBN 13: 978-1-59869-829-9.

ISBN 10: 1-4405-3139-0
ISBN 13: 978-1-4405-3139-2
eISBN 10: 1-4405-3140-4
eISBN 13: 978-1-4405-3140-8

Printed in the United States of America.

10 9 8 7 6 5 4 3 2 1

Library of Congress Cataloging-in-Publication Data
is available from the publisher.

This book is dedicated to the people who trade their goods, money, time, and expertise; they provide the markets with the grease that makes the world go round. I would also like to dedicate this book to my mother, Cynthia, and my brother, Teddy, who listened to the ideas I spouted while writing this book.

Contents

Acknowledgments

I would like to thank my editor, Ross Weisman, for his very important insight and input into the content of this book. I would also like to thank my family members who stayed up late with me while I read the broker's reports, studied the central bank websites, and set up overnight trades, all in the process of researching this book: They know who they are!

The Top 10 Keys to Trading Currency

1. Always combine fundamental and technical analysis to arrive at your best trading ideas.
2. Always use the pyramiding method of building up a position in a currency pair. Use the same pyramiding method when you are closing out the position.
3. Go long commodities currencies and short safe-haven currencies when the overnight markets are up big.
4. Use carry trades to reduce risk and capture a steady stream of income for your overall investment portfolio.
5. Use your smart phone or iPad to keep on top of your open trades and account balances.
6. Learn to walk away from your trading desk after a really good day (or week) in the currency markets.
7. Learn to read between the lines and see what the central bank websites are really saying about their currencies' future prices and interest rates.
8. Always trade your currency portfolio at the same leverage ratio; use the same one that your demo account is set at and you are used to managing.
9. Know that it is okay not to trade during times of market upset, as these times can be very difficult to trade and make a profit in.
10. Use diversification of different currencies even if your overall FX account is aimed toward the same overall market direction.

Introduction

WELCOME TO CURRENCY TRADING! As a beginning investor, this book will introduce you to the world of Forex markets and currency trading. Currency trading (also known as FX trading and Forex trading) is different from day trading—instead of buying and selling stocks for profit, you buy and sell the money of the different countries of the world. Though it is similar to buying stocks and mutual funds, the actual investment vehicles you use are digital money. You can trade this money or currencies with an independently owned retail account, much like an online brokerage account.

The mechanics of currency trading are also a bit different from stock trading. Leverage ratios are much higher—which means you can trade more money with a smaller cash balance in your account. The trick is to manage your funds safely. If you trade carefully, as many Forex traders do, you'll begin to see profits sooner than you think. The tips, tools, and techniques available in this guide can be used to keep your FX losses to a minimum and your gains to a maximum!

This all-in-one guide discusses the basics of currency investing, from macroeconomics and global concerns to technical analysis, and details many of the strategies that successful traders use in trading currency. There is a heavy emphasis on usability, with various trading strategies and outlooks grouped by budget amount and risk appetite. For instance, if you're looking to spend $1,000 aggressively trading Forex, you'll be directed to different strategies and currencies than someone with $25,000 looking to supplement his retirement and hedge his stock positions.

Above all else, this book will give you the skills you need to trade wisely—and lucratively—in this high-risk, high-profit business. With this guide, patience, and practice, you can begin a successful career of currency trading. Good luck!

CHAPTER 1

Currency Trading: The What, the Why, and the Rewards

It would be best to know a bit about currency trading before you look at your first chart, read your first broker's report, or place your first trade. You first have to learn what it means when someone says they trade currencies, and why they do it. You can then evaluate your investing goals and determine if the rewards of currency trading are worth the added risk to your overall investment portfolio, plans, and goals.

What Is Currency Trading?

Currency trading (also called FX trading and Forex trading) is when you buy and sell the money of the different countries of the world. It is a form of trading similar to buying stocks and **mutual funds**, only the actual investment vehicles are digital money. You can trade this money or currencies with an independently owned retail account, much like an online brokerage account.

The preparation you would take to make a trade in the FX market is similar to the research you would make for a stock purchase. You would spend time reading **brokers' reports**, seeking out information from websites, and looking at technical charts.

The difference between stock and FX trading is that with stock trading you are betting that a company will increase in perceived value against the perceived value of other stocks, and therefore the other people in the stock market will pay a higher price for your small slice of that company (represented by shares of stock). With currency trading you go about buying or selling the relative value of one country's home money in relation to another country's home money. In stock trading, a company must have a good (and you hope increasing) stream of income to rise in value against its peers. FX trading is different. In order for the money of one country to rise in value against another country's money, there has to be a wider mix of positive news and expectations.

Traders **going long** on a currency (placing bets that the money will rise relative to another) usually look for a combination of rising interest rates, increased positive economic activity, political and social stability, and the home country's debt levels. Other considerations include commodities demand, and that country's **central banking stance** and comments. Lastly, a currency trader will consult brokerage reports for an opinion, and consult a chart for technical indicators.

The mechanics of currency trading are also a bit different from stock trading. With stock trading you are usually allowed a 1.5:1 to a 1.75:1 ratio of leverage. This means that if your account has a balance of $10,000, a brokerage house will allow you to buy and trade an additional $5,000 to $7,500 worth of stock. This would bring your possible trading position size to $15,000–$17,500 all while having only $10,000 worth of your actual cash in your account.

With currency trading, the leverage ratios are much higher. Most FX brokerage firms allow you to trade with leverage ratios of 10:1 up to 50:1. With this kind of leverage you would be able to trade $100,000 to $500,000 worth of currency with a cash balance of $10,000 in your account.

ALERT

Don't let the availability of the high margins in currency trading make you say "No" to getting started in FX! You can learn to use the margin in your account safely by limiting position size, and using automated take-profits closing triggers. These can be used to keep your FX losses to a minimum and your gains to a maximum!

Another characteristic of FX trading is the ability to make a good profit with a small account. Some currency brokerage firms allow balances as low as $100, which would allow you to trade $5,000 worth of currency (with your leverage set at 50:1).

Finally, since people all over the world trade currencies, the market is open longer than the U.S. stock market. It is possible for you to trade Forex twenty-four hours a day, from Sunday afternoon eastern time, until Friday afternoon eastern time.

Why Trade FX?

You might be asking yourself, "Why should I trade currencies?" The answer is simple: for profit (and fun!). Whether you are a big player or a small account holder, the combined elements of studying economies and political climates, using high leverage, and maintaining unconventional hours can add up to a very enjoyable and profitable pastime. Whether you plan on FX trading to earn your weekend fun money, or you plan on drawing a paycheck against your profits, Forex trading can allow you to use your knowledge for real gains.

Currency trading allows you to bring your knowledge of economies, countries, central banking, technical indicators, and research into an arena that provides a chance to profit from these skills. If you feel as though you do not have the skills or are unsure about your skill set, this book will get you up to speed at analyzing market conditions and news, and executing successful FX trades safely.

This book will also guide you through the benefits of starting small and risking nothing but your time, by teaching you to trade in a practice-demo account that you can sign up for at FX brokers' websites. Downloading trading software for these demo accounts is easy. They offer the same charts and market pricing of a live account, and they will offer you the opportunity to get a feel for the analytical and order-entry skills required for successful and profitable trading. Whether your account is large or small, and whether your risk appetite is high or low, with practice you can gain the skills and knowledge to seek out, recognize, and place successful currency trades.

FACT

With the low account minimums and the high chance of success, many people consider currency trading a kind of high-stakes video game. With all of the graphs, charts, information, and fast action, it is easy to see why so many people enjoy FX trading as a video hobby or sport!

You might be asking yourself, "What else can currency trading do for me?" The answer is multifaceted. For one, when played correctly, trading in the currency market can lead to gains in your overall portfolio beyond your usual stock dividends, **capital gains**, and bond income. If you have a traditional portfolio that includes equity and bond mutual funds, stock and fixed income, the addition of FX trading to your overall portfolio acts as a return enhancer to an otherwise conservative portfolio.

It is also possible to build the bulk of your overall portfolio to an almost risk-neutral position by investing in a very conservative mixture of treasuries, **investment-grade corporate bonds**, and other high-quality, low-yielding investments and accent the return of your portfolio by actively trading in the currency market. This strategy is one that is often recommended by financial advisors to their high net-worth clients. Financial advisors usually recommend **options** on the Standard & Poor's (S&P) 500 as the risk portion of such a portfolio. In this case you would substitute trading the euro,

British pound, Australian dollar, Japanese yen, Swiss franc, and Swedish krona instead of S&P 500 options.

If the return enhancement weren't enough for you to want to trade FX for yourself, then consider the diversification properties of currency trading. It could be (and often is) a time in the market that the U.S. stock market (represented by the S&P 500 index) is underperforming, moving sideways, or just plain going nowhere. It also might be true that your portfolio of bonds, mutual funds, and stock is heavily weighed to a U.S. perspective, with the bulk of the assets relying on a good economy in the United States in order to show any positive gain. Lastly, it could be difficult to structure a portfolio that gains in an economy that is doing poorly or one that has a stock market that is moving downward. In these situations, FX trading can diversify your overall portfolio away from a "good fortunes in the U.S. only" stance and into a worldwide trading arena where you can profit from good news and bad.

While the stock markets might be retreating or stuck, you can build a bond portfolio that preserves capital and enhances its return by trading a small percentage of that portfolio in the currency markets.

What Are the Risks and Rewards?

Before you begin your career in currency trading you will first have to see if the rewards of FX trading outweigh the added risks that it brings. While it is true that currency trading involves the use of high levels of margin, there are a few risk management techniques that can help limit your risk.

It is true that you will be trading with leverage ratios of 10:1, 20:1, or even 50:1. It is also true that things can happen fast at this leverage ratio. It is common for a position to move upward around 1 percent during the heaviest trading times of the day. If you have a big trade in that currency at a high leverage amount and the direction of the trade moves against you, then it is also possible for your whole account to get closed out due to a **margin call**, which is when your broker will automatically close out your positions before your account gets a negative equity balance. If this happens, you have **blown up** your account, as the professionals say, and your money will be permanently lost into the great electronic money abyss.

Many people new to currency trading have had this blow up happen to them; this is precisely why currency trading has such a bad reputation in certain circles. On the other hand, the currency market is the biggest, deepest, and most widely traded market in the world—not all those traders can be losing big. Quite the opposite! Most of the FX traders of the world are making a living at it, trading in office buildings with posh addresses in New York, London, Zurich, and Tokyo. There is money to be made in trading FX, and if done right, the money can be made with such consistency that you can earn and draw a paycheck out of the profits in your trading account.

ESSENTIAL

You can scale your currency trading to any level that suits your needs. If you would like to learn about the world's economies and markets, currency trading is for you. You can trade with a practice account, or you can trade with your extra money. You can even go full time and use FX trading to earn a living.

With the right amount of knowledge and training you can make sure that the size of the paycheck that you earn from your currency trading endeavors is in proportion to the size of the balance in your account, and is *not* related to the amount of risk you have taken in your account.

You can run your trades in such a way that the risk is the smallest required to earn the largest returns. You can also assure yourself that your gains can result in proportionate gains: the larger your account, the larger your gains. It should never be a practice for a trading method to squeeze out the highest level of earnings by pushing the risk level beyond what is acceptable to you. You might be happy with a lower, steady yield from your trading, all while assuming a very limited risk level. On the other hand, you might have the perspective that you and your portfolio can tolerate (and enjoy!) a higher level of risk, and that you relish the bigger gains that those trades offer. Your account can be highly tuned for profit with added risk, or de-tuned for lower gains, but reliability: the choice is yours. Either way, if done right, only FX trading offers the highest level of payoff per dollar invested, along with manageable and adjustable risk levels per unit of return.

Who Trades FX?

Currency trading is an endeavor that is pursued by people and investors all over the world. Some investors are hedge funds that operate in an unregulated environment. These hedge funds work much like a mutual fund with sales of shares and calculation of value. The difference is that only accredited investors, or investors who meet a certain minimum of net worth and annual income, can purchase hedge funds. Other investors of hedge funds include institutional investors such as school endowments and pension funds. All these types of investors are trying to obtain the same thing: a wide diversification of total invested assets, with measurable uncorrelated returns.

While there are many different types of hedge fund investment strategies, many **macro funds** (a strategy that looks at and invests in the entire investment universe) involve currency trading and currency hedging techniques. Macro- and currency-only funds trade with the same leverage and trade on the same observations as you, the retail, individual FX trader.

QUESTION

What does it take to open a FX account?
You can open a practice account with just a login name and a password. In order to open up a live account and put money into it, you usually need the same information as opening up a bank account: photo ID, proof of residence, social security number, etc.

International Banks

Other players in the market include international banks that buy and sell currencies on behalf of their major customers. These customers might be manufacturing companies with factories or sales that are overseas. A bank might assist these customers in setting a currency hedge to help offset the risks associated with accepting foreign currency payments or paying bills in a foreign currency at a future point. For example, if an auto parts company knows that it will have to pay 10 million Danish kroner to a company based in Denmark in three months, they might lock in the price of the payable DKK with a Danish krone position in the currency markets, much like a form of a simplified derivative.

Central Banks

Still other participants in the Forex are the **central banks** and treasuries of the nations of the world. While not common, a country or coalition of countries can act in the currency market to put pressure on a currency. If, for example, the Swiss National Bank (SNB) thinks that the Swiss franc has appreciated against the euro too much, or that they feel that the exchange rate between the euro and the franc is beginning to slow the economy in Switzerland, the SNB might intervene. The bank could do this by using francs to buy up short-term government debt issued in euros. This would put more francs in circulation, and also create a demand for euro-denominated debt. The combined effect of more Swiss francs and less euro debt would effectively cause the franc to get cheaper (because of **liquidity**) than the euro (because of scarcity).

This type of intervention can be a major undertaking by a country's central bank and is usually done only in extreme circumstances. It can be an effective management tool though: Once a central bank announces its intention to act with a goal of influencing its home country's exchange rate, the market can react suddenly. These kinds of announcements make even the most seasoned trader nervous, as the weight of an entire country's reserves will soon be used to move the markets. Sometimes, when an announcement of intervention is made, the market will react with such intensity that the exchange rate will move on its own, as FX traders around the world begin to price the currency differently. This market reaction can have the effect of reducing the upcoming work of the central bank in its goal of moving an exchange rate.

Does FX Fit in My Investing Goals?

There are only two goals in the whole investment universe: capital preservation, and capital gains. When an investment vehicle serves the purpose of capital preservation, it acts as a way to store your money for future consumption. Capital-preservation investments are usually low-risk investments. You pay for this low risk and safety by accepting a lower potential for interest paid and gains. It is simply that a return on that part of your investments is not as important as the requirement that the invested principal be there when it is time to take it out and use it for consumption.

On the other hand, if an investment is one that is expected to produce capital gains, the investment is expected to move up and down along a gently upward-sloping path. When you invest for capital gains, what you are expecting is that the investment will be worth more sometime in the future then what it cost you. The price you pay for this potential upward movement in price (gain) is the risk that the investment might not be worth more when you sell it than when you bought it. In the future, it might even be worth less than when you bought it. It is this risk of the unknown future price that you accept as a price to pay for the chance that the investment will pay a capital gain in your favor.

Before you invest or trade any of your assets, you should ask yourself, "Should this money be put in an investment vehicle that offers a safe but small return, or should I put it into a vehicle that offers a higher return, but is riskier?" This is the question that you must ask yourself when it comes to currency trading: "What are my investing goals, and are they met by opening a currency account and trading in the FX market?"

If you trade in the FX market you can meet several goals. You can design your overall portfolio to have a majority of assets in very low-risk, capital-preservation investments. You could then take a small percentage of your overall assets and place them in a FX account and trade that money with higher (or lower) risk strategies. These currency strategies can then serve as a return enhancement to the otherwise low-risk, capital-preservation portfolio.

A Currency Trading Risk/Return Model

A $100,000 portfolio can be invested in $95,000 AA-grade bonds with the remaining $5,000 being placed in a currency portfolio trading with a 50:1 leverage. If the AA bonds paid an average of 2 percent per year (with very little risk), the FX side has the potential to earn an additional 21 percent per year with an ultraconservative, part-time trading style. A conservative FX trading style yielding these annual returns would mean limiting your open position size to no more that 10 percent of total margin, and seven 1 percent gain trades per month. To simplify the math a bit, you are risking the total loss of 5 percent of your portfolio for the potential of gaining 23 percent in returns. This equates to a 1:4.6 risk to return ratio. For every dollar that has the potential to be lost (the full value of the FX account, or $5,000) there is a very high chance of making $4.60 in gain.

ESSENTIAL

You should begin thinking of why you are getting into currency trading and what you expect to gain from it. Whether or not you are looking for recreation, extra income, or drawing a paycheck, it is best to keep your goals in mind when reading the examples shown in this book.

To look at this another way, the typical 60 percent stock–40 percent bond portfolio (one that is considered well-balanced for risk/return payoff) is much riskier. A $100,000 portfolio would be 40 percent or $40,000 in AAA bonds paying 2 percent. The remaining 60 percent or $60,000 would be invested in an S&P 500 stock index fund. The S&P 500 historically has a return of 10 percent per year. Carry out the math, and you have a total potential of 6.8 percent total return on this bond/stock portfolio. This number is achieved by:

$$.40 \times 2\% + .60 \times 10\% = 6.8\%$$

The risk-return ratio for this portfolio is 1:0.11, or for every dollar that has the potential to be lost (the full value of the stock part of the account, or $60,000), there is a chance of making 11 cents in gain.

While this is a simplified model of **VaR**, (VaR, or Value at Risk, is a mathematical formula to determine the day-to-day risk of a professional trader's account), it can help you see the difference in unit of returns per unit of risk. Using these simplified models, you can see that if played properly and managed well, a currency account can actually offer less risk to your portfolio than a more traditionally balanced portfolio of 60 percent domestic stock and 40 percent AAA-rated bonds!

CHAPTER 2

The Basics of Currency Trading

The basics of FX trading include the basic trading mechanism and the currency pair or FX pair. In this chapter you will learn the mechanics of the FX pair and what its quote represents. You will also get a grip on what it means to trade the major FX pairs, the minor FX pairs, and discover the benefits of trading the currency crosses. Lastly, you will learn the hours of the currency market, and the overlapping times of the world's money center trading hours.

The Mechanics of the FX Pair

When someone says he is trading currencies, what he actually means is he is betting that one currency will get stronger in relationship to another currency. For example, an FX trader might set up a trade that the euro will get stronger against the U.S. dollar, the Australian dollar will get stronger against the Japanese yen, or that the Swiss franc will get stronger against the British pound.

The concept that one currency will move and get stronger against another currency is the basis of FX trading. A currency trader will place trades in what are called FX pairs. **FX pairs** are two currencies and their prices relative to each other. As the overall currency market participants buy and sell a currency against other currencies, their prices move up and down against each other. These prices are reflected in the quote that is shown in your trading platform for that FX pair.

Sample Trades to Consider

As an example, after studying the overall economic conditions, fundamental country information, and other factors, you might consider that the value of the U.S. dollar is underpriced against the relative value of the euro. You might reach this conclusion after a big run-up in the euro, geopolitical events, etc. The difference and movement in the relative values of the U.S. dollar and the euro are measured and traded in the currency pair EUR/USD. In this case the EUR part of the pair stands for euro and the USD part stands for the U.S. dollar.

ESSENTIAL

In the currency pair EUR/SEK, the first part, EUR, is called the base currency. The second part of the pair, SEK, is called the counter currency. Additionally, the first two letters of the symbol of a currency "SE" stand for the country (Sweden) and the last letter "K" stands for the currency (krona).

The FX pair EUR/USD represents the value of the euro relative to the U.S. dollar. At any given moment during trading hours the euro will be worth a more or lesser amount in dollars, depending upon trading conditions. If, during the trading day, the value of one euro is determined to be worth a certain amount in dollars as determined by market participants and conditions, that value will be reflected in the quote of that FX pair.

For example, if during trading hours one euro is determined to be worth $1.31, the quote for that FX pair would be EUR/USD 1.31. In another example, in the pair Australian dollar/Swiss franc (AUD/CHF), if one Australian dollar bought 0.9340 Swiss francs, the quote for the FX pair would be AUD/CHF .9340. When the AUD gets stronger against the CHF, the quote of the AUD/CHF will move up. If at one moment the AUD buys .9250 CHF, the quote will be AUD/CHF .9250. As the AUD gets stronger and the exchange rate changes between the AUD and the CHF, the one AUD buys incrementally more CHFs. If in the next moment the market determines that one AUD should buy .9300 CHFs, then the new quote that currency traders around the world will see is AUD/CHF changing from .9250 to its new value of .9300.

The Major FX Pairs

The currency market consists of four divisions of pairs: the major pairs, the minor pairs, the cross pairs, and the exotic currency. The majors are the group of pairs that have the heaviest trading volume and are often the mainstay of professional traders and trading houses. Due to the massive amounts in U.S. dollar terms that are traded each day worldwide, these markets are usually the most quoted in news reports, both online and on cable news stations such as CNBC and Bloomberg TV. The major pairs consist of the big currencies: the EUR, USD, Japanese yen (JPY), and to some extent Great Britain pound (GBP) and the CHF. There are major players involved in trading the EUR/USD, EUR/JPY, and the USD/JPY. Some of the groups that take positions in these pairs are international banks and brokerages. Other players are large, independent hedge funds. Still others are the reserve banks of the world, as they hold these currencies in their reserve portfolios. These central bank–reserve portfolios are often used to stabilize a country's home currency value against both sudden and gradual moves against trading partners' currencies.

FACT

Even though the United States has trading partners all over the world, its central bank holds only JPY, EUR, and gold in its reserves. It also holds SDRs which stands for "Special Drawing Rights," a form of "potential claim on currencies used at the IMF," as quoted from the International Monetary Fund website (*www.imf.org/external/np/exr/facts/sdr.htm*).

Because of the large amount of volume, analyst, and media coverage, the majors are a good place to start to get a feel for how the currency markets move over the days, weeks, and months. If you are following the major pair EUR/USD, you can see how the value of the pair moves up and down as the market conditions change. These market conditions might be a new round of bad news about European Union sovereign debt, a change in interest rates, or a change in overall **market risk appetite**.

The Often Predictable Major Pair Directions

Since the major FX pairs are so heavily traded, they have a tendency to move in smooth up-and-down movements over medium periods of time. These medium periods of time are anywhere from several weeks to several months; when seen from the perspective of a technical chart set to "one hour" or "daily" (meaning the increment of time for each point on a technical chart), the ebb and flow of the value of these pairs can be seen clearly. Major FX pairs are often range bound, meaning that they move up and down in value between two value points, and never quite seem to break free from these constraints. This range-bound tendency is from the perceived value of the pair by the market participants as a whole. For example, as the U.S. stock market moves up and down along a gradually increasing value path, the value of the EUR/USD can often move in the same gradual up-and-down movement. The major currency pair EUR/USD sometimes moves up with the rising fortunes of the U.S. stock market. That is, the EUR sometimes becomes stronger against the USD in good stock market conditions. This is true because a long EUR/USD trade (a position of betting that the EUR will increase in value against the USD) is a riskier trade than the opposite trade, a short EUR/USD, one in which it is expected that the USD will get stronger than the EUR.

As someone who observes the U.S. and world stock markets, you can trade the pair EUR/USD going long or short depending upon the direction of the market. The major pairs can earn you your daily paycheck as you switch from loving the EUR against the USD when the stock markets are good to loving the USD against the EUR when things don't look so good. This switching of sides of the major pairs, whether it is the EUR/USD, EUR/JPY, or USD/JPY, can be an FX trader's mainstay of trading ideas. There is a drawback to these major pairs: they can be predictable, chartable, and swing back and forth, but often those movements are almost too pendulum-like, and sometimes they do not follow any pattern at all! This breaking of patterns, like any other FX trade, can cause harm to the value of your FX trading account and to your net worth if proper risk management techniques were not used in setting up the position.

The Minor FX Pairs

The minor currencies consist of country currencies that are traded heavily, but are in less quantity in the world market. For example, the Australian dollar, AUD, is very heavily traded in what are called carry trades. Worldwide, it is popular to go long on the high-interest paying AUD by selling a low-interest charging currency such as the JPY or USD. Profits can be made by the interest differential of the pair, i.e., the profit comes from the interest earned on the long position in the AUD, subtracting the cost of the position from the low-interest charging counter currency.

Other minor pairs include the **euro proxies**. The euro proxies are currencies from a group of countries that trade heavily in Europe, but which have chosen to stay out of the European Union's EUR for economic and political reasons. Taking a position in these currencies often results in a stronger gain (or loss!) against the USD than a straight long EUR/USD position. This is true because these countries are independent from the European bloc, and therefore their economies can grow at different rates from the EUR bloc nations. Due to economics, when a country's growth rate exceeds that of its trading partner, its exchange rate can get stronger against that trading partner's currency. This is due to interest rates, national debt, and current account deficits (or lack thereof). Minor currencies consist of AUD/JPY, AUD/USD, USD/SEK, USD/NOK (Norwegian krone), (Canadian dollar) CAD/USD, and USD/CHF.

ALERT

Don't make the mistake of thinking that trading minor FX crosses offers only minor returns! Trading minor pairs can offer your FX portfolio quite a percentage bounce in profit on a daily and weekly basis. Due to their market risk sentiment-following behavior, the direction of these minor FX crosses can be very easy to predict, meaning higher probability of profitable trades.

Minor FX pairs can add a degree of stability to a trading portfolio because the minor currencies in the FX pair have a tendency to move in a unidirectional path. As an example, the Norwegian krone has had a long, slow, steady climb against the USD. As with all FX pairs, there can be many reasons for this longer-term movement. In the case of NOK, the country of Norway has enjoyed the benefit of a positive currency account, surplus budget, and other strong economic fundamentals. In addition to this, Norway exports the crude oil that comes from its offshore oil rigs, and sells this oil in the open market. These sales have been increasing in dollar terms, mainly due to the weakening dollar and subsequent rise in crude oil prices.

ESSENTIAL

Commodities such as gold, silver, and crude oil are priced and traded throughout the world in U.S. dollar terms. As the relative value of the USD goes down, the price of an ounce of gold or a barrel of oil goes up the same percentage. In this way, commodities such as these are in effect a currency to be traded the world over.

▼ **TABLE 2-1: COMMODITY COUNTRIES AND THEIR MINOR CURRENCIES**

Country	FX Symbol	Commodity Produced	Export Partners
Canada	CAD	Gold, Copper, Oil, Grains	USA, UK, Europe, Asia
Australia	AUD	Gold	India, China, USA, UK, Europe
New Zealand	NZD	Wool, Grains, Cotton	India, China, Japan
South Africa	SAR	Gold	India, UK, Europe
Norway	NOK	Crude Oil	Europe, UK, Asia, China

Many of the minor currency pairs are what are often referred to as **commodity currencies**.

Commodity currencies refer to the home currency of countries that mine, drill, grow, or raise raw materials for export onto the world market.

Currency Crosses, Are They for You?

The third type of FX pairs is called the currency crosses. Currency crosses, or the cross pairs, is a term that refers to pairs that are made up of either minor currencies or other infrequently traded groups. A good example of these is AUD/GBP. When you trade this pair, profit can be made off the movement in each, usually caused by actual or planned interest-rate movements of Great Britain and Australia. Other factors that come into play are the different growth rates of the countries, and, of course, actual or expected inflation rates of the countries. While it can be quite difficult to predict the movement of this particular cross pair, the movement of others can be easier to predict, and therefore easier to trade successfully.

Trades that involve FX pairs of the euro and euro proxies can be very successful. This success is because the euro proxies such as SEK, NOK, and CHF and their home country's economies are independently monitored by the relative country's central bank. This freedom and separateness from their main trading partners can offer a wonderful opportunity to observe, read, and predict the current and future economic conditions of these countries that neighbor the euro bloc. This observing can be best done by reading and studying brokers' reports, and the commentary and guidance put forth by the English versions of the Swedish central bank (*www.riksbank.com*), Norway's central bank (*www.norges-bank.no/en*), and the Swiss National Bank (*www.snb.ch*). By contrast, you as an FX trader can look for conflicting economic, interest rate, balance sheet, and economically political significant information on the European Central Bank website (*www.ecb.int/home/html/index.en.html*).

With a bit of patience and insight, an FX trader such as yourself can train to spot the exceptional setups and trading opportunities that trading euro-proxy crosses offers. While it is true that the economies of Sweden and the like are small, it is that very fact that makes the krona, krone, and franc such market darlings in the post 2008–2009 banking crisis world.

FACT

In 2008–2009 the world's economies suffered from a near failure of the banking systems. Recovery came at the cost of an increase in the quantity of money supply by the world's central banks. The increase in monetary base was historic, and by some estimates, it increased in the United States by four times the amount before the crisis began!

These independently monitored and managed economies and currencies are free of some of the problems of the **big four**: the USD, EUR, JPY, and GBP. These big four economies and currencies have suffered the most from the most recent worldwide-banking crisis, while some minor countries (and therefore their home currencies) have economically recovered at a faster and more widespread rate then the big four. This is a newer development in the FX trading environment, and if studied, understood, and acted upon, can offer you very profitable trades with a relatively high percentage of trading successes.

Other crosses include all of the big four, USD, EUR, JPY, and GBP traded against the commodity currencies such as the New Zealand dollar

(NZD), AUD, and CAD. Of course it is possible to study, monitor, and predict the movement of FX pairs that are crossed with the euro-proxy minors and other minors. Such a trade might include CAD/NOK, with perhaps the idea of trading the difference in the price of crude oil in the two economies (as North American-produced oil can and is often priced differently than the oil of the North Sea). Perhaps you could also exploit the fact that the NOK trades a high amount of its oil with EUR nations, (therefore increasing its balance sheet position in EUR) and the fact that the CAD's main trading partner is the United States of America (increasing CAD's balance sheet position in USD resulting from Canada's net export of oil to the United States).

Overlapping Times of Money Center Trading

The currency market is one that is open twenty-four hours, from Sunday afternoon New York time to Friday afternoon New York time. These trading times reflect the changing time zones of the major world money centers that trade currency. Whether it is Tokyo, Sydney, Zurich, London, New York, or Chicago, throughout the trading week there is always a major trading house, bank, or hedge fund that is trading FX in the market. While it is true that the thinnest trading is in the late afternoon New York time (due to the not yet fully opened Asian markets), the FX market is deepest and in fullest swing during the time of the twenty-four-hour day that major money centers are open and overlapping. For example, you as a currency trader will find it easier to find setups and exit out of profitable trades in the times when the Asian markets are in their late-in-the-day hours and the European markets are just starting to open up (rather than in the late afternoon). This period of heightened market activity is around midnight to 2:00 A.M. New York time. Many U.S.-based traders find that it fits in their overall trading program to trade into the wee hours of the morning, move in and out of the AUD, EUR, JPY, etc., and close up shop by 3:00 A.M. to 4:00 A.M., with the next day's sunlight hours spent living life outside of the currency-trading world.

Another time of trading-center overlap is in the 4:00 A.M. to 9:00 A.M. New York–time period. It is during this time that the brokerage houses, banks, hedge funds, and individuals are working in Zurich, Paris, London, and New York, trading away to make their fortunes. These early morning trading hours can be the heaviest trading hours of the day. This is because the news that happened overnight in the Asian markets is met with the developments of the European markets, and then digested by the then-awakening New York markets.

It is also true that on big news days, or days that central bank announcements, interest rate changes, inflation numbers, etc., come out in Europe, there is a good chance that similar news will be reported in the morning hours of the North American countries. The effect can heavily weigh on the direction of currency pairs, especially the majors and the euro proxies.

ESSENTIAL

The currency trader's work day can be quite different: reading news, looking for setups, all while the sun is down and the moon is out. On the other hand, life can be quite exciting when you make a day's salary in the FX market, all before the kids get up to get ready for school, or while the late-late movie plays in the background.

For example, the inflation numbers for Sweden might come out, along with rumors about the state of the European Union and its debt, only to be followed by a drastically down U.S. S&P 500 futures report—all before the sun even comes up in New York, Chicago, or San Francisco.

This is an example of a heavy news day, and you could find it to be a day full of opportunities to make profits in your trading account. Sudden movements of 1 percent to 1.75 percent are not unheard of on these days. While that might seem manageable or even small, you must calculate into that equation that it is possible to trade FX at a 20:1 or even 50:1 margin ratio. With this said, such a dramatic news day could result in a movement of 87.5 percent in either direction for a FX pair that moves 1.75 percent at a 50:1 margin. Quite a lot to be sure, and if you played carefully, you could generate a profit by risking a small percentage of your overall FX portfolio, and yet yield a week's worth of gain for your account. If this happened, you would then have the option to take minimal risks for the rest of the week, keeping your trading account intact and safe, all while knowing that your profit goals and requirements for the week have been met.

Early morning hours and late nights are the best times to trade in the currency markets. Keep this in mind when working out your personal-trading plans.

CHAPTER 3

What Exactly Am I Trading?

When you are thinking of trading currencies, it can help immensely to get a proper feel for what is happening with the actual FX pair before you commit to it. You have to get to a level of understanding—you must understand that FX is not actually money, but rather a relative value of two expectations. Additionally, currency pairs exist with nontraditional assets such as gold, silver, and oil, and can be traded as such for added returns in your FX portfolio.

Is It Money? Or a Pair?

Currency trading, and trading in general, is best viewed as a kind of sport. The sport of FX trading requires the viewpoint that the market is a moving force, and that your computer trading terminal is your playing field. To carry the analogy further, it can help you as a FX trader to think of the cash balance and open trades in your account as pieces on a chess board. As in chess, each piece moves differently, and by different amounts. The pawn moves only forward, and one square at a time, while other pieces have greater power, range, and directional possibilities. Even though each piece is different, you, while playing the game of chess, have the chance to pick which piece to move, in what direction, and by how much, all toward the end goal of winning the game.

This is the way that cash and currency pairs work in a trading account when you have the perspective that you are not trading money: You are in fact moving playing pieces around the chess board of the computer screen.

ESSENTIAL

Professional trading houses and hedge funds often hire former college competitive athletes such as football and rugby players to work at their trading desks. Other skills they look for are knowledge of economics and mathematics. Trading houses also look for strong computer skills, including programming and aggressive video-gaming experience.

Trading for the Score

If you have the idea that you are not trading money, but rather a currency pair, and that you are trading for the score, then you are starting to have the perspective of a professional trader. Professionals trade with the idea that they are in it for the score, for something almost like a points system. Think of each dollar you gain in your account as a point in a computer game that you are really good at: play the game with a vengeance, and read the books about the secrets of the game (how to score higher, etc.).

Thinking of your gains as points can go a long way in helping you evaluate your setups, enter into trades, and know when to exit. When you think of your points competitively as something to covet, you will not fall in love with a trade or country's currency and overtrade it. The opposite will happen: You will look for trades that will increase your points, and you will not even consider a trade that carries too much risk of having your point score erode or go into reverse. You will begin to think that, unless you know at the end of the day your score will be higher, you will just not play the FX video game that day.

While it is money in your account, you are actually playing a computer game with FX pairs as your playing pieces. Too often people are willing to risk money on a losing trade because sometimes money can seem easy to come by. Believe it or not, Hollywood movies sometimes portray that it is somehow romantic to lose in the market, or to have risky, wild swings of fortune. Thinking of the money in your account as your score and the profit that you earn every day as your points will go a long way in keeping you away from an easy come–easy go mentality. Think of it as a computer game that you play competitively online, picking up points here and there, never risking your status as the big winner by playing the game in a market that is too choppy, risky, or unprofitable.

Thinking of Relative Values

In order to trade currency effectively you will first need to realize that what is being traded are currency pairs. Each currency pair consists of one currency sold into another currency. For example, a short EUR/NOK trade is when one unit of EUR is sold and the proceeds are used to buy an equivalent unit or units of NOK. It is good to think of units when trading currencies other than the U.S. dollar, as that idea can help you keep the perspective that what you are trading is the relative value of euros to Norwegian kroner. It is easier to think in unit terms rather than, "how much is a Norwegian krone worth?" It can be daunting to go through the procedure of mentally converting one Norwegian krone into your home currency (about 18 U.S. cents) and then converting one euro (about 141 U.S. cents), and then proceeding to determine if one is overvalued against another in U.S. dollar terms. In this

EUR/NOK trade, each end of the pair's USD value can really confuse your idea of which way to trade, either long or short.

If you think of the elements of the EUR/NOK trade in relative value, you can think in units of EUR and units of NOK. You can take the unit of relative-value concept for further evaluation when looking at a potential trade. Then you can evaluate market sentiment and questions of a fundamental or technical nature more clearly. You are effectively horse trading, and when you look at trading in this fashion, you begin to see major, minor, and cross pairs as a form of bartering. Think of the difficulties of a monetary system of barter: someone offers to give you three chickens for your one baby piglet. You have to decide and evaluate: the chickens lay eggs and are laying eggs right now; the baby piglet has the potential to become a full-grown sow. What is each worth? If there were no money, this type of decision making is what would go on in each economic transaction, whether you were paying for rent or paying for coffee.

Currency trading is much the same. You are constantly forced to evaluate the value of each end of a pair in relative terms. Play with the idea that there is no money: Euros, kroner, and francs are not money. Play with the idea that they are the chickens, pears, and bushels of grain of a moneyless world. This perspective will help when evaluating a currency pair: He wants to give me eight kroner for my euro? No way! It's worth at least nine kroner!—She wants to give me eight bushels of wheat for my one baby goat? No way! It's worth at least nine bushels!

ALERT

The relative value of an FX pair might be different than when you studied it last. News happens fast, and a currency can be revalued by the market, taking it to a new semipermanent rate. If you haven't looked at a pair in a while, give yourself time to digest its fresh valuation before trading it.

Keep in mind that relative values are for each separate currency pair. For example, the Australian dollar might be moving in an upward trend against the U.S. dollar and in relative terms getting stronger, therefore a short USD/AUD trade would be best. On the other hand, the Australian dollar might be getting weaker against another commodity currency, the New Zealand dollar. It might be the case that New Zealand is undergoing rapid growth, growth that is stronger than that of Australia. Not only might these fundamental elements be in play, but the technical elements might say the same story. In this case the relative value of the AUD is less than that of the NZD, which would warrant a short AUD/NZD trade. Each currency is valued relative to each other in units.

Looking for FX Pair Directions

In order to trade profitably, it will be necessary for you to get into the right currency pair, in the right direction (long or short), before the rest of the currency traders of the world recognize the same currency pair should be valued at the same price at which you are set to make a profit. In order to do this effectively you should train yourself to look for and place your trades with an idea of the where the overall market will be expecting the FX pair to be soon.

To profit by currency trading you will have to buy a pair at one price and then sell it at a higher or lower price than you paid for it. To do this you will have to trade the expectancy of the market. This is where the skill comes in with currency trading: looking for opportunities where a FX pair will be moving soon, whether up or down. This determination is done with analysis of the **fundamentals**, the **technical** indicators, or a combination of both.

FACT

When you are actively trading it is not always necessary to be in the market with active trades all of the time. In fact, most professional traders spend as much time searching fundamental information and performing technical analysis as they do actually placing trades in their FX trading platform.

For example, as a currency trader, you might have spent the early part of the week monitoring the news of the Swiss franc. After spending time on the Swiss National Bank's website, (*www.snb.ch*), looking at brokers' reports, and looking at the charts (and related news) on Big Charts (*http://bigcharts*

.marketwatch.com), you notice that the Swiss franc has been gaining steadily against the euro for the past eighteen months.

Looking into it further, you could switch to your trading platform and set up a technical analysis chart. Currency brokers such as Windsor Brokers (*www.windsorbrokers.biz*) have trading platforms that allow you to choose from a variety of technical indicators and imbed them right onto your active trading chart.

You could decide to imbed a **200-day moving average** line into your EUR/CHF daily chart. A quick analysis of this chart leads you to see graphically that the pair is well below its trend line, leading you to concur with the broker's report that the EUR/CHF pair is due for a **correction**.

After seeing this graphically on the charts, you explore it further, only to notice that your trusted full service broker mentioned the EUR/CHF pair in a report last week. He reported that the value of the Swiss franc was so high that it was beginning to impede on the general economy of Switzerland. This was due to the fact that Switzerland's high franc value was making the country's exports expensive in Europe, therefore slowing export trade, a key part of the Swiss economy. In a situation like this, it would be safe to assume that the EUR/CHF pair is something to be watched closely.

You Spotted a Trade, Now What?

Before you begin to trade the EUR/CHF pair, there needs to be a catalyst, an event that gives urgency to the trade and urgency to the trade in other FX traders' eyes. In this scenario, one last look at the Swiss National Bank's website reveals that the bank's leaders have a rate meeting scheduled on Thursday of this week.

This is a great opportunity to place your trades ahead of the news. It is good to remember that the whole market is looking at the same indicators as you; it is also good to remember that that is the only information they have. Due to its size, the FX market is very deep and liquid; this means that it is very difficult to manipulate and control to one's advantage. The charts you look at are the same ones that others have access to: You are on equal information footing with all. While you can't predict the exact direction that the EUR/CHF pair will take, you can know that it will be moving around quite a bit in the next few days. You can feel certain that in this type of scenario, this FX pair will be bouncing back and forth as the currency market players try to get a footing, a feeling of where the FX pair will be after the Swiss National Bank announces future actions regarding the direction of the Swiss franc.

FACT

Professional currency traders often sit out the day-to-day trading when there is little news in the FX markets. Some FX traders take the approach that more infrequent, but more carefully placed trades on big news days can offer a greater risk-adjusted return than having positions on a daily basis.

In this scenario, a good bet is that the franc will get weaker against the euro, even if for just short moments at a time. A long EUR/CHF bet with higher leverage and a small position relative to your overall trading account would be the best bet. Other things to consider would be the volatility of such a developing news story. You wouldn't want your trade to close out too soon automatically without the chance for the pair to move in the opposite direction. This whipsaw motion of the market can work against you or for you. To make it work for you, go against wisdom: Place your predetermined profit-taking point at one-third the value of your loss point.

In other words, you can set the software in your trading platform to close the trade automatically at a profit three times as often as the trading platform will close the trade at a loss.

Use Caution to Trade Successfully

Remember, you are trading expectancies: the market expects something to happen, it just doesn't know what. Neither do you. All you know is that the world's FX traders who are following the EUR/CHF developments will be entering into that trade, both long and short, in a tug of war that will have the effect of pushing the Swiss franc up and down, right up until the Swiss National Bank makes a formal announcement. There is money to be made with this type of trade, in this type of market, and when a currency pair is in the news and in play.

Using your trading software correctly, you could set up automatic selling points at a ratio of win to loss of 3:1. After each winning trade and after the trading software automatically closes out your position, you would then re-enter the trade, at the same ratio, repeating the process over and over, until you made your paycheck for the week.

QUESTION

What math skills are required to trade currencies?
To trade currencies effectively it would be good to know how to do the basics: add, subtract, multiply, and divide. Knowing a bit about ratios would also serve you well, as positions are best made using a system of predetermined ratios to your total account value.

As you can see, trading expectancies are a process of reading brokers' reports, digesting the news, and looking at the technical indicators. Taking it to the next step would include spotting situations in which the world's currency traders will be wondering what direction to go in for that FX pair: long or short. Lastly, you would then place trades with automated profit and loss points that would allow you to capture profits at a ratio suited for the volatility of that particular currency pair.

Trading Gold Like a Currency Pair

Although FX trading by definition involves the paper currencies of the world's economies, the trading of spot gold can also be considered to be a form of currency trading. This is because gold itself if a form of money that is traded the world over. Prices of gold are set in euros, Great Britain pounds, and U.S. dollars. Additionally, like currencies, gold is traded from Sunday afternoon New York time until Friday afternoon New York time. These hours and crosses are equivalent to Gold/EUR, Gold/GBP, and Gold/USD. With this in mind, gold is and can be traded like a currency.

Many of the inputs in the overall currency pair equation are absent in the gold currency pair equation. When you evaluate an FX pair for a potential trade, you might consider each currency's home-country economy, political climate, geopolitical problems, expected interest rate changes, as well as technical indicators. Evaluate each input in relation to the other side of the currency pair. Gold FX pairs, on the other hand, are missing half of the inputs that go into a usual trade evaluation. This is because gold does not have a home country, interest rate, or even a meaningful control to its supply. Gold is the ultimate international currency, with its supply increasing only very minimally yearly.

FACT

The popularity of gold exchange-traded funds (ETFs) such as SPDR Gold Trust (GLD) has increased the ability of the average investor to add gold to her portfolio. Gold ETFs are claims on the physical gold that is held in the vaults of the ETF. Some gold ETFs hold as much physical gold in their vaults as the treasuries of some small countries!

On the other hand, the overall money supply of EUR, GBP, and USD is changing with each of these countries' central bank management techniques. This is one of the reasons gold moves up and down against these currencies. In other words, if the market believes that there will be an increase of the number and supply of USD while the amount and supply of gold will remain constant, then gold will gain in value relative to USD. This is because the market would be expecting the effect of the increased number of dollars in the money supply to bid up the price of the limited gold supply. In effect, the increased number of dollars would cause an inflationary effect on goods that are in limited supply.

There are other elements that go into the price of the gold FX pairs. These include the increase in the price of gold beyond the loss of the value of the USD, EUR, or GBP due to trading demand. Other factors include news of major central bank gold purchases, and the anticipation of a strong upcoming Asian holiday season.

You can study the technical indicators for Gold/USD the same way as you study the indicators for other FX pairs. Information is readily available too: You can use the brokers' reports published by full service brokers and consult the World Gold Council's website (*www.gold.org*).

Many forex trading firms such as Oanda (*http://fxtrade.oanda.com*) and Windsor Brokers (*www.windsorbrokers.biz*) are set up to allow spot trading with Gold/USD on the same platform as your regular currencies. Forex brokers such as these allow you to trade the metals with an adjustable margin ratio from 10:1 up to 50:1. Units are small, usually around lots of 100 ounces; due to these small-sized lots, an open position will move into and out of profit at a very slow, manageable rate.

Are Silver and Oil Like Currencies?

You might be wondering if other investment products can be traded like currency pairs. The answer is yes, and the trading of spot silver and oil come to mind. Like gold, silver and oil are priced in relative terms to the U.S. dollar. This dollar pricing opens the way to beginning to think of Oil/USD and Silver/USD as currency pairs with all of the fundamentals, supply, and technical indicators of other FX pairs including Gold/USD.

Silver, on the other hand, acts like gold with its reaction to inflationary indicators, and relatively constant supply (although the supply of silver is much more elastic than gold). The spot silver market is much smaller than the spot gold market; this often leads to more volatile and dramatic price movements throughout the trading day. It is not unusual for gold to move 0.75 percent to 1 percent per day, while silver moves 3 percent to 5 percent per day. As with gold, some Forex brokers allow spot silver (Silver/USD) trading with 10:1, 20:1, or even 50:1 leverage.

FACT

Gold, silver, and oil are traded in dollars; this is why they can be considered currencies. The same might also be said of other widely traded financial products that are denominated and block traded in USD. The S&P 500 Index comes to mind as a kind of currency of the U.S. stock market.

In addition to the high leverage, the minimum order with Silver/USD is usually 5,000 ounces. This combination of high percentage movement, high leverage, and large lot size can lead to huge gains in your account if the conditions are right. It is possible to have a large percentage of your FX account in silver, and after a strong run in silver's price, triple the overall value of your FX account when your silver positions are closed out. This can happen in a matter of a few weeks (most likely in the winter months during the Indian wedding season and the Chinese New Year, or an overly active upward swing in the gold market). Silver prices follow gold prices, and trading spot Silver/USD is often recommended by advisors as a form of a return enhancement for spot Gold/USD traders.

The Oil/USD Pair

Although Silver/USD is much more akin to Gold/USD and other currency pairs, Oil/USD is less so. If you allow the thought that Oil/USD is a currency pair, then you would analyze it the same way as others. You would look for economic factors, geopolitical tensions, and technical indicators much like Gold/USD. The one difference is that while the supply of gold remains relatively constant as the supply of USD moves up and down, the supply of oil often moves up and down with changes in the Organization of the Petroleum Exporting Countries (OPEC) quotas. Other factors are sudden changes in weather, such as when severe hurricanes and tornadoes affect the areas where oil is drilled for or refined. Oil/USD does have some predictability in its direction, though. The summer months in North America usually mean increased vacation and holiday driving, often leading to a run-up in the barrel price of oil.

Trading currencies means trading the relative value of each element of a FX pair. These FX pairs consist of the traditional paper-based currencies of the world. FX pairs can also consist of other forms of money, such as gold, silver, and even oil. USD pricing and worldwide electronic trading of these three acts and trades just like other currency pairs.

CHAPTER 4

Moving the Currency Markets

One of the factors that goes into the perceived value of a currency is its interest rate as set by that nation's central bank. In addition to a central bank's intervention and control of interest rates, and the talking up or down of a currency, you must consider that government's debt levels and its money supply before pricing a currency in a pair. Other factors include whether or not that economy is moving along at a slower or faster rate than the counter currency of the pair. Read on to learn to identify these key factors.

What Is Money and How Much Is There?

Money can be defined as an object or unit of measure that can be used to pay for goods received or services rendered. In this way, money can be the paper bills that you use to pay for your double shot espresso, and it can also be the electronic balance in your currency brokerage account that you use to buy positions in the FX market. This type of money is backed by the ability of its issuing government to raise taxes and pay its bills. When you are buying a currency, you are buying a commitment from the issuing government that the money is sound, and that the finances of the government are such that it has now and will have in the future the ability to find sources of capital to pay its day-to-day and long-term debts. This commitment is why a government with a strong balance sheet, a strong and united political environment, and a strong taxable workforce (or other source of funds) will issue a currency that will be perceived as sound. Strong economies mean the ability of a government to pay its bills without the issuance of more money today (altering the money supply) to pay yesterday's debt.

The value of currencies will depend somewhat on the amount of **money supply** in the system. Money supply is divided into three basic parts, called **M1**, **M2**, and **M3**. M1 is the amount of the money supply owned by the public and held in the bank, including savings accounts and checking accounts. It also includes traveler's checks and the amount of actual paper and coin currency in circulation.

ESSENTIAL

A listing of the amounts of M1, M2, M3, and L is available on the Internet and also is published in the *Wall Street Journal* once a month. You can go the Federal Reserve website to get the latest figures called *Money Stock Measures* (*www.federalreserve.gov/releases/h6/current*).

The M1 money supply is usually the amount of money that can actually be used to buy something with, and to pay bills. It is the amount of money that can be used for an exchange of goods and services.

The M2 includes the amounts of money that are in M1 and also savings deposits in money markets and money market mutual funds held at brokerage firms. Other elements of the M2 calculation include some overnight ultra-liquid moneys that are in overseas banks, such as Eurodollar deposits. Whereas M1 includes the amount of money that is intended to be used to pay for goods and services, M2 is the measure of how much money is in the system that can be used as a store of value.

ESSENTIAL

A listing of the amounts of M1, M2, M3, and L is available on the Internet and also is published in the *Wall Street Journal* once a month. You can go the Federal Reserve website to get the latest figures called *Money Stock Measures* (*www.federalreserve.gov/releases/h6/current*).

The third level of money in the markets is M3. The M3 consists of the cash products that large banks and business have on deposit. It includes CDs and other structured time deposits in both domestic and Eurodollars. The main purpose of the M3 calculation is the amount of money that is used system wide as a unit of account for that currency. The last measure of money supply is L. L refers to all of the other liquid cash-like equivalents including ultrashort-term commercial paper, T-bills, and other structured cash equivalent letters of credit, etc.

The Role of the Federal Reserve

The central bank of the United States is the Federal Reserve, also known as the Fed. The Fed performs many roles, but most importantly its function is that of a bank. Its main clients are not individuals or small business, however. Its main clients are other U.S. banks. Lately, the role of the Fed has been expanded to include the coordination of swaps and reverse repurchase agreements (repos) that involve other central banks and some of the largest and most influential banks of other home countries. In this fashion, the central bank of the United States can act as a "lender of last resort," a bank that other banks can turn to in times of need. This need was most apparent during and after the economic and banking crisis of 2008–2009.

During those years the strength of the U.S. Federal Reserve was tested to the maximum. The Fed was called into action, and it provided liquidity to banks of all kinds by offering the exchange of "toxic" assets in place of "good" assets. The Fed did this by taking these rapidly deteriorating assets onto its inventory and exchanging them with the much-needed liquidity that the banks and investment banks of the United States required at that time. There is even evidence that the central bank of the United States offered and provided liquidity to foreign banks, including the largest Swiss bank, UBS.

FACT

If you are interested in the role that the U.S. Federal Reserve played in the crisis of 2008–2009, then you can do a bit of research on the subject. A good place to start is the Federal Reserve's website (*www.federalreserve.gov*) and the website of its biggest player, the Federal Reserve Bank of New York (*www.newyorkfed.org/index.html*).

Keeping the United States on Track

In addition to acting the role of lender of last resort, the Fed sets a few key policies that can have a heavy influence on the U.S. economy. These key policies can go a long way in keeping the United States on track or giving it a nudge in the right direction if its economy is too slow or too strong. First, the required reserve ratio is set by the Fed, and it refers to the minimum amount of money that retail banks are required to hold on tap for customers' withdrawals. The reserve ratio acts as a limit on how much a bank can lend out in relation to its deposits. The lower the required reserve ratio, the more the banks can lend out per dollar of deposit. Lending out more has the effect of increasing money supply.

The Discount Rate

The second policy is the monitoring and setting of the discount rate. The discount rate is the overnight interest rate that the Fed charges the retail banks to borrow short-term money. If the rate is low, or goes lower, then retail banking institutions will borrow more from the Fed at a cheaper rate, and will then be able to lend the money out at a cheaper rate. The increased lending also has the effect of increasing money supply.

Open Market Operations

The third method of monitoring and controlling the money supply is through **open market operations**. Open market operations involve the purchase and sale of T-bills, T-notes, and T-bonds on the open market through a system of dealers, such as the nation's largest broker dealers and banks. It is often considered the most effective and most mysterious tool at the Fed's disposal. Purchases and sales can be done during different times, with or without notice to the public. The buying and selling of these instruments is a function that goes on every day. The Fed takes a reading of the market by contacting its sources: investment banks, brokerages, and other major players. It then enters into the process of buying securities if there is not enough money in the system and selling securities if there is too much money in the system. The whole process is usually done in secret, but lately there have been public announcements of such activity.

Monetary Policy

In the United States, the Federal Reserve is the independent body that has the power to make and enforce monetary policy. As with many other central banks, its main goal is to regulate the supply of money and interest rates in such a way as to preserve price stability. The Fed does this through a combination of controlling money supply, setting interest rates, and determining the amount of available credit to banks.

This regulation of the economy through the methods of the Fed is referred to as **monetary policy**. At the opposite end of the spectrum is **fiscal policy**. Fiscal policy refers to the efforts of lawmakers to raise taxes and spend those funds in such a way as to spur growth of the economy. There is some argument as to which method works best, but in the past decades, monetary policy has been at the helm of the economic ship of most developed countries.

Regulating Economies: Sweden and the United States

Since most central banks have keeping price levels stable as one of their main goals, the banks will use the same types of methods to regulate their home economies. There might be slight variations, such as using a "repo-rate" to set the base interest rate of the country. Such a method is used in Sweden. Looking at the Swedish central bank website under monetary policy, (*www.riksbank.com/templates/SectionStart.aspx?id=10602*), they explain: "According to the Sveriges Riksbank Act, the objective of monetary policy is to 'maintain price stability.'" The Riksbank has a secondary goal of an inflation target: "The Riksbank's objective is to keep inflation around 2 percent per year, as measured by the annual change in the consumer price index (CPI). In order to keep inflation around 2 percent, the Riksbank adjusts its key interest rate, the repo rate."

In the United States, the goal is to keep the inflation rate in a range from 0 percent to 3 percent. The inflation rate in the United States is measured by the CPI. The CPI is a periodic measurement of a predetermined basket of goods. The elements of the goods are measured against the prices at the prior term, and any differences are noted. The result is a gauge of how much more it costs for basic living expenses period to period.

FACT

It takes a bit of time for the actions of the Fed to work their way through the economic system. If the Fed adjusts the money supply, the effects of the adjustment might not reach the average household for several months. This delay is called forward-lag.

When the CPI comes out and it shows a large jump in the prices of basic goods, the central bank of the United States—the Fed—takes notice. It will then react by a series of tactics such as selling securities in open market operations, raising reserve requirements, or raising interest rates. Whatever method the Fed uses, the result will be the same. The money supply will decrease, money to lend will become harder to obtain, and the economy will begin to slow.

Reading the Economy

The time it takes to get a reading from the CPI and other indicators as to the heating up or cooling down of the economy varies. Some say that it takes up to six months for the CPI and other indicators to get a good reading of the economy. This is why you often hear "we are already in a recession" or "the recession is over" from the market commentators and famous fund managers who are interviewed on news stations. These market experts are reading the market and looking at their own information. They are often privy to the temperature of the economy well before the official numbers come out. If you hear the experts speak like this, take heed. They are usually quite right with their observations.

A Brief History of Fiscal and Monetary Policy

In recent history there has been the coordination of fiscal policy and monetary policy. The determiners of fiscal policy lowered tax rates and this action left more money in the taxpayers' wallets. Since the average taxpayer was paying less in taxes, there was more money in her household budget to spend on goods and services. Money spent on goods and services put money in the pockets of the businesses and business owners. The business owners and business then had to pay less tax on the income, which in turn left more money in their checkbooks. The process was repeated when the businesses and business owners spent the money on goods and services. A larger proportion of this money was then left in those business owners' pockets when they, in turn, paid less tax. The overall effect was a growing economy.

While this was being done, the Federal Reserve offered a coordinate policy of increasing the overall money supply by keeping interest rates low. This easy money policy, coupled with the lower taxes, had the net effect of growing the U.S. economy quickly and strongly. One of the most effective uses of this low tax–easy money policy was in the 1960s.

The 1960s and 1970s

The growth created by the combination of monetary and fiscal policies was very strong and carried much momentum. The slower economy of the late 1950s was turned into a raging economy of the 1960s. The economy was so strong that it overheated in the 1970s, leading to an inflationary era. The price of commodities such as gold and oil went up seemingly overnight, while the producers were just beginning to corral their sources. The best known case of this was the formation of the OPEC oil embargo, when the world's producers of crude oil worked together to raise the price of oil by limiting supply. The lower supply of oil to the world caused even greater inflationary pressure. The result was very high inflation across the spectrum of goods and services.

e! ALERT

Inflation can creep up suddenly and unexpectedly. You can measure the effects of inflation by looking at a good that has both material and labor inputs. For example, a fully loaded 1974 Ford Crown Victoria station wagon cost $4,300 when it was released. The same Ford station wagon cost $7,300 in 1977!

The 1980s Recession and the 2008–2009 Crisis

Other experimentation with fiscal and monetary policy was done in the early 1980s with the election of the new U.S. President, Ronald Reagan, and the idea of future tax cuts. The chairman of the Federal Reserve took a different approach and used the discount rate as his mechanism to control the economy. Interest rates were hiked up. The overall effect was a severe recession and huge amounts of new government debt by the United States.

More recently there has been the coordination of fiscal and monetary policy in reaction to the recession that followed the 2008–2009 banking and housing crisis. This most recent recession has proved to be the deepest and most severe recession since the Great Depression of the 1930s. This recent recession has been felt worldwide, and its secondary effects are still not known. From the huge amounts of added money supply to the added debt levels of governments, the outcome is yet to be finalized. Perhaps it will be a repeat of what was seen before: a combination of the inflation of the 1970s and the recession of the 1980s.

Economically Contrasting China and Switzerland

China has become one of the fastest growing economic zones of the last twenty years. Because of its growth, it sucks in massive quantities of monetary surplus, which it then turns into investments. These investments are mainly U.S. government debt. China has become the largest holder of United States T-bills, T-notes, and T-bonds. These debt instruments act as the currency reserves of the Chinese government.

Some say that one of the main reasons for China's stellar growth is its artificially low exchange rate. Since the government of China controls the exchange rate, the government has effectively created a flow of surplus funds into the country. To understand more easily how this works, consider the following: A neighbor is an accountant and has a staff of five in his office. He charges the going rate of $105 per hour for staff and $275 per hour for supervisors. Due to his going rate, he must compete on other factors besides price. You are also an accountant. You have a staff of five, but you pay them less and charge only $55 per hour for staff and only $125 per hour for supervisors. With this scenario you have effectively set your "exchange rate" artificially lower than that of your neighbor, even though it is the exact same type of work. By the law of economics you will naturally have created a positive inflow of surplus cash into your business. This holds true when the products are identical but one supplier's price is considerably lower than the other's. This is the effect that China has created by keeping its exchange rate low. China has, in effect, lowered the labor rate of the products its workers produce.

ESSENTIAL

Both China and Switzerland's economies are somewhat similar. One of the main similarities is that while both China and Switzerland do well at providing the labor inputs in manufacturing, they are both heavily reliant on imported raw materials to make those same goods.

Switzerland, on the other hand, has allowed its currency to float freely against its trading partners. When there were problems in Europe, the

United Kingdom, and the United States, many found the Swiss franc to be the ultimate safe-haven currency in times of upheaval in the markets. The Swiss franc was touted as being the paper version of gold. Its price moved to record levels in currency pairs. This increase has, in turn, caused the Swiss economy problems that are the exact opposite of China's growth issues.

The high franc has had the effect of slowing the economy of the small Alpine country. The higher currency acted like a price increase on the goods produced by Switzerland, and began to stunt its economy. This was mainly because Switzerland relied so heavily on the service sector (banking) and already expensive luxury goods (that were slated for export). As the price of the Swiss franc went up, so did its goods in the eyes of people outside the country. Soon all of Swiss goods were priced 20 percent to 30 percent greater than then they had been three or four years before. The net effect was a slowing economy and efforts by the Swiss National Bank to regulate more actively its exchange rates.

A Bit about Bubbles

The world's economic history abounds with stories of bubbles. A bubble is when a popular item or commodity falls under the force of speculation. Once this speculation takes place at the everyman level, the price expands upward. The prices of the speculative bubble increase to the point where there is no longer any available cash to support its continued upward movement. At this point the bubble is formed, and soon thereafter, the bubble pops.

FACT

According to Charles Kindleberger's classic work *Manias, Panics, and Crashes: A History of Financial Crises*, there were thirty-five speculative bubbles between 1618–1982. It seems as though this type of boom-bust is a natural part of the economic cycle, and very difficult to prevent even in the modern day.

According the economist Hyman Minsky, a speculative bubble usually starts with an economic shock to the otherwise normally operating financial system. Historically, this triggering event has ranged from famine, excessive credit regimes, and even the implementation and widespread use of a new technology such as the railroad. The net effect is that of a created rush of investment capital into the new situation. In the past, most booms have been allowed to happen with some form of added money supply.

The Great Tulip Bubble

In 1636 in the Dutch republic, there began one of the most famous bubbles, the Great Tulip Bubble. This was the time when the Netherlands was one of the world's most sophisticated business centers. With the boom that arose out of a war with Spain, there came added abundance to the lowlands of Europe. The average Dutch homeowner began to buy up exotic tulip bulbs, and soon there was "tulip-mania." A year later, the whole industry collapsed, and many households lost their life savings.

The 1920s Bubble

In the 1920s there was another bubble. This one was a bubble in the equities markets. The stock markets across the world were going up and up daily, which led to more and more people investing in the market. Liquidity was available as many people who speculated in the U.S. stock market bought their stock on margin. In the 1920s an investor was able to use 10:1 gearing on his stock purchases. This means they could buy $10,000 worth of stock for $1,000 in cash (currently the margin on stock purchases is 1:1.5, or $1,500 worth of stock for $1,000 in cash). In the end, the stock markets of the world came tumbling down in value. As they crashed, they brought economic destruction to those who had their life savings invested in the stock markets.

The 2008–2009 Bubble

In 2008 and leading into 2009 there was another bubble. This one hit closer to home as it not only involved the U.S. and world stock markets, but also was rooted in the falling values of the U.S. residential housing market. Before this fall in value, the U.S. residential housing market was going forward in full force. It seemed as though anyone could get a mortgage and it seemed like everyone had a home of his own. Through a series of unfortunate events, the housing bubble burst, leaving many "underwater" in the debt/equity ratio of their mortgages.

Speculative bubbles are seen in almost every form of trade instrument. Some develop slowly; others come and go in a year or less. Bubbles can be very hard to detect when they are ascending, and many can get caught up in a quickly deflating or popping bubble. Bubbles happen in the Forex world too, as a currency pair can be a market darling for quite some time, and then all of a sudden, it is no longer in favor. Sometimes it is the whole market that is under the influence of a bubble; other times it is one sector, or in the case of currencies, one economic region or group of currencies.

CHAPTER 5

Methods of Valuing an FX Pair

You will need to look at the value of each FX pair at the beginning of each trading session, by seeking out and using information. To establish the value of a currency pair you should always start with a fresh perspective as to the value of this FX pair. You can use fundamental or technical analysis, or a combination of the two to come up with a good idea of what is the proper value of an FX pair to help you determine entry and exit points of trades.

Review Before Each Trading Session

You should begin each trading session with a fresh perspective as to all of the FX pairs that you are trading. You should also get into the habit of looking at the FX pairs that you are thinking about getting into with the thought that the market might have reacted to news developments since the last time you evaluated such pairs.

For example, you might have closed out all of your trades late on Thursday afternoon after a profitable week of trading. Looking at your profit and loss statements, you decide that while the week wasn't spectacular, you still earned enough in your account from the last two weeks of trading to make a withdrawal and issue yourself a paycheck. You have met your goals: you have realized enough gain in your account to earn a living. You have determined ahead of time how much you need to earn in order to make a living that is equal to working a full-time job.

You go to the screen in your account that is labeled "Withdraw Funds" and place an order for your FX broker to use the Automated Clearing House Network (ACH) to credit you your predetermined paycheck amount. This action will leave enough of the previous two weeks gains in the account to allow it to **grow organically**, which means the money in the account is able to grow on its own, building on its profits. You decide you've done well in the last two weeks, and especially well in the last two days. You give yourself permission to take a four-day weekend, starting Thursday at two in the afternoon. After a weekend trip spent cross-country skiing with your family, you come back to your home office early the next Tuesday morning.

ALERT

When setting up your Forex trading account for the first time, choose your method of funding the account carefully (wire, ACH, PayPal, or check). This is because some Forex brokerage firms will only allow one method of funding and only the exact same method for you to withdraw your funds.

Review Your Currency Pairs

In this scenario it is best to perform a systematic review of all of the currency pairs that you regularly trade. You might start off with the Anglo currencies, such as the GBP, the NZD, and the AUD. You should then move into the other big players, such as the Japanese yen, the euro, and the Swiss franc. Spend some time going over these currencies' central bank websites first. You would be surprised as to how in tune you can get with a currency if you spend a few minutes looking at the website of the bank that is issuing that money. You can also use the little secret of looking at the part of the central bank websites that discuss the current designs of the paper-based currencies you are trading. This can help you get a feel of that money beyond the electronic trading screen, as you can use the pictures to see what the inhabitants of those countries hold in their hands and use to buy an espresso and a newspaper at the local hangouts in Budapest, Zurich, Oslo, and Paris.

Always Check News Reports

After this, move on to any brokers' reports that have been issued over the weekend, and search the Internet for any news that has developed over the past twenty-four- to forty-eight-hour period. This can be done by going to *www.google.com* and typing in something such as "Swedish krona to dollar" (for USD/SEK) or "British pound to dollar" (for GBP/USD), and then selecting any news options. This will bring up all of the most recent news that is published on the public access side of the Internet, including stories from *www.marketwatch.com* and websites that are of a more mainstream or general nature, including foreign websites.

Upon a full review of the news, proceed to move on to your trading-news journal to review what was developing with the FX pairs before you left for your long weekend. Then, finally, move on to looking at your live-trading screen, with all of its flashing green and red lights, and ever moving charts. At this point, you will have completely refreshed your view on the value of a pair that you may have been looking at, and will not (you hope) react too strongly to seeing a quoted price that is far from where you remember it, whether strongly up or down. This procedure, if undertaken at the beginning of every trading session, can prevent you from jumping into a trade when the FX pair has been revalued by the entire market, and you are the last to know.

You Are Always Starting from Scratch

Reviewing the information that is available before you begin to trade is crucial to protecting that balance in your account and keeping your FX trading profitable. As you look at each bit of information before you begin to trade, keep in mind that you are trying to establish a new value for a currency pair. You should always start from scratch with your evaluations of the market's perceived value of a currency pair, and you should always begin with a new perspective if the currency pair is set to make a move that would allow you to make a profit with a trade.

Foreign Market Movements

For example, it might be that while you were away for the weekend (with no trades on your books) that the market's risk appetite developed considerably. Good news might have come out of the European Union (EU) regarding a wide sweeping deal, and that reform deal might serve as an ointment to that economic area's woes, which in turn will calm market participants all over the world. The development might have happened early Saturday morning when all of the major markets were closed. The good news didn't wait for Monday morning to travel though, and traders have been gleefully waiting to up their inventories of risky assets. They have been spending all of their weekend thinking of how they would like to have more stock and other higher-yielding assets. As the markets open in the beginning of the week, the world's stock markets gain. Other assets that go up on positive news gain also. In the currency arena, this means that the SEK, the NZD, the EUR, and the AUD will gain, while the low-risk currencies such as the USD, JPY, and the CHF will fall in value.

Since news coming from such a large economic block as the EU can be so positive to the markets, there can be movements of 1 percent to 1.25 percent or even greater in these FX pairs. If you have been away from your trading desk for any length of time before the EU's developments came about, your *before* valuations will be much different from the market's *after* valuations.

ESSENTIAL

While it is best to get refreshed and walk away from your trading desk after a few good days in the FX market, you should still stay at least a tiny bit connected to the trading world. This connection might come from checking your favorite financial website on your smart phone or iPad while away from your office.

After news such as this, it is quite possible that the Paris market's CAC40 has gained over 1.6 percent, and London's FTSE100 has gained over 1.1 percent. These European stock market gains can be very positive news to the trader of the euro versus the Swiss franc. In fact, it may be that the value of the Swiss franc has been gaining against the euro as the negative European news has been developing, and now the pressure has come off the euro versus the CHF since the problem has come to a positive conclusion. The major cross might have gone from a previously valued EUR/CHF 1.15 to a new stronger valued EUR/CHF 1.168, a nearly 1.5 percent gain over the past two days!

Evaluating FX Pairs with the News

It is clear with this example that it is necessary to re-evaluate where the new value of the FX pair stands in relation to the developments in the news. Although it is true that this particular pair has a good chance of moving from its current level, it might also be that it will move in the opposite direction from when you last observed it. You might have been anticipating an appreciation in the EUR versus the CHF on Thursday when you left for your weekend of skiing, and fully intended to go long the EUR and sell the Swiss franc. Upon returning from your trip, you would re-evaluate. Considering the up and down nature of FX pairs, you might decide to look at the opposite trade, going long the Swiss franc and selling the EUR, all in anticipation of profit taking in the world's stock markets and the inevitable swinging back of the EUR/CHF pair as the world scales back its risk appetite (which it always does at some point).

Overview of Fundamentals and Pair Valuation

There are several ways to evaluate the price of a currency pair. One of the easiest to understand methods is called fundamental analysis. When you read the fundamentals, what you are doing is getting to know the economic and financial situations of the areas of the world and countries that use the different currencies to trade. Most countries allow their currencies to move relatively freely against the other currencies of the world. They allow the market to determine the exchange rate between their home country and their trading partner. These exchange rates are determined by a combination of supply and demand and speculation. In any case, most central banks allow the currency they control to adjust up and down in an ever-moving wave pattern. They know that if a currency becomes too strong against a trading partner, economic forces will naturally lower the price of the currency over time, even if it takes a few years. With this system the central bankers of the world usually do not artificially manipulate the price of their currency in the market, and prices are allowed to set by the give and take of the market forces.

QUESTION

Are the central bankers of the world your friend or foe?
Even though it is true that the currency market is the largest, most liquid market in the world (and therefore free from participant manipulation), the central bankers of the world play a huge part in the pricing of a currency. When central bankers give a speech, just a hint of their intentions can cause a currency to move up or down.

This type of nonintervention is also called a **floating rate system**. It is the method of nearly all currencies of the world: in fact, if a currency is not on a floating rate system, then it most likely will not be a choice of yours (and others) to trade in your FX account, as its movement is linked to another major currency. This link is called **pegging a currency**. Developing nations oftentimes peg their currencies to a more stable currency in an effort to stabilize their home-countries' currencies in outside investors' eyes. Needless to say, there are quite a few times that this pegging has been tried, but the pegging of a developing country currency to a developed country currency often leads to economic problems. When the problems become too great, the developing economy will de-peg and revalue their home currency in an effort to relieve building pressure on the home economy. The de-peg often means a devaluing of the home currency. While this can often offer immediate relief to a developing economy, it can wreak havoc on that country's investors and currency holders.

When a country is on the floating rate system, its price is always changing due to supply and demand and the market's analysis of the home country's economic condition (growth or recession) and any future interest rate adjustments that will be set by that country's central bank. Lastly, any news that would make the market change perceptions about a country's money supply or any chance that the currency's exchange rate will be adjusted by a central bank or a group of central banks will also greatly affect the price of a currency in the market.

Overview of Technical and Pair Valuation

Fundamental analysis is often referred to as a security-selection approach, and technical analysis is often referred to a security-timing approach. While fundamentals can help you determine which FX pairs to trade and which currency is likely to go up or down against another, technical analysis can help you determine when is the best time to get into a trade (of those currencies) and when is the best time to get out of a trade.

Using technical analysis to determine a currency's valuation uses the philosophy opposite of fundamental analysis and is of different complexity. Technical analysis is the process of consulting charts, averages, and indicators to help you the trader determine the best time to enter and exit out of a currency trade. A FX trader who uses technical analysis will use these charts and indicators to help her analyze the markets and look for setups. Most charts and indicators can be accessed from your trading platform, and you can even adjust the inputs to add the indicators for the whole market or just one currency pair.

Technical analysis is a graphic representation of the price and number of trades (commonly called volume) of a currency pair over time. The most common chart is called a **bar chart**. A bar chart shows the high and low points of a FX pair at time intervals that are preset by you on your trading software. For example, you might be looking at a one-hour chart to get an overview of EUR/NOK while reading the news, websites, brokers' reports, and other sources of fundamental analysis. By setting your chart parameters to show EUR/NOK's movements in one-hour intervals, you would be able to see a chart that traced the history of the cross pair back about five weeks.

FACT

It is good to use a few of the key technical indicators while evaluating setups in your currency trading program. There are over 200 different ways to use technical indicators in your analysis from an advance/decline line to a zero-lag, exponential moving average and everything in between, all providing different levels of quality information.

Once your observations about the possibility of going short EUR/NOK being a good trade were confirmed, you could then switch to a five-minute or even a fifteen-minute chart to help you further determine a proper entry point to short the EUR and buy NOK. The modern software on most FX brokers' trading platforms can allow for multiple time frames to be viewed, and some even allow for multiple time frames to be viewed at the same time.

Some Currency Trading Technical Indicators

Other information that you could use in your technical analysis could be to draw moving averages onto your chart. It is easy to go to a drop down box and go to "Moving Averages" and enter a number of days to be used in the computer's calculation. A useful and popular line to draw is a 200-day moving average. When you ask your software to calculate this line, a contrasting colored graceful line will trace its way across the otherwise choppy bar chart. A chart drawn on Windsor Brokers (*www.windsorbrokers.biz*) Windsor Direct 4 platform can show a Spot Gold/USD one-hour chart. The irregular line is actually separate lines showing the open, close, and movement for spot gold once per hour. The wave is a 200-day moving average line, and the spikes at the bottom of the chart are volume indicators.

There are others, including support and resistance lines, and 50-day moving averages. Some indicators are currency pair specific. Examples of these are the Fibonacci series and Elliott waves, or the law of fives. Some technical analyses look at where the 200-day moving averages touch the 50-day moving averages; the convergence is considered a strong indicator.

ALERT

If you are having a difficult time understanding how technical analysis works, don't worry! Many Forex traders at proprietary trading houses leave the actual analysis up to the research department. You can use your FX broker or full service broker's reports as a kind of private research department of your own FX trading house.

Other technicals are for the market as a whole, and include stock market indicators (remember, the up-and-down movements of some currencies are directly related to the market's risk appetite, and are indirectly linked to the world's stock markets' ups and downs). These technical indicators include the Chicago Board of Exchange (**CBOE) Volatility Index**, more commonly known as the **VIX Index**. The VIX Index monitors the volatility of the market, and is used to measure stock and stock-option traders' emotional feelings about the market. If this VIX Index is higher than normal, then the world's stock markets are usually falling (or free-falling as sometimes happens!). If this is the case, it would be best for you to short high-yielding currencies such as the AUD and NZD and go long safe-haven currencies such as the USD, JPY, and especially the Swiss franc. This is because some currencies such as the AUD and others (SEK, for example) have their up-and-down movements very closely timed to risk sentiment. Others have their performance tied to bad times: the worse the market does, and the more people are afraid of losing money, the more they will go up. This is the case of the lower-yielding currencies such as USD and JPY. The Swiss Franc also holds a safe-haven status, as its country's central bank and economy are able withstand harsh times.

Using Both Fundamental and Technical Indicators

Using a combination of both fundamental and technical indicators can yield you a very strong trading system. For example, things might look promising after reading the Norwegian central bank's Norges-Bank website (*www.norges-bank.no/en*). Some of the information that you read on the Norges-Bank website might lead you to believe that the currency has the chance to get stronger.

▼ TABLE 5-1: FUNDAMENTAL INFORMATION TO FUNDAMENTAL ANALYSIS

What You Are Looking for in Fundamentals	Questions to Ask
The Currency's Rate of Return	Are current interest rates relative to other currencies?
Current Account Is Balanced or in Surplus	Is the country taking in more foreign currency than it is sending out through trade?
Governance	Is the central bank consistent and well managed?
Economic Policies	Is the central bank implementing constructive methods of growth with limited inflation?
Interest Rates	Is there a hint of an interest rate hike in the near or medium term?
Growth	Are there any economic indicators (or proxies for indicators) that are showing economic growth in the country?

You might decide that the Norwegian krone has a high likelihood of strengthening against the euro. You decide to look at the technicals before you commit any money to a trade against the euro and for the NOK. Switching to your charts on your trading platform, you use the technical indicator software provided by your Forex broker.

You draw lines; some look like waves, others look like mountains and valleys, still others look like upside-down icicles. After notating all of your observations relating to the technicals, you take one final review of the fundamental information. All the information gets written down in your trading journal before you trade. Just before you commit to the trade, you decide how much to buy compared to your overall FX account size. Lastly, you decide on an appropriate exit point, both if there is a profit and if there is a loss.

ESSENTIAL

Although the currency world can be fast paced, it is best that you take your time to learn and evaluate all you can about entering into a currency pair before you commit money to a trade. Remember, a few good trades at the beginning can go a long way at giving you confidence to continue your Forex trading endeavors!

All your information is determined, and then you place the trade. The information you read might lead you to think that a short time frame of overnight is your best bet. In that case you would have a larger percentage of your account in the trade and exit out at a very close profit point with an automated take-profit command programmed into your software. If you determine that it will take a bit longer for the currency pair of EUR/NOK to move in your favor, then a trade with a smaller portion of your overall account balance would be best, with a much larger take-profit point set in your automated trading platform.

Either way, you have used both the fundamentals and the technicals to decide on a trade, and you've used the both of them to help you determine an appropriate time frame to be in your EUR/NOK trade for maximum return with minimum risk.

CHAPTER 6

Fundamental Research: What, Where, and How

In order to get ready to make your first currency trade you will first have to have a grip on the basics of what is known as fundamental research. With a strong knowledge of fundamental research you can begin searching through central banking websites on your own and cross-reference your observations with that of news sources and brokers' reports. You can then take these cross-referenced ideas and plan what currency pairs you will trade.

A Starting Point for Fundamental Research

Good research is the key to spotting setups when currency trading. It is generally not good to go around throwing money at your trades without some sort of idea of what is a good trade and what is not a good trade. Remember the idea is that you are undertaking currency trading for pleasure and to make money. While it might be fun to act in a sort of Wild West-gunslinger fashion and place your FX bets wildly and loosely, it can be much more fun to properly research a currency pair. You can then move on to place an order in your FX trading platform—a trade that is well thought out rather than just a haphazard bet on the markets.

Once you agree that it is actually possible to have a good idea as to what direction certain currency pairs will take in the future, you will then discover that the careful study of economic indicators, central bank websites, brokers' reports, and news data is a good place to start. These sources and this type of information are called fundamental information and the study of it is called fundamental analysis.

ALERT

> Fundamental analysis is the procedure of looking at a country's growth rate, inflation rate, current account surplus or deficit, and other information. Sometimes a separate study of economics is required to understand the full picture gathered from the fundamental analysis of a central bank's website.

Fundamental analysis is the key to a well-thought out and therefore a well-run trading system. When you allow yourself to study the fundamentals, you are allowing yourself to look at the big picture. When you look to fundamental analysis, you look at the actual central bank websites of Switzerland, Sweden, Hungary, Europe, the United States, etc., with an eye for hints and suggestions as to the state of a particular country's economic well-being. You would search through all of the announcements and reports for signs that their home economy is doing better or worse, i.e., growing or slowing (and at what rate). You would then compare these growing or slowing signs, suggestions, and hints of the counter currency you are considering trading.

For example, for the currency cross of the Swiss franc and the Hungarian forint, CHF/HUF, you would visit the Swiss National Bank (*www.snb.ch*) and the Hungarian central bank (*http://english.mnb.hu*) websites. You would then read the past news releases and make note of any sign that the separate banks are speaking about an economy that is on course or overheating or stagnant. Look for key words that can help you decide if that country's central bank thinks that the economy is going fast, slow, or steady.

A hint of a fast economy would lead you to think that there might be a possible interest rate hike in the future. Conversely, a hint of a slowing economy would lead you to believe that will be a loosening or lowering of interest rates. This is true because most central banks regulate the rate of their home economy's growth by raising or lowering interest rates. A slowing economy would need lower rates to increase lending (and therefore spending, leading to growth), and a speeding economy would have to be slowed by raising interest rates to limit lending (and therefore slowing growth).

Taking this information to the next step, you would then search through your broker's reports for a mention of the same rate-change direction, and also get the market sentiment of where the interest rates are going. You could look at news services such as DailyFX and FXstreet for back up of this information. Remember, you are looking for one interest rate of one currency to move up and the interest rate of another currency to move down. Sometimes the expectation that the currencies will move interest rates against each other will be enough to be the catalyst of a good FX trade. As long as the market thinks that the interest rates (and therefore the relative value of each currency against each other) is about to change, the players in the FX market will place their bets, and the weight of the world's FX traders will cause the currency pair to move in that direction.

This studying of the world currencies' central bank websites should be the beginning of any study of the fundamentals of all of the currency pairs you are considering trading. Whether it is the EUR/NOK, the EUR/SEK, or the EUR/CHF, (or any other combination of any currencies) the European Central bank website (*www.ecb.int/home/html/index.en.html*), the Norges Bank (*www.norges-bank.no/en*), the Riksbanken (*www.riksbank.com*), and the Swiss National Bank (*www.snb.ch/en*) should be visited and studied. A list of the world's national and central banks can be found on the Bank for International Settlements (BIS) website (*www.bis.org/cbanks.htm*). There is plenty of information at the BIS website, including a good idea of the movement of money among the banks of the world and reports on inflation (*www.bis.org*).

The Use of Fundamental Indicators

Once the basics of a country's economy are determined from looking at the central bank website, you can delve deeper and look at some of the current and future economic indicators. The following is a list of indicators on the U.S. Economics and Statistics Administration's website (*www.esa.doc.gov/about-economic-indicators*).

▼ **TABLE 6-1: FUNDAMENTAL INDICATORS**

Economic Indicator	Website link
Advance Monthly Retail Sales	*www.census.gov/retail*
Advance Report on Durable Goods	*www.census.gov/manufacturing/m3*
Current Account Balance	*www.bea.gov/newsreleases/international*
New Home Sales	*www.census.gov/const*
Personal Income and Spending	*www.bea.gov/newsreleases/national/pi*
U.S. Trade Balance	*www.bea.gov/international*

Current and future economic indicators are a bit more complex to digest and assimilate into good trading information. Don't allow yourself to get caught up in the numbers. Remember, what you are looking for is any indication that a country's economy is steady, slowing, or growing too quickly. After looking at this information and its equivalent on the non-U.S. central bank websites, you can build upon your knowledge base of what is expected in the direction of interest rates of that currency through its current and future growth rates.

Additionally, you can cross reference any of the information you may have noticed with the currency-news websites and any broker's reports you may be receiving as part of your trading platform's information news feeds. It would also be good to make note of your observations in your trading journal, keeping note of where and when you observed the hint or suggestion that a trade might be developing.

FACT

Economic indicators are used by economists as well as stock, bond, and currency traders to predict where a country is financially heading. Some of the economic indicators tell a story of what has already happened, called lagging indicators. Others tell where the economy will be soon; these are called leading indicators.

Gathering Fundamental Information

Fundamental information develops slowly: It is considered the longer-term information and therefore a medium- to long-term analysis of where a currency and a currency pair are moving. Often, your broker might report a current price and a medium- and long-term range for a particular currency pair. What these investment banks are doing is having their currency analyst departments look at the fundamentals of a currency and compare it to the fundamentals of a counter currency.

For example, the currency analyst might look at the NZD/USD for a possible trading opportunity. The FX analyst at the investment bank that is providing the report would study all of the written reports on the Reserve Bank of New Zealand (*www.rbnz.govt.nz*) for any indication of growing, slowing, or steady economic development. This would indicate a change in the interest rates of currency as set by the Reserve Bank of New Zealand to control the growth (or lack of growth). The FX analyst would then look for any information on money flows into and out of the country and other statistics (*www.rbnz.govt.nz/statistics/econind/index.html*). She would then make note and compare these to the same type of information on the related U.S. central bank website. This information would be matched with the information and observances of the NZD/USD technical indicators, and if she has an idea that there will be a widening or convergence of the interest rates of the two currencies, she would take a long, short, or neutral stance.

Interpreting the Information

If the analyst thinks the NZD will raise interest rates and the USD will be steady or lower interest rates, then she would issue a long NZD/USD buy signal in the report. A long NZD/USD would mean you are selling USD and using the proceeds to buy NZD. The trade would make money when the NZD crept up in value against the USD over time due to other traders pushing its price up. This pushing of the price of the NZD would most likely be due to the world's FX traders engaging in the time-tested practice of carry trades, or making money selling short a low-interest currency (in this case, the USD) and using the money to invest in a high-interest currency (in this case, the NZD). Additional information as to actual entry and exit points of the NZD/USD trade would be given, and the report would be checked out by a senior banker. That NZD/USD broker's report would then be sent out over the Internet to the bank's customers and clients.

Interest Rates and FX Pairs

The most important factor in FX pair valuation is the interest rates of the two currencies. Before you learn why that is true, you must realize that forecasting the change in the difference of interest rates between two currencies is the key to trading successfully and profitably. Your estimates of the direction of each element of a currency pair's interest rates will give you a bearing as to the best way to trade that pair: long or short. If you think that a currency pair is going to have its interest rate widen, then you would go long the currency that is increasing interest rates and sell the counter currency that is staying the same or reducing rates.

ALERT

> A good carry trade can be profitable for years. Traders all over the world put more and more bets in the carry-trade direction. It can seem too good to be true—until the point when the carry trade gets stretched too far. It will then collapse with a vengeance, crushing all long positions in its path!

Money is basically made with FX trading in two ways. The first is through capital gains; this is the money made from buying low and selling high. The second method is through **interest**. With this method, traders are entering in what is commonly called a carry trade. This carry trade is where a low-yielding currency is used to fund a buy into a high-yielding currency.

The FX trader pays interest in the low-yielding borrowed currency (anywhere from 0.25 percent to 0.05 percent annually) and can invest those funds at a higher rate (from 0.75 percent to near 7.25 percent historically). This makes for a kind of money machine where money is churned out through the **interest rate differential**. If you borrowed USD at 0.75 percent and used it to buy NZD at 7.25 percent, you would make 7.25 percent minus your borrowing cost of 0.75 percent for a yield of 6.5 percent. Not only that, but you would be making this investment at a leveraged amount, from 10:1 to 50:1. This means that at the high end of the leverage scale (50:1), you would make 325 percent annual interest (6.50% × 50). Also, since most FX trading platforms offer continuous compounding, you receive a daily payout of accumulated interest. This money can be added to your position for even more compounding!

With this in mind, a well-thought out idea of where a currency pair's interest rates are heading can give you the time advantage to get your trades in early enough to capture the inevitable movement of a FX pair that is changing its interest rate differential.

Your estimate can be supplemented with the information that is obtained from your broker's website, brokers' reports, and the **word on the street**. The word on the street refers to the thoughts that are being written and spoken about on news sources such as CNBC and Bloomberg. As you can see, the idea of where the interest rate for a currency is heading is key to making good trades.

More Currency Fundamentals

There are three forms of currency management that a central bank can undertake to regulate and control its home currency. One method is to forcibly link the value of the home currency to the value of a stronger currency. This method is called pegging and is done in many developing countries, such as those in Latin America and Asia. When a currency is pegged to another, its exchange rate is fixed. Not only that, but its growth rate and volume of money in circulation can also be related to the like amounts in the other country's economy. This is true because the home country's money value will be related to other currencies in the same up-and-down fashion as the movement of the assumed currency.

For example, China has long pegged its currency's exchange rate to the U.S. dollar. This means that the Chinese yuan is always the same value of a certain number of U.S. dollars. Since the value of the two is fixed, if the value of the USD goes down against the EUR, the value of the Chinese yuan will go down against the value of the EUR by the same amount. This technique of pegging the Chinese yuan to the USD has worked especially well for the Chinese economy. This is partially because the USD is the largest currency in volume of all the traded currencies in the world (over 62 percent in 2010) as reported on the Bank for International Settlements website (*www.bis.org/publ/rpfxf10t.htm*).

ESSENTIAL

Some currencies are managed in a monitored float that is similar to one that is pegged. The difference is that the currency is constantly adjusted to the benefit of the home country. A committee will usually adjust the rate of exchange up or down according to the home country's immediate needs. This is often called a "dirty float."

Many people believe that the reason the USD/CNY peg has worked so well for the Chinese economy is that the peg has historically been set at an artificially low rate, which in turn, many believe, has helped make China more competitive in the world market. This is one example of an effective use of a pegged currency.

Dollarization

The second method of monetary management that central banks can put into place is a method of **dollarization**. This is the method where a country's central bank gives up all control of its currency to the point of adopting the currency of another nation. The home country will usually adopt the currency of a neighbor that is a heavy-trading partner and has a history of economic stability. Examples of this would be the Caribbean Netherlands using the U.S. dollar, the Cook Islands using the New Zealand dollar, and Liechtenstein using the Swiss franc.

This method allows the greatest stability to these economic centers, but the use of a dollarization regime reduces the control of the central bank of these nations to next to nothing. They are at the full will and whim of the assumed currency and all of the interest rates and money supply growth and shrinkage that the assumed currency is assigned by those foreign central bankers. For all of its downfalls, the system works for smaller countries or ones with near and direct ties to their neighbors.

The Gold Standard and FX Trading

The third method is one called the floating rate system. This is the method of currency management that you should be most concerned with while you are looking for good FX trades to develop. Before you learn what is the floating rate system is, it would be best to go back about 150 years to the development and usage of a different system, the gold standard.

The gold standard was a method of monetary management that was initially developed and adopted by the Bank of England in the mid-1800s. This system was one in which a certain amount of the face value of paper money could be directly exchanged with a certain amount of gold. The amount of the paper money face value was essentially fixed to an amount of gold that was defined by weight and fineness.

Countries all over the world issued gold coins. In some of these countries the gold coins were only used to transfer wealth, not as a method of payment in everyday situations. There were, among others, Netherlands 10 guildens, .1947 ounce gold; Belgian 20 francs, .1867 ounce gold; and India 15 rupees, .2354 ounce of gold. These different monies were directly convertible into each other by the weight and fineness of each gold standard coin that the country issued.

In 1944, the world adopted an international gold standard that was based upon the convertibility of the currencies of Europe into the U.S. dollar, which was then in turn pegged to a certain weight and fineness of gold. The convertibility was simply $35 per ounce of .995+ fine gold.

The idea was simple. Instead of gold coins being circulated throughout Europe and the rest of the world in trade, they could be melted down, formed into 400-ounce bars, and stored at various vaults throughout the world. A home country would then issue paper money, and convert it into dollars, and then convert those dollars into gold, resulting in a kind of U.S. dollar/gold standard.

FACT

Pre-1944 foreign gold coins continue to be bought and sold to this day. It is common for investors to hedge stock, bond, and FX portfolios with a long gold position. These investors often buy gold coins because the coins are usually sold at only a few dollars above their gold value. This gold value is called a melt value.

This system of currency management was called the Bretton Woods Agreement, and came out of the aftermath of the heavy indebtedness caused by countries entering and fighting in World War II. The system was locked in place, and worked for some time until it became apparent that more gold was flowing out of the U.S. treasury than was flowing in. In fact, gold was flowing out at such a fast rate that on August 15, 1971, the President of the United States, Richard Nixon, effectively stopped the U.S. dollar/gold standard by halting all convertibility of U.S. dollars into gold, and therefore halting all shipments of gold out of the U.S. reserves.

The Floating-Rate Mechanism and Currency Trading

After the closing of the gold window by Nixon and the breakdown of the Bretton Woods Agreement, the world's main currencies began to move against each other based only upon supply and demand. This unmanaged (or only slightly managed) system is called the floating rate system. This means that the exchange rates between currencies and currency pair prices are not set by central banks. The central bankers of the home countries might have a target amount that they would like the currency to trade at; however, central banks that use the floating rate system usually do not put forces into motion to change the current market determined exchange rate.

This means that the exchange rate between the AUD and the NZD will be determined by currency markets alone, as well as demand for the goods and services between Australia and New Zealand. The same goes true for Europe, the United States, and most other countries. Most of the time, the market forces, supply, demand, and trade factors between the two countries will determine the market price for the EUR/USD pair, and other Forex pairs.

Sometimes a central bank will buy and sell its own currency in the FX market to change the price of its currency relative to a trading partner. This type of buying and selling was happening in Switzerland in late 2010 up until mid-2011. The Swiss National Bank was using its reserves to buy up massive quantities of euros in the open market. It also entered into derivative agreements such as repos and reverse repos to cool the price of its franc. The franc at the time was gaining nearly every week against the euro, mainly because of the worsening sovereign debt situation in Greece and other euro-bloc countries. At the time, FX traders looked at other safe, low-yielding currencies such as the JPY and the USD, but these too seemed as if they were not very good alternatives. Consequently the Swiss franc became the ultimate safe-haven currency, and was even touted as being safe as paper gold by some news sources.

ESSENTIAL

Safe-haven currencies are usually the lowest-yielding currencies in the world. The idea is that the lower yield of the currency usually equates to a lower price in the market. To carry the idea further, if the currency is already lower priced, it has less room to fall against other higher yielding currencies.

This trying time brought a rapid increase in the EUR/CHF exchange rate in favor of the Swiss franc. The Swiss National Bank thought it would be best to use its power and reserves to bring the franc to a more manageable price level. The methods used by the bank worked for a while, and the price of the franc lowered against the euro. The pressure became too great and the SNB gave up the fight: The Swiss franc continued its climb to record levels against the USD and the EUR.

This process, while rare, is called **intervening in the markets**. It is not a good idea to trade into an FX pair while a central bank is intervening in the markets, as the force of such intervention can be massive and sudden! Just the idea that a central bank will get into the markets should be a warning to you to stay clear of that currency until notice that the intervention has stopped. Most of the time with a floating rate currency regime, an FX pair will move up and down as the market moves. These are the best currencies to trade. Their movement is smooth, and can be tracked and predicted through fundamental analysis.

CHAPTER 7

Managing Margin and Risk Management Techniques

When you are trading currencies you will be setting your margin ratio much higher than with a normal stock margin account. Since these margin levels are so high, you will need to understand the dynamic of how to use your margin account for maximum effectiveness. You will also need to know how to prevent a margin call by dismantling your positions one trade at a time. Lastly, this chapter will also cover some risk management techniques such as position pyramiding and the 2 percent rule.

Think of It as a Cash Account

In order to safely navigate the world of currency trading, you must first get the perspective that your Forex account is actually a cash account. In other words, you should be thinking of your Forex account as a bucket of money that can be used for trading. If you are always in a trade, your account never quite gets back to being in full cash.

You must always keep hold of the idea that cash is where you started and cash is where you will ultimately end. Thinking this way, you will soon get the idea that you will only get into a currency trade if there is a very good chance of getting out of the trade with your cash intact and, you hope, with a bit of interest or capital gain to boot.

One of the best ways to think of FX trading is to remember that your account is a cash account that *temporarily* goes out of cash and into a currency trade. Your risk appetite can be taken from this perspective. This will also give you the perspective needed to think of your Forex trading endeavors in a way that will allow you to build up enough **free-cash flow** to make withdrawals. These withdrawals can then be used to pay your bills, etc.

Free-cash flow is the amount of money that your account generates beyond the additions of cash that you have put in. In other words, free-cash flow is the organic growth of the account. It is the same as the balance in the account minus the amount that has been deposited by you. This free-cash flow is the ultimate goal of the professional currency trader.

FACT

> The term *free-cash flow* is an accounting term that is used in when preparing a cash-flow statement. Just as in a normal business, you can prepare a cash-flow statement for your currency trading business. Cash-flow statements comprise the money generated from operations (trading) minus money expenses, plus money deposited in your account.

Professional currency traders usually borrow the money that they use to deposit in their accounts. They might put up a small percentage of their own money, but the majority of the money is borrowed against other securities in other accounts. If the currency traders have high credit worthiness and the quality of the collateral is very good, then they will pay a lower interest on the borrowed monies. If they have a lower credit rating or the quality of the collateral is lower than the best, the professional currency trader will pay a higher interest rate on the borrowed funds.

These borrowed funds act as the trading capital of the professional Forex trader. If the trader has the average collateral that includes stocks, bonds, and CDs as her collateral, and her credit rating is above average, the rate is most likely the same rate as it would be to borrow on margin at a stock broker's firm. This rate is usually 5 percent to 7 percent more than the prime rate. If the prime rate (the rate for the bank's best customers) is 3.5 percent, then the professional Forex broker will pay 8.5 percent to 10.5 percent yearly interest on the borrowing of the funds for trading.

You divide the yearly interest rate into a daily rate and you consider this daily rate an expense to be deducted from the free-cash flow. This is one form of funding and expensing of a Forex account. You can use your own expenses to determine the free-cash flow that your Forex trading delivers on a weekly and biweekly basis.

Keeping Your Cash in Perspective

Once you understand that your currency trading goal should be to produce free-cash flow, you then see that cash flow can only be made from being in cash. With that said, the more you are returning to cash after a trade with your gains intact, the more safe your account will be and the more you will be reassuring yourself that your trading account is acting as a cash account.

You must remember, Forex trading can be a source of income for you, and you can produce a steady stream of paychecks coming out of your account. In order to send yourself a paycheck you will have to think of your trading as a source of income primarily and as entertainment secondarily.

With this in mind, you would do well to consider your account as a cash account first and a trading account second. A cash account's main goal is to be in 100 percent liquid cash. The cash is ready to be used for any purpose needed, including buying into a trade when the time is right. After trading for a few weeks and months, you will most likely find yourself in positions where you would love to have more cash and more margin available to buy into that day's best trade.

ESSENTIAL

Keep your Forex trading objectives in mind when you are thinking of your cash account. Whether you are trading for some extra cash, for enough profit to buy a new car, or for enough profit to live off of, keep these trading goals in mind when you consider that your account is a cash account first.

Keep Your Money in Perspective

You will go a long way in keeping your trading account intact if you consider that the money in your account is just that, real money. All too often it seems that traders get away from the fact that they are trading with actual money, and that this is the same money that can also be used for needs that are more basic than trading (such as paying rent, etc.). You will have to realize this when you have a big balance in your account. It often seems that a $1,000, $1,500 or $2,500 balance in some form of trading account is not really that much. The fact is, if someone handed you an envelope stuffed with $2,500 worth of $20 bills, you would most likely think you had a lot of money. It is sometimes hard to grasp the same feeling for the same amount of money when the money is in an electronic format.

With this in mind, you should work to keep a good perspective on what the balance in your trading account actually is (money) and what you can do with it in the world outside of currency trading. A well-rooted idea of cash/money/margin/Forex can keep your account and your currency trading viewed in a positive light within yourself. It can also help you when it comes time to review your trades. It is common to think of your profit as never enough, and to think that you are not earning enough with the money you have invested.

All Gains Add to Your Cash Account

If you are thinking of the money in your account as cash that can be used in the outside world to pay bills and enjoy, then you will view your trading gains as tiny little gifts that add to your cash balance. In this way your cash account will be growing little by little, and the primary focus will be to create just that: a cash account that has very good returns. If you do keep this perspective, you will view a night of trading that earns you $25 (or some other number that is otherwise unacceptable) as a profitable night. There are times that you will feel lucky to earn only $25 dollars that trading session. Perhaps it is a night of really bad news that has caught you off guard and on the wrong side of the trade. Perhaps the markets went south during the overnight session and you had most of your account in short U.S. dollar and Swiss franc trades. Either way, there are many times when you will feel lucky to walk away from a trading session $25 (or sometimes less!) richer.

If you do not have the perspective that your FX account is basically a cash account and that you are trying to enhance your returns, then you will be losing the perspective that your account is cash first and gains second. Further, you will begin to think of your FX account as a cash account that will have buying power. Buying power is related to what utility can be had from the money in the account, whether it is used to pay bills, buy a new car, or buy loads of a carry trade for a well-run and tightly managed investment portfolio. With this in mind, you should always be thinking of the value of your FX account as a cash account: This perspective will go a long way in keeping your account safe and profitable.

ALERT

Look for all of your returns when considering how much you have made with Forex. Sometimes you are making very little cash, but you are gaining in other ways. You might be gaining by working the risk bug out of your system; this can then get you to the point that your main portfolio is invested in super-safe securities!

How to Think about Margin

When you put money in your account and you are leveraged up 10:1, 20:1, or 50:1, you are multiplying the amount of money you put into the account by the gearing of the margin number. If you put in $1,000, and your margin ratio is set at 50:1, you are actually able to purchase $1,000 × 50 = $50,000 worth of currencies in that account. The margin acts as kind of a loan against your balance. Much like when you put money down on the purchase of a home, you will be putting money down on the purchase of the currencies.

Most home purchases require 5 to 20 percent down, and the remaining 80 to 95 percent of the balance is financed. The banks that are in the business of giving home loans are not in the business of losing on the mortgages they give out. This is precisely why they ask for money down. This is the amount that the home will fall in value if the bank has to take over the mortgage and sell it at what is often referred to as a fire sale. Fire sale prices are the prices that the homes will sell for in a one-day auction. If the market is bad, then the reserve or the down payment will be hiked up to cover any potential losses by the bank.

The same idea exists in the Forex business. The required ratio at 50:1 is actually 2 percent cash down on the loan to buy securities (currency pairs.) At 20:1 the deposit is 5 percent, and at 10:1 the deposit is 10 percent. As you can see, by nature and mathematics, a 10:1 ratio is safer than a 50:1 margin ratio strictly because you have more money as a deposit.

As you put more money in your account, you will be able to trade with more capital, as the loan is extended further and further up to the limit of your cash balance. You will also earn interest at the prevailing rate on the cash balance in your account (as well as any interest on any trades that have a positive interest differential).

Margin Call Basics

After you have deposited money into your Forex account, you will then have to set the amount of margin ratio that you would like to trade at, whether it is 10:1, 20:1, or 50:1. Once you establish your margin ratio, the next thing you will have to do is determine how much of that margin amount you will use at any one time. If you are setting up a long-term trade, you might only use 10 percent of the available margin. If you are doing an overnight-hedged trade, you might use 33 percent of your available margin, and if you are setting up a short-term scalping trade, you might decide to use 50 percent of your available margin. This means that if you were trading at 50:1 and you had a balance of $1,000 in your account, you would be able to use $16,666 at a time (this is using 33 percent of your account for an overnight trade). Shown mathematically it looks like this:

$$\$1{,}000 \times 50 = \$50{,}000 \times 33\% = \$16{,}666$$

While more profit can be squeezed out of your account when you utilize more of your available margin, the more you use, the more chance you run of getting a margin call. Most Forex brokerage firms have a set floor as to the amount that a trade can reach before it is automatically closed out in what is called a margin call. A margin call is when the cash equity in the account falls below a level that is sufficient to keep the trade liquid. It is usually 5 percent to 10 percent the value of the open trades. If this level is breeched, then you will get a margin call. When you get a margin call, the Forex broker will not actually call you and give you time to get new money in the account. They will just automatically close out all trades that you have on the books, whether they are gainers or losers.

FACT

Your cash balance to margin amount ratio is often called your skin in the game. When you have skin in the game, you will be taken very seriously by other investors. When you have your own money at risk when trading, you are considered to be in the big time, no matter what your balance.

Getting a margin call can be very disruptive to currency trading. This is because the positions are closed out before they have the chance to return to a point of profit, or at least return to the point that they can be closed out at a zero. Since this is a very bad and unprofitable thing, many experts recommend that you set your Forex trading software to alert you when that margin level is getting close. This alert is easy to arrange. You can set up the software to e-mail or text you when a margin call is getting close, and the warning gives you time to get more money in the account.

If you notice that you are close to getting a margin call or the broker notifies you by e-mail or text that a call is near, you have two options. The first one is the easiest. You can simply make sure that you make a cash deposit into the account before it is automatically closes out. Depending upon the overall size of your account, it may not take that much more deposited money to get your account back in the safe zone. Since depositing more money in your Forex account might be easier said than done, the next best thing to do is to close out of one of your positions.

Margin Call Management and Prevention

It can be very unprofitable to be in a series of trades and have your Forex brokerage account drop to a value that you are close to having a margin call. If you have a large account and three, four, five, or more trades on the books, and you are forced into a margin call, you are running the risk of completely destroying your entire account. A margin call can be prevented by putting more money in the account. If this can't be done, then the next best thing to do is to begin to dismantle the trades you have in your account in an effort to free up margin.

One of the best ways to do this is first to analyze your positions and close out your winning trades. This would be the best first step, as most professional money managers, traders, and currency traders know that the first thing you sell when you are close to a margin call is your winners. Begin selecting the trades in your account that can be sold off in a step-by-step fashion, starting with the oldest first. Once you have selected the oldest trades, the next thing is to select the trades that are anywhere near profitable. Choose the most profitable ones first and close out of them.

ESSENTIAL

> Some of the rules of currency trading have changed lately. The U.S.-based regulators have gotten in on the picture and have changed some of the basic rules of FX trading to better protect U.S.-based traders. Lower margins, better reporting, and fuller registration requirements of Forex money managers are some of the recent changes brought on by U.S. regulators.

If you have several trades building up on one currency pair, the possibility of a margin call will force you to close out the oldest one of the grouping first. In the United States, closing multiple trades in the same currency pair must be done in a first-in, first-out basis. This means that you will have to close out the first trade that you used to buy into the currency pair first, *even if it is at a loss, and later trades are gains.* This rule is one of the reasons that it is best to pyramid your trades in a multistep method of purchasing. If you go all into a position in one swoop, you are running the risk that you will have to dismantle the whole trade at a loss sometime in the future.

After selling off your winners, take notice of the amount of margin available you have posted on your trading screen. You will undoubtedly have noticed that the amount has gone up considerably, and most likely you are out of the danger zone. The next best thing to do now is to wait. Wait for the trades to turn in your favor, if even by just a bit. Every cent matters in currency trading. A cent on a trade can mean a lot when you are trading at high margin–ratio levels.

With this idea in mind, you can see where building up a position in smaller sections can really help out when it comes time to close out those same positions. If you have used the pyramid method of one-third, one-third, one-third, or better yet, one-fifth, one-fifth, one-fifth, one-fifth, one-fifth of your margin goal building up a position, then you will have greater flexibility when it comes time to dismantle the same position at the time of a margin call.

The method of **pyramiding** a position can also be very helpful when it comes time to close out and dismantle a position that is profitable. You can switch to the part of your trading software that gives the status of your positions. It will tell you the net number of units per pair (grouped together) and it will also tell you your net profit for the group of trades that are all in the same currency pair. If you are in a profit point that is good for you, then you can start to dismantle the position one trade at a time. It might be that you want to reduce your exposure to a currency pair by a third or a half. When you have built up the position in smaller bites, you can reduce your position in the same smaller bites, and get it down to the size you would like and feel more comfortable with.

The 2 Percent Rule and Risk Management

One of the ways that you can set up your account to prevent any chance of a margin call is called the 2 percent rule. The 2 percent rule is a method of setting your stop losses to be no more than 2 percent of your total margin balance. Setting stop losses is when you program the software to close out of a trade at a predetermined point automatically. Once you set up a stop loss it will fire automatically when that price level is breeched. The use of stop losses is one of the best methods of preventing an all-out disaster in your account. Setting stop losses can be one of the best methods to keeping your Forex account intact during harsh market conditions.

When you are going to set up your stop losses you can use the 2 percent rule. By nature, if you are trading with a smaller amount, you would be able to place your stop losses at a further price difference away from the original purchase price. If you have a large position on the books, then the placement of the stop loss would be that much closer to the purchase price. To explain this further, if you have a total of $10,000 available margin, 2 percent of this would be $200. You would keep this number in your mind when you were going to the order entry screen. When you are buying into a trade you would then set the amount of units (money) that you are to buy at that time. Before you click the "Submit" button, go to the "Stop Loss" part of the order-entry screen and enter in a price level at which you would like the trade automatically to close out. Take notice of the amount of money that you will lose if the trade goes through at that level and closes out at that price point. Keep adjusting the price of the stop-loss level until it reaches "loss amount = $200." Once you find this price level, you are ready to go. Next, you need to confirm the amounts mentally, and then click "Place Order."

ESSENTIAL

You can get familiar with using the 2 percent rule when you are using your practice demo account. Practice many of the ideas presented in this book by working out your skills in a demo account that is the same type you intend to trade with. Learn the skills required for currency trading by practicing often!

You should do the same thing for any amount of currency that you buy. If you purchase a smaller amount, then there will be more room built into the length that the pair can travel before triggering the $200 loss. If your purchase is a large amount, the price will naturally have to move less to trigger a $200 loss.

Using the 2 percent rule and keeping your losses to within 2 percent of your total account value is doing two things. One, it is keeping you within a range of profit and loss that is easy to visualize and gauge with each trade. Second, keeping your losses to 2 percent for each trade means that you will lose a maximum of 2 percent of your margin with each trade; or in other words, you will never lose more than 2 percent of your account if a trade goes bad or against you. Carrying this out further, if you used the 2 percent rule for each and every trade, you would be able to lose 50 trades in a row before your account was closed out with a balance of zero (100% × 2% = 50). The idea of losing fifty trades in a row is almost inconceivable, and would rarely happen. It would be more likely that you would win a number of those trades, and this would add to your available margin.

Either way, understanding how your margin works and using stop losses effectively will help you keep your account in profitable territory. If you can work in a bit of risk management by using position pyramiding and also the 2 percent rule, you will be going a long way toward keeping yourself net positive over the weeks and months. You will also be giving yourself a proven method of risk management that goes beyond what most Forex traders work into their trading systems.

CHAPTER 8

Technical Analysis

Technical analysis is the study of the currency pair in its graphic form. If you can learn to look at the charts and use your trading platform to plot and draw some basic technical indicators, you will be well on your way to developing a rock solid trading system. This chapter will get you started into the whys and hows of basic technical analysis and show you how to use it to help you make strong currency trading decisions.

Charts, Graphs, and a Bit of Magic

After you study the fundamental information and begin to look at three or four ideas for trades, you should shift your perspective to the technical analysis of those currency pairs. Technical analysis is the reading of charts and market-trading indicators and assessing the optimal time for getting into a currency pair. It is often used for looking at short-time trading patterns, and if used properly, will enable you to get a feel for the best time to enter and exit the trades that were previously confirmed by your fundamental analysis.

Technical analysis uses a combination of statistics, regression analysis, charts, and graphs to allow you to look at the market and trading pairs in a graphic fashion. It is also based upon the theory that you should trade on the charts and graph indicators only and totally ignore what the fundamental information is telling you. Traders who are experienced or certified in technical analysis are putting their faith in their craft based upon three ideas.

There is usually a lot of noise in the information that is presented in currency trading. This noise is the information that, if followed, can lead you into the wrong trade times even though you have the right idea of what to trade. The idea behind technical analysis is that you allow the charts and graphs along with the fundamental information to filter out the noise, and allow you to hear a clear signal as to what to trade and when to trade it.

FACT

If you learn to use technical information and like to produce your own technical analysis, then you might want to study and apply for the Chartered Market Technician (CMT) designation and qualification. To qualify for the CMT, you need to pass three exams based upon technical analysis. Information can be found at *www.mta.org/eweb/StartPage.aspx*.

There are several basic charts and indicators that are used in technical analysis. Whether you use a candlestick chart, regression analysis, Elliott wave principles, resistance levels, or moving averages, the ideas are the same: You take the mathematics behind the currency pairs and either draw lines or use statistics to come up with estimates as to when is a good time to trade.

Some charts can be drawn quite easily on your FX trading platform directly. In order to do this, go to your trading platform and go to the section marked "Technical Indicators." You can then select the indicator you would like to use, and that technical indicator will then be drawn on your chart. Other indicators are more active in nature; you draw them on the chart by selecting the indicator, and then drawing the line from the points you are trying to analyze.

An Example of Charts and Indicators

This is a picture of a chart from Windsor Brokers showing the EUR/CHF pair in a fifteen-minute chart. As you can see, the euro is getting stronger against the Swiss franc. At the end of the time frame the Swiss franc has gained strength, shown by its drop below the fifty-day moving average line (the thick graceful waving line).

You can also see the manual drawing of **Fibonacci series** lines that are drawn from the lowest point of the chart, when the euro was weakest (shown by the fan-like grouping of three lines). As you can see, the chart has come back up after just touching the bottom Fibonacci line. At this point the euro is regaining strength against the Swiss franc (remember, the chart will go up when the first of the pair, or EUR, gets stronger against the second of the pair, or CHF).

ESSENTIAL

You can use your trading platform to practice drawing Fibonacci series lines on your charts. To do this, simply call up a chart and click on the "Technical Indicators" section of your software. You can then drop a pin at the lowest valley in the chart and drag a Fibonacci series line to the most recent time on the chart.

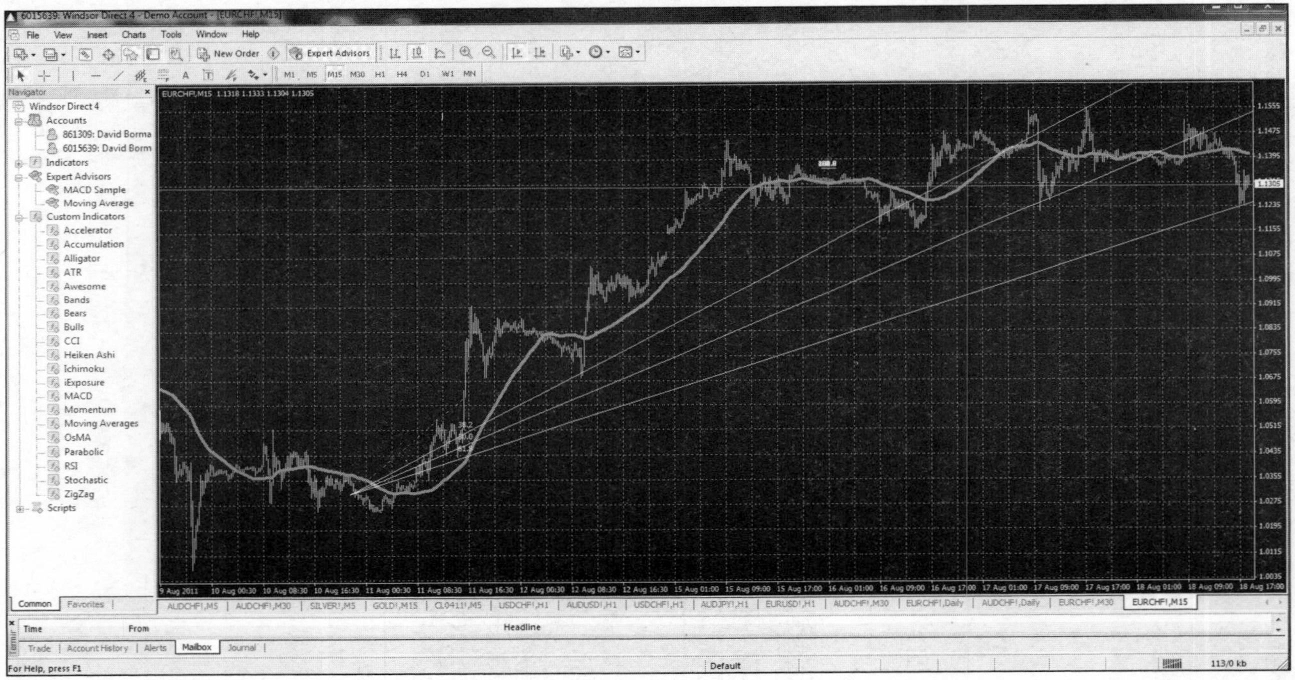

A fifteen-minute chart from Windsor Brokers, showing the EUR/CHF pair.

This upward movement has happened for many reasons, and one of the reasons is that the Fibonacci series is a technical indicator that traders use to determine reversal points of currency pairs. In this case, the mid-line is the average of the EUR/CHF pair, and the lower line is the support point of the pair. Technical traders use this bottom line to determine the point that the pair (in this case the EUR/CHF), will have difficulties breaking through. In other words, there is a support at this level. In fact, this is what your broker's reports will be referring to when they give advice about an FX pair: Your FX broker will issue a report that will say, "The EUR/CHF has support at this level, etc." These are two examples of using technical indicators to help you determine the timing of an otherwise previously determined currency trade.

The Theories Behind Technical Analysis

You can learn to use technical indicators to strengthen your conviction as to when it is the appropriate time to get into a trade and get out of a trade. If you allow the three basic ideas of the professional technical traders to be true, you would accept the reading of the charts to supplement your fundamental analysis.

▼ TABLE 8-1: THE THREE THEORIES BEHIND TECHNICAL ANALYSIS

Theory Name	Description of Theory
Crowd Psychology	Crowds move in the same direction
Efficient Market Hypothesis	All information is reflected in the pair's exchange rate
Pairs Revert to the Mean	History repeats itself

The crowd psychology idea allows you to accept the fact that if an FX pair is moving along a path, then it will most likely continue to move along that path in the same direction. With crowd psychology, the thinking is that the pair will continue to move along the path in the same direction until there is an event to change the ideas of the people in the crowd (the other

FX traders in the market). This continuing along the same path happens because everyone in the FX market has access to the same information (efficient markets hypothesis).

FACT

The development of the efficient markets hypothesis (EMH) has a long history, starting with a financial model designed by a French stockbroker Jules Regnault in the 1860s. Around 1900 that model was developed further mathematically by Louis Bachelier, and then finalized by Eugene Fama in the 1960s.

With everyone following everyone else, a huge momentum can develop. This is true because as the FX pair starts to move (up or down), it will gain strength and speed as the rest of the world's currency traders jump in and place their trading bets in the same direction. This has the effect of pushing the FX pair further into the direction, which further strengthens the idea of the movement in the minds of the FX traders, who in turn pile on more currency bets in that pair's direction. This constant addition will go on and on until a change in the crowd psychology comes along, whether based upon fundamental or technical information. The crowd will all get the same idea at once and the FX pair will begin to reverse itself (the idea that pairs revert to the mean), and begin to pick up steam moving in the opposite direction. This movement will continue until the process repeats, and the crowd, again, goes in the opposite direction.

With a few charts and these theories, you can use the technical data like a form of magic to help you determine if and when to enter into a trade. You can predict when the trade is about to reverse, and when it is a good time to take your profits and run (before the crowd shifts its sentiment of the currency pair you are trading).

Candlestick and Line Charts

When you are first getting ready to build a FX technical chart you will need to choose the currency pair. Say, for example, you are going to look for indicators in the EUR/CHF pair. You have read the brokers' reports and finished studying the fundamentals. Some of the fundamental indicators that helped you decide on a long EUR/CHF trade were a reading of the Swiss National Bank (*www.snb.ch*) website and a reading of the news reports on the website DailyFX (*www.dailyfx.com*). You have decided that the Swiss franc has appreciated quite a bit against the euro, and that the euro will regain strength, if even for the short term.

In order to look at this EUR/CHF pair on a chart, you would first have to draw one. Most Forex brokers will allow you to call up either a **candlestick chart** or a bar chart. Some will allow you to do both. If that is the case, you can go ahead and switch between the two at the click of a mouse, and then you can decide which one best works for you.

The candlestick chart, also known as a Japanese candlestick chart, appears as a series of vertical lines on the graph, representing prices, and time of days across the bottom of the chart. For example, if you are going to draw a fifteen-minute EUR/CHF candlestick chart, the computer software of your trading platform will show the prices of the pair up and down on the chart and the time over several days in fifteen-minute intervals along the bottom of chart. Additionally, the actual prices of the EUR/CHF pair will show up, one for every fifteen minutes of trading. Small lines of red and green will indicate not only the price of the pair for each fifteen minutes, but also the range of the trading, which will be indicated by the length of the red and green lines. A red line indicates that it moved down, and a green line indicates that the pair moved up during that fifteen minutes.

Line charts are a bit easier and more intuitive to use than a bar chart. With a fifteen-minute line chart, each open and close of those fifteen minutes will be indicated by a notch at the left and right of the longer up and down line. If the pair had moved up and down along that opening price, the line will show its range by being longer or shorter to cover the prices that the pair was at during those fifteen minutes. At the end of the fifteen minutes the close price will be indicated by a notch on the line to the right of the longer up and down line. On a full-size laptop computer with a 15- or 17-inch screen, the lines on a fifteen-minute chart may be ½ to 1 centimeter long to indicate the movement of a pair, such as the EUR/CHF, within that time frame. Each fifteen-minute range line is close to another, and the total effect is a semismooth line across your computer screen showing your trading platform and its EUR/CHF chart.

ALERT

It sometimes helps to look at a range of time frames on your bar charts. You can look at a one-day chart to get an overview of what direction the currency is moving, and switch to ever-shorter time frames. At the very end you can use a thirty-second chart to time your FX trade precisely.

Using Moving Averages to Time Your Trades

After you have signaled your trading platform's software to draw a bar chart for the currency pair EUR/CHF, the next technical indicator that you can use is the 50-day moving average and the 200-day moving average. These moving averages use statistical formulas of the openings, closings, or averages of the EUR/CHF pair for the past 200 or 50 days on a rolling basis. This means that 200-day moving average will drop day 201 and add day 1 the next day you look at the chart. Also, the chart is rolling as to time; i.e., if you are on a one-hour chart, the 200 days × twenty-four hours will be looked at, and then in one hour the 199 days plus twenty-three hours will be factored in plus the most recent hour of the trading week. The same is true for the 50-day moving average.

Once you have the fifteen-minute (or other time frame) bar chart drawn on your trading platform, you can easily use one of your drop-down boxes in the "Technical Indicators" section of the commands in your software. You will most likely see a series of commands in the "Add Technical Indicators" drop-down box: Select the one that is marked "Moving Average." You can draw any number of days for this indicator. First make the selection of a 200-day in a contrasting, colored thick line, and then in a different colored thick line make the selection for a 50-day moving average.

This will draw two lines across the chart. In this example, the EUR/CHF is shown on a one-hour chart. The jagged up and down line with the valley are the effect of the one-hour bars showing up in the chart all compressed together. The 50-day and 200-day moving averages are shown by the graceful lines that somewhat follow the curve of the one-hour bar chart.

Since the 50-day moving average is more sensitive to changes in price, it more closely follows the bar chart: It is shown in the example with the lighter line. The 200-day moving average is less sensitive and moves in an even more slowly sloping pattern. The 200-day moving average is shown by the darker line.

After you have used your trading platform to draw a one-hour bar chart, a 50-day moving average, and a 200-day moving average, you can then use the moving averages as indicators. The easiest way to use the moving averages is to draw the 50- and the 200-day upon each other and look where they cross. As you can see, in this example, they cross in three places. At each point where the 50-day and the 200-day moving average cross, the direction of the EUR/CHF pair is changing direction, and that new direction should continue for a length of time.

You can see in this example the theory holds true: the direction change is indicated by the crossing of the two moving averages, the 50- and the 200-day moving averages. At the end of the chart, you can see that the 50- and the 200-day moving averages are beginning to converge again. If you allow you chart to be "live" and set the 50- and 200-day to move along with the chart as time progresses, you will eventually see when the 50- and 200-day moving averages converge once again. When this happens, it would be a good time to consult your fundamental information (brokers' reports,

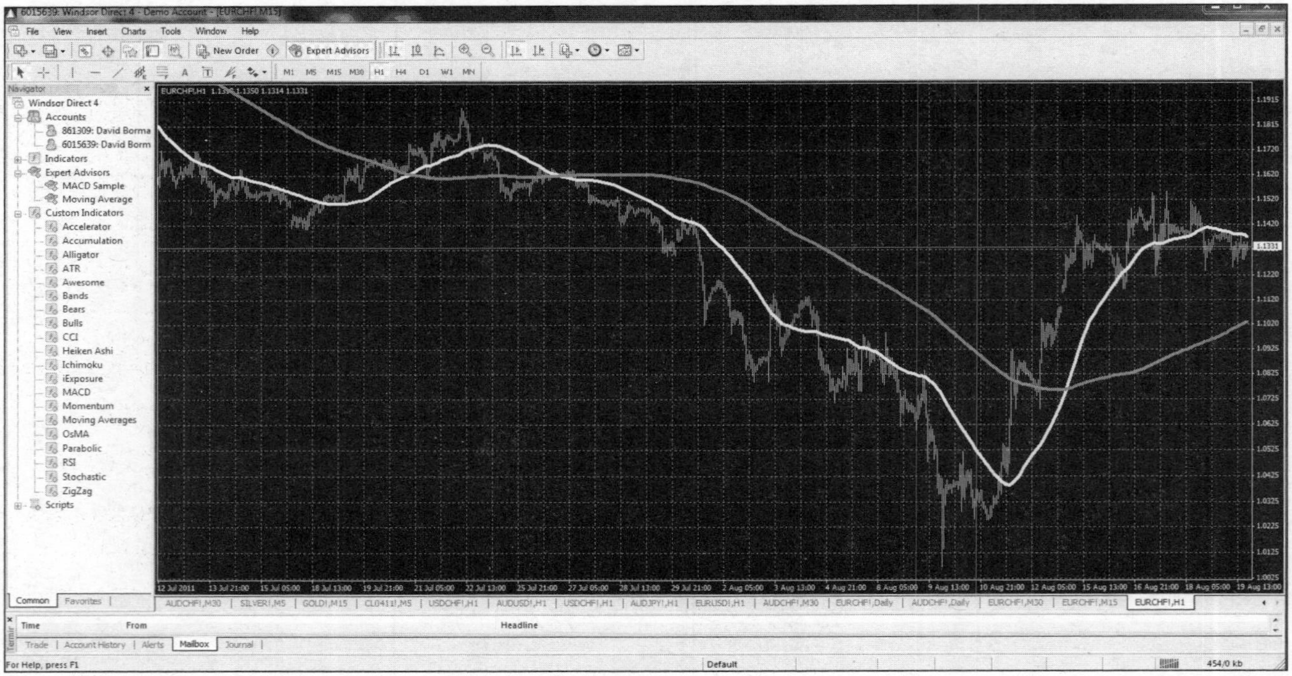

A one-hour chart showing the EUR/CHF pair.

economics, interest rate expectations, etc.) to reconsider changing the direction of your bets. If the fundamentals reconfirm it, and the technical indicator of the 50-day and 200 day-indicators are also telling that same tale, together you have what can be a very strong signal that the direction of your currency pair is changing. The direction of the currency pair might change for only a few days, but as you know, all it takes is a few days of movement to make a week's worth of salary trading currencies.

ESSENTIAL

Once you have noticed the establishment of a crossover point between the 200-day and 50-day moving averages, you can back up your observations by looking for crossover points between a 100-day moving average and a 20-day moving average. If they tell the same story, you are in luck! A trend is definitely developing.

Support and Resistance Indicators

Another set of indicators that you can use is called the support and resistance indicators. The idea behind the support and resistance indicators is the thought that there is a mathematical and statistical price level of all currency pairs that is difficult to pass through. Most brokerage firms offer information as to the mid- and upper-support and resistance levels of the FX pairs that they cover. A broker's report or news service such as DailyFX (*www.dailyfx.com*) or FXStreet (*www.fxstreet.com*) can give you quick data as to these support and resistance indicators.

Support and resistance are price levels that are not only difficult to pass through, they also offer a psychological indicator for FX traders. Support and resistance indicators are mathematically calculated places for a particular currency pair to naturally stop its downward (support) or upward (resistance) movement. These lines are estimates taken from historical closing levels for the previous several months, psychologically significant levels, and graphic lines called Fibonacci lines.

It is more important to know how these support and resistance lines are created than how to create them yourself. If you know the basics of what they mean, you can jump right to using them in your trading plan. Sometimes it is just as good to know how to use a statistical or technical indicator rather than to spend a lot of time trying to run a lot of scenarios and then trying to come up with your own fresh information. The idea is similar to knowing how to drive, or first having to know how to design a car: if you really want to get somewhere, then just turn the key and go; you don't need a degree in mechanical engineering to drive your car to the grocery store!

FACT

Some Forex news-feed services offer excellent quality technical analysis. It usually costs to have access to these reports, but paying for this high-quality information can help you get on to actually trading FX, or at the very least help back up your own technical analysis.

The same is true for resistance and support lines. Since almost all news feeds, brokers' reports, and FX trading websites will be publishing first and second support and resistance lines for every currency pair, spend your time learning how to use the information instead of creating the information. After getting to know how to use this type of technical information to time your trades effectively, you might want to consider reading and studying how to create your own data. In the meantime, use the sources of information you have. Since technical analysis is somewhat of a science, most professional technical analysts will be coming up with the same information and will publish the same support and resistance levels (give or take) to their readers. That is one of the advantages to subscribing to higher-end news services and having access to full-service brokers' reports: Much of the work is done for you!

More on the Technical Indicators

Fibonacci lines are taken from a theory that there are three levels of a currency pair's peaks and valleys. Lines are drawn from the lowest to highest point in the time frame. The three levels are then drawn at preset, statistically significant levels. Entry and exit points are then determined from these numerically significant levels. Modern FX technical analysts use software to draw the line directly onto trading platform charts. These levels are observed by currency traders all over the world: that is precisely why some support and resistance levels have such significance. The world's traders know that if a level is breached that the other traders will observe it and react strongly either positively or negatively, depending upon the direction of their positions.

FACT

For a bit of background, the theory of Fibonacci lines and its three levels of resistance is based upon the golden ratio and was first introduced by Fibonacci (also known as the Leonardo of Pisa) in a book he wrote in 1202 called *Liber Abaci* (Book of Calculation).

Once one level is broken through, in theory there will soon be a breach of the second level, and then after the second level is breached, there will be quick movement to the third level. These quick movements through levels are true for support and resistance: It is the breaching of the level that is important, not the direction, as there will be winners and losers to each upward or downward movement of a currency pair. Once you understand and begin to use the support and resistance indicators in your trading, you will be well on your way to using one of the strongest technical indicators to supplement your fundamental research.

Draw and Interpret Your Own Charts

You can learn to take the main technical indicators and draw charts on your trading platform's software. You can learn to use candlestick and bar charts to get a graphic visualization of where a currency pair has been and is heading. You can use the chart to watch the FX pair move up and down over time, and choose between long- and short-term time horizons. Longer-term time horizons such as one-hour and one-day charts can be used for an overall picture of what is happening to a currency pair. Shorter time frames such as fifteen-, five-, and one-minute charts can help you on the tactical, immediate timing of when it is a good time for an entry point.

Once you have your basic chart drawn, you can then move on to using the moving averages. Use your software to draw a 200-day and a 50-day moving average in different colors. Take note as to where the moving average lines cross: these are where the direction of the FX pair is likely to change, whether up or down. Take this information and cross-reference it with the information you have gathered from your trading journal. Make note in your trading journal of when the 200-day and 50-day moving average will cross again. Some Forex brokers allow you to plot a free-form line on your chart. If this is the case with your broker's software, use the option to sketch lines to arrive at an estimate where the 200-day and 50-day will again cross in the future. Draw a line across and down. Make note of what that time is and at what price the cross will most likely take place. Use your software to drop a permanent pin at this point on the chart, and make a note in your trading journal.

Become a Proactive Trader

This is one method of actively looking for entry and exit points using a bit of math and logic, and being proactive in your trading, not being reactive. Observe your predictive results. If it seems that you are getting good at this type of predictive analysis, then take it to the next level and begin to place the appropriate long or short trades in your demonstration or practice account. Observe again, and take notes as to how the market reacts at this time and at this price of the FX pair.

You can learn how to use technical indicators as a form of a hard science to bolster your observations in the fundamental information universe.

The combination of learning through planned observation and then moving on to place experimental trades in a demo account coupled with fundamental analysis can really get you a strong trading system that can predict and allow you to be proactive in your trades. As you know, a strong trading system is the foundation for keeping your FX account in the profit range over the developing trading days, and will keep you in the Forex trading game.

CHAPTER 9

Developing a Trading System

Trading systems use a combination of past trading data and computer modeling as a form of decision science to help determine the quality of a potential FX trade. After looking at a currency pair's fundamentals and the economic data, and performing technical analysis, you can use a trading system to help confirm a potential profitable FX trade. This chapter will show you how to build a statistics-based system on Microsoft (MS) Excel using data found on the Internet. You will then learn how to modify and tune your new trading system to your needs.

Finding Data for Your Program

The most basic of trading systems use past data to test the probability of future events. You can set up a very simple system that can help you determine the potential for a currency pair to move in an either up-or-down direction using a combination of past closing prices of currency ETFs and economic indicator ETFs. You can build a system such as this using information (called data points) off websites such as Yahoo! Finance and Google Finance. Once you have the required information, you can arrange the data points on MS Excel and perform simple regression analysis to build a model that can predict with a high degree of accuracy the direction of your target currency pair, and to a lesser extent, the percentage of that FX pair's movement.

The programming of MS Excel isn't hard, and the real value is the part where you find your own data to fit into the model you are building. This means that although anyone can learn how to build a system such as this, the real challenge lies in finding combinations of data that have meaning and influence in the direction and percentage movement in the target currency pair.

FACT

Regression analysis is usually the place where many hedge funds begin their numbers-driven, quantitative-trading programs. These highly automated, highly tuned funds use historical data, mathematics, and lightning-fast computers to create trading systems that can be adjusted, updated, and refined continuously during the trading day.

To begin, you are trying to find which combinations of ETFs influence the target ETF. In essence, you might ask your model how much the JPY ETF, SEK ETF, EUR ETF, S&P 500 ETF, VIX ETF, Dollar Index ETF, TIP Index ETF, or any combination of other ETFs influences (and if so, by how much) a target currency ETF.

The first step in building any trading system using regression analysis is to find as many factors that might possibly influence the target ETF or currency pair. In this case, the more the merrier, as at your first run at spinning the wheel you will learn with precision which inputs have a say in the direction and percentage movement of your trading target.

ETFs as Prepackaged Data Points

With this in mind, you should first determine your target currency pair, which will be represented by proxy in the corresponding currency ETF. The second step is make a list of four to seven or even more possible factors that influence the target currency pair. The key is to find proxy ETFs that track or duplicate the direction and percentage movement of that potential influencing factor. You know that fundamental, economic, and technical indicators influence the direction of a currency pair. Many of these indicators are prepackaged in ETF investment vehicles for the public to track and trade. With a little research (by searching "ETF list" in Google), you will find listings of many ETFs that track indicators that you can use as inputs in your model. There are ETFs for VIX, Inflation, T-bill prices, the S&P 500, gold, overseas indexes, and other currencies. After performing a search, you can choose a number of ETFs that are traded in the U.S. markets that you can use to build your trading system.

ESSENTIAL

The greater the number of observations you have in your regression analysis model, the more accurate it will become. The minimum you should aim for is 100. Finding this many observations should not be a problem: most ETFs have been around for more than 1,000+ trading days.

As an example, you will learn how to build a model using ETF data and regression analysis that uses decision science to help you determine the potential direction and percentage movement in the AUD/USD currency pair. Your first task is to select the CurrencyShares Australian Dollar Trust ETF (FXA) as a proxy for the AUD/USD pair. The second task is to go through your list of ETFs that you found with a Google search and choose which ETFs serve as proxies for a group of potential influencers in the price movement in the FXA ETFs.

▼ **TABLE 9-1: ETFS TO USE AS DATA POINTS**

Influencer of Target FX pair	Symbol
Dollar Index	UUP
USD/EUR	FXE
USD/CHF	FXF
USD/JPY	FXY
U.S. Treasury Inflation-Protected Bonds	TIP
U.S. S&P 500 Index	SPY
USD/SEK	FXS
U.S. S&P 500 Volatility Index	^VIX*

**Not an ETF, but the actual Option Index Symbol*

After selecting the above list of potential influencers and noting the symbol of the ETF that tracks them, your next step is to gather the data. In this example, you would find the data points for your financial model by looking up the individual symbols on a website such as Yahoo! Finance.

Steps to Retrieving Data from the Web

After you have decided on what indicators you would like to use in your model, the next step is to begin downloading the information into a useable format. The easiest format to download into is MS Excel. You can easily look up the historical closes of any indicator or ETF in the world, convert that data to a spreadsheet, and download it into your Excel program on your laptop.

1. Go to a site such as *http://finance.yahoo.com.*
2. Enter in the symbol you are seeking data for in the "Get Quotes" box. In this case enter "FXE," the Currency Shares Euro Trust ETF.
3. Click on "Historical Prices" to the left of FXE's market information.
4. On the "Set Date Range," pick a date at least four and a half years in the past.
5. Select "Daily," and then click "Get Prices."
6. At the bottom of the webpage click on the line "Download to Spreadsheet," then "Save" to your desktop, and label "Table_FXE."

Continue steps two through five with the other ETFs you are gathering data points for, making sure to label each one with the appropriate ETF symbol before saving. After you have saved all of your ETF historical price data to your desktop, open each file, and click "Save as Excel Workbook." This will create a workable Excel copy of the downloaded data that you can manipulate later. Delete the original Excel files, leaving only the newly saved documents. In this example you should have created a total of eight MS Excel tables, all with the different ETF labels. Perform steps two through five and the "Save as Excel Workbook" for your target currency pair, or in this case AUD/USD, which is tracked by the proxy ETF FXA.

Adding Formulas for Meaningful Data Points

Now begins the tricky part: you will begin using MS Excel formulas to find the percentage change of each indicator ETF's close from the day before. For this example, open your FXE workbook. In the blank column next to the "Adj. Close" column, type in this formula: = ($G2- $G3)/$G3.

Copy the formula down the entire column of data by clicking on the cell with the first formula, grabbing the "cross-hairs" in the corner with the left button of your mouse, and dragging down to the end of the column of data, all while holding down the left button of your mouse. The "$" signs keep the formula's cells relative to each other. After this is completed, change the entire column to percentage to a few decimal places. This is achieved by clicking on the "%" and then the 0.00 buttons at the top of your Excel workbook.

By using this formula, copying it down, and converting to percentage, you have created a listing of the change in the percentage movements in FXE from one day's closing price to the next day's closing price. These percentages will serve as the "Data Points" of your system and will become the inputs in your regression analysis. Follow along with the instructions for all of your ETF Excel workbooks separately, all the while making sure that the first date of the data is the same on all of the spreadsheets.

The Last Step of Gathering Data

The last step of this part of gathering the data is to take each ETF workbook and copy the entire columns that have the percentage-changed information that you created with the formulas and paste them all into a newly created Excel workbook. To do this, highlight the column you wish to copy, click "Copy" and then place your cursor in the topmost cell of the first column, and click "Paste Values." This will make sure that the formulas do not copy over, which would cause your data to read false, as the formulas would overlap with unrelated data. Continue this process with each column of "Percentage-Changed" data, pasting the values of each column right next to each other with no blank columns in between.

ALERT

> Depending upon what version of Excel you are using, you might not have the additional add-ins to perform regression analysis. Go to *http://office.microsoft.com/en-us/excel-help/load-the-analysis-toolpak-HP010021569.aspx* to load the "Data Analysis Pack" on your Excel program if it hasn't come with it or you haven't installed it already. It's free!

The last column you should copy and paste values for should be your target currency pair. In this case, your target currency pair is the ETF FXA. Be sure to make certain that the dates line up correctly.

After you have all of your information on the spreadsheet in columns of information, the next step is to spin the numbers using regression analysis. Go to the tab in Excel that has the "Data Analysis" section. Click on "Data Analysis" and select "Regression" from the info box that appears. Follow the instructions on the regression section of Excel to fill in the areas that you would like to analyze. After all the fields have been filled in, click the calculate button. The Excel program will then offer a formula that includes each data point as input in a formula.

Using the Regression Analysis

Your regression analysis is now complete. You have used Excel to determine which of the eight factors affects the price of the AUD/USD currency pair, and by how much. Depending upon what eight factors you have selected (or however many you use), some will have a high degree of influence and some will have a lower degree of influence on the price of the AUD/USD pair.

To carry the experiment one step further, you could track the inputs at the close of each trading day. You could then enter in each of the eight inputs you have chosen into the model you have created and then calculate the expected direction of the AUD/USD pair the following morning. Depending upon the quality of your inputs, your model will be more or less accurate.

It will take a bit of time getting used to selecting and gathering data points to build a good model. Professional trading houses that use regression analysis usually employ math majors to work on setting up the experiment and analysis to determine what indicators to use. You will have to learn how to do both. When you get good at it, you will be building models that can predict the direction of currency pairs with precision. Take your time learning how to use regression analysis and don't be discouraged programming Excel.

In order to learn how to fully employ statistics and regression analysis into your trading, you should read books on data analysis for Excel. These books are available at your bookstore and are available for any version of Excel you may have. When you get a copy of a book on data analysis, look up and read the sections on regression analysis. These books usually offer examples of how to program Excel in easy to follow formats. Most of them have a great number of pictures, and some of them have CDs to download most of the work directly to your computer.

Once you get the basics down, you can build a model and analyze it in an hour or two. Once you get to this level of proficiency, the next step is to discover what ETFs and other data points you can use to build models that are strongly and accurately predictive of the direction of FX pairs.

CHAPTER 10

Looking for Setups

Currency trading can be profitable if you take the time to look for good setups. These setups are the times when either the fundamentals, technicals, or both are telling you that it is time to get into a trade because an FX pair is about to move. Though spotting setups takes a bit of plotting and planning, sometimes trading news happens fast; it is during these times that a quick analysis of the situation can put you into a position to reap quick profits.

Different News, Different FX Pairs

It is important to trade the FX pair that is in the news during that time. Movement in the market is what allows you to make money. A nonmoving or stagnant currency pair will only tie up cash with no gains, all while still having that amount of cash at risk. You will do well to trade with a long and a short time horizon, but above all, trade the news. Trading the news is the process of scouting for setups, or opportunities to make money in the market. Looking for setups is your currency trading job while you are not actually in a trade.

It is possible to look for an appropriate and profitable setup for days before one develops that has your risk tolerance and an appropriate return potential. In fact, the scouting for setups is the process of keeping your money safe and *not* in a trade, and allowing yourself to trade only when you have a very certain chance of getting your money back intact, along with a profit for your risk taking. You should get to the point where you actually *prefer* to be in cash, and not in a trade. Only begrudgingly should you enter into a trade, and only if the setup offers a reasonable chance of profit.

FACT

It is possible to build a short-term trading system for maximum safety by being in cash over 90 percent of the trading week and be in a trade less than 10 percent of the time. This equates to about twenty-four ultrashort-term trades a week. Limiting your cash exposure to the market can keep your account safe and secure!

If you are going into a trading week, look for points that might develop into trading opportunities. If you find them before the week starts, (if you spend an early Saturday morning reviewing charts and fundamentals), that is good. Sometimes, however, things can change (for the better!) and a clearer directional trade will present itself. You would then switch gears and change your focus and money to the new FX pair that is in the news.

At any time during the trading week, information regarding economies and the currencies those economies affect will be in the news. Not only that, but the news story that you have been following over the weekend and into the beginning of Monday and Tuesday might fall out of importance as a bigger story in a different country or part of the world develops. You might have been following the first story in your broker's reports and on the news wire, and may have been getting ready for a chance to enter the market on the winning side of that trade.

It might be that the Hungarian forint is gaining too much value against the Swiss franc. A story might be developing that the HUF is just about to change direction against the CHF. Upon further examination, you determine that the CHF/HUF is at the top of its 200-day moving average. Not only that, you determine that there is a resistance point at the current trading level, and that volume has been building. Under these circumstances, a small, highly leveraged, long-term trade would be your preference, and you begin to look to entering the trade later on in the week.

A Scenario of Developing News

While you are scouting around looking for a CHF/HUF entry point, another news story might develop. This one is about the economic and employment numbers coming out of the United States. The data is announced and is worse than expected, which makes the risky assets of the world retreat. The U.S. stock market will be affected badly by such news, as investors change their risk appetite to match the developing news.

ESSENTIAL

Things can happen fast in the market; riskier investments can fall out of favor. With currencies, the AUD, SEK, and NZD will fall relative to the safer USD. If you do not have a position in these pairs, this would be in a good time to pick up the risky sides of the pairs at a cheap price.

You would then change your focus from a long-term trade of CHF/HUF to a shorter time frame, high-yielding currency risk trade. These high-yield, high-risk trades are the ones that react positively to good worldwide stock market gains. It is known that after a big news announcement and when the stock market has a big reaction, there is a good chance that a few days later the market will change direction for a day or two. This is due to the fact that traders in the stock markets of the world are either bargain hunting or profit taking. Either way, the stock markets will eventually move in the other direction: this is a wonderful opportunity to capture the gains by having a position in a high-yield, high-risk trade.

In a bad news scenario, you would diversify your portfolio into three positions totaling 18–21 percent of your total portfolio. This means a combination of positions of USD/AUD, USD/NZD, USD/SEK, and EUR/CHF consisting of 6–7 percent of the total cash value of your currency portfolio.

If the market were reacting to the news in a dramatic or negative way, these FX pairs would also fall suddenly. Any down movement beyond 1.25 percent from the point the news was announced represents a good entry point for these pairs. The idea is not to be precise as to entry points but rather just to get the orders in before the market reverses (as this could happen fast!).

After you have the orders entered, then go back into the "Modify Order" screen and place your automated exit points, at 0.65 percent to 0.75 percent profit points. This will assure a good, fast profit from the trade. Then, walk away. Take the rest of the day off. Have a cup of coffee with your significant other, or play with your kids at the park. Your work is done. Let the computer finish up for you, as you have entered into a fast-turnaround trade and you have used automated trading to take a profit and to ensure the exit trade is executed at the right time.

This is a fine example of looking for setups, keeping ahead of the news, and, in the end, being flexible enough to jump on a chance to make a solid profit when a new, quickly developing news story and FX pair comes into play.

The Market Is Always Reacting

The market is always reacting to the news developments of the day. Because of the fact that the markets are open twenty-four hours a day, nearly six days a week, there is always a chance that there is some news that is developing somewhere in the world. This news also has a strong chance of affecting the currencies of all the countries involved.

For example, it is possible that fresh news can come out of the Asian money centers such as Tokyo or China when the European and U.S. markets have not yet opened. It might be a story about China's growth figures being higher than expected. This news would affect not only the currency markets of China and the commodity currencies, but also those of its main trading partners.

Additionally, good news from China also means good news for the developing economies of Southeast Asia such the Malaysian ringgit, the Singapore dollar, and the Thai baht.

This is true because China is beginning to outsource some of its labor and light manufacturing to these developing economies in Southeast Asia. Therefore, when capital flows from the United States and Europe to China to pay for increased Chinese goods, some of this newly acquired capital will be exported to the emerging markets that China uses to outsource labor. Because of the fact that the growth of China is also related to its future consumption of commodity inputs such as steel, copper, and the soft commodities such as cotton and wool, the commodities currencies would be affected as well.

ALERT

Some news is planned to be released after peak trading hours (5:00 P.M. to 7:00 P.M. eastern time). This timing is to give currency traders time to digest the information while the market cools off after a trading session. News releases are just one example of how information can be published at any time of the trading day to control currency traders' reactions.

News will also develop at scheduled times during the week and month as the central banks of the world issue reports or otherwise have conferences that happen at prepublished times. Just about every currency that is regularly traded has a website that is in English, and the site is updated by the governing body of that currency. Whether it is the Riksbank of Sweden (*www.riksbank.com*), the Reserve Bank of New Zealand (*www.rbnx.govt.nz*), or the Magyar Nemzeti Bank (the central bank of Hungary, *http://english.mnb.hu*), these sites will publish the dates and times that rate adjustments, economic numbers, and other guidance will be officially announced. If you are trading a particular currency pair, whether the EUR/SEK, the USD/NZD, or the CHF/HUF it would best if you get to know the websites of the central banks that manage the currencies that you are trading.

Keeping a Trading Calendar

Because the market is always reacting to the developments of news, and news is happening at all times, it is best to keep a desktop calendar in which you can keep track of the dates and times of the news and information that develops in regard to your frequently traded FX pairs. This way, you can keep track of the developments that you know are scheduled to happen.

One type of information that you can use your trading calendar for is to keep you from forgetting about an upcoming interest-rate announcement from a currency's central bank. You could monitor the FX market and have your trading calendar remind you that the U.S. Federal Reserve, (*www.federalreserve.gov*), will be making an announcement about a jobs report or other information that is important to your open or future currency trades with a USD side.

This trading calendar can also keep track of the market sentiment of currency pairs as it develops over time. If you regularly trade a pair that includes currencies that are in a state of flux and moving up and down, then this calendar can help you to keep focused on the developments in the market's commentary about the pairs you are trading.

You could use it to make note of your broker's recommendations as they develop over the months and weeks leading up to a possible change in the economic numbers of that country. Your calendar could serve as a record of the market chatter you are hearing about the stock markets of the countries, their leading indicators, etc. Lastly, if you are already in the trade, or thinking of getting in the trade, you can use the notebook as a form of a record of your own market sentiment.

While it is true that markets are always reacting to the news, it is also true that you as an FX trader will also react to the news. This is especially true if you are in a trade. It is quite common to fall in love with a pair, wait for the perfect time to enter the trade, and then have buyer's remorse after your money is on the table. This is normal! While it is said that you should get out of a losing trade before it becomes an investment, you can use your calendar to look over the developments of that trade before you jump ship and possibly exit it too soon. The feeling of getting out of a trade minutes after it moves the wrong way can be overpowering.

ESSENTIAL

You should not be using emotion when looking to exit a trade at a moment's notice. It would be best to use automated stops to program into your trading software the best time to exit a trade. With a bit of practice, you can learn to rely on technical analysis, fundamental analysis, and math instead of emotions when currency trading.

The market will always move to the news. This works both ways: While the currency market is always moving, it will move in both directions, both up and down. With this in mind, if you are in a trade with good reason, only exit out of it with good reason.

You can go further with your trading journal and allow it to take on the properties of a news journal. This will help you grasp how the news for your pairs has developed over the past months and weeks. This will help you get a grip on the fact that your FX pair has most likely moved up and down as the market reacted to developing news. Upon a second look, you may even notice that market sentiment went back and forth over time. When you record these observations you then have a historical reference to ask yourself, "Am I reacting to the news just like the market, and being led around like a lamb?" and then ask yourself, "What has it (the currency pair) done before in these situations?" Finally, you will have the ability to have a point of reference to help answer the question, "Will the market come back (if you are under water with the trade and it is in a losing situation) or will the market swing back to the point where the trade can be closed out at break even with zero loss?" A trading or news journal can help you keep yourself on top of developments before they happen, and it can help you determine if now is really the right time to get out of a trade.

Trading with the News

Reading the *Wall Street Journal*, (*http://online.wsj.com/home-page*), *The Economist*, (*www.economist.com*), or *Market Watch* (*www.marketwatch.com*)

gives you access to the news of the day that is in relation to the economies of the world. The news of the economies and markets of the world in turn affects the ideas that the traders of the world have on the future capital inflows into an economic region, the future growth rates of an economic region, and even the future interest rates of that region's central banks. It is a give and take: The economic news causes a reaction in the FX markets, and the FX markets cause a reaction in the economies of the home (and trading partners) economies. With this in mind, it is best to keep ahead of the news and plan your trades to work with the news.

ESSENTIAL

> Some currency brokers will allow you automatically to subscribe to two or even three different FX news feeds. These currency brokers will also allow you to have a news feed window open directly on your trading platform which can give you instant access to the information.

The news can be a currency trader's best friend, and certainly ranks up there with fundamental analysis and technical analysis to help select and time good FX trades. Ultimately, it is the addition of the process of watching the news to a strong fundamental analysis and knowledge of technical indicators that can make your trading system lock tight; the news can make your trades statistically more profitable in the short, medium, and long time frame.

There are several factors that can cause a currency pair to move in either direction. These factors could be macro events such as a banking crisis, or they could be events that are isolated to a particular country, such as surprisingly good (or surprisingly poor) economic news about one of the ends of the currency pairs. Between these extremes is almost every bit of event and news development imaginable, from a country's leader making a televised speech, to hurricanes and isolated skirmishes. Whatever the event, in today's connected world, the development will be reported by the news agencies.

Like it or not, people react to developing news stories. A common saying is that "the news rules!" A typical scenario is that you have spent the time studying the Reserve Bank of Australia's (RBA's) website and you have read your broker's reports for the AUD/USD pair. Additionally, you have been watching the stock markets around the world, and have monitored the VIX index.

OBSERVATIONS BEFORE MAKING A LONG AUD/USD TRADE

- ☑ The Reserve Bank of Australia hasn't raised rates in two terms.
- ☑ The Reserve Bank of Australia is scheduling a meeting in two weeks.
- ☑ Your broker's reports suggest the RBA will raise rates by 0.25 percent at the next meeting.
- ☑ Another commodity currency, NZD, had its rates raised by its central bank last meeting.
- ☑ The world's stock markets have been steadily rising (suggesting increased risk appetite).
- ☑ The Swedish krona has been moving steadily higher against the EUR (suggesting increased risk appetite).
- ☑ The VIX has been lower recently (suggesting a calm, reassured market with increased risk appetite).

After looking over your notes and sensing an increased risk appetite coupled with the chance of an increase in the interest rates set by the Reserve Bank of Australia, you decide to place a long AUD/USD trade that will make money when the AUD goes up against the USD. You know this trade will make money if the stock markets continue to rise, the market continues to feel good about risky assets, and the RBA raises rates.

A Good Trade, but Bad News

You might have a longer term, smaller trade on your books. It might be only 7 percent of your total portfolio; it might be that you entered into the trade with the thought of using the trade as a sort of carry trade for the next few weeks until the Reserve Bank of Australia meets and raises rates (when you will capture a capital gain). Your carry trade is one that is set at a 50:1 margin. You have the intent to hold for two weeks and then sell. Since you are long a currency that pays a higher rate of interest than the currency that you are short, you will accrue an interest on the AUD/USD trade. The amount of interest is deposited into your account every night. It can accumulate rapidly, as it continuously compounds, and is measured in seconds and minutes in the trade (unlike regular time accounts which compound monthly or quarterly). The AUD/USD trade is a risk trade. The more the market likes risk, the better it will do. It is a well-thought out trade.

The trade is logical, but sometimes the market isn't. News happens fast. There are any number of things that can happen to make the market suddenly reverse course and send the world running for cover and out of risky assets. It might be a snow storm on the eastern part of the United States (New York traders would stay home and not be at their trading desks) or a negative development in a euro-bloc country. Either way, there is a chance that some news could happen that would send your well-thought out long AUD/USD trade into a spiral, as the USD would gain since it is considered a safe-haven currency.

In fact, you could use the market's reaction to increase your long holding of the AUD/USD at an even cheaper rate than before. Reading the news helps you to keep on top of trades. It also allows you to keep on top of opportunity: the reaction is most likely a temporary setback in the world's risk appetite. It is also most likely that the Reserve Bank of Australia will still raise rates that 0.25 percent since they will be looking at the long term (and the news often looks at the ultrashort term).

ALERT

One of the best things an FX trader can do is learn how to walk away from her trading desk. If well-thought out, automated take-profit points and stops are built into the software, then just let the market and the computer do the work. Do not become impatient or worried! Your trading system will do the work for you.

You could hold on to your original observations. Watching the news could alert you to a chance to add another position to your AUD portfolio. You could use a risk management idea to break your additional position into three entry points over the next two or three days. You could set your exit points at a nice 1 percent (average) price movement to the upside. At this point, it would be best to walk away from your trading platform for a few days. Keep checking the price of the AUD/USD by looking at the FXA on your iPhone or iPad during the next several days to keep abreast of the developing price. Let the computer exit out of your long AUD/USD trades automatically when the time comes. The time will come. Risky assets will be back on people's minds as something to have in their portfolios. The AUD will come back. It always does!

CHAPTER 11

Fast- and Slow-Happening News

One of the secrets of getting into good currency trades is the practice of aligning your FX trades with the direction and development of the news. Some news is quick happening and some is of the slower type. Either way, if you can identify the direction that the markets will be moving before, during, and after the news develops, you will be making a good effort to get your Forex account into a profitable trading situation.

Interest Rate Changes

It is true that the news moves the currency markets. It is also true that there are two types of news, fast-happening news and slow-happening news. An announcement of an interest rate change can be the source of the most sudden of currency pair movements. If you are invested in a currency pair and one of the ends of the trade is changing its interest rate, you can rest assured that there will be a wild ride coming soon.

Use Interest Rate Announcements and Your Spare Margin

Central banks give the markets ample time to get ready for an interest rate announcement. All it takes from you is to look at the websites of the central banks that are related to the trades you are in at the time. If you think the stock market will be going down and you are in a long EUR/SEK trade, and the Riksbank lists on their website that they will be making an announcement regarding any change on their repo rate at the end of the week, then you should be wary of this and scale back any trades. At the very least, you should have enough unused margin to absorb any downturn in the market if the Swedish bank raises its repo rate: If it does raise it by any amount, this will throw off the prices of that currency pair and your profit to boot.

A second method that you can use to help prevent a totally disappointing trade is to have enough spare margin to buy into the currency pair at the new price if it moves against you. In this way you can lower the average cost of your FX pair to include the new price. This staged building of the position can go a long way in keeping the trade at a point that money can still be made off it once the stock markets do fall, and the SEK goes with it.

Monitor Interest Rate Changes

Interest rate changes are very big in the Forex trading world. This is true because one of the elements of determining the fair price of a currency pair is predicting the growth rates of countries. If a country looks as though its growth rate is more than that of another country, there is chance that the home country will raise the level of its interest rates in an effort to control the economy.

The opposite is also true. If there is an expectation that a country's economy is slowing, then there is a good chance that the home country's central bank will either lower interest rates or take other measures to make money easier to borrow. By allowing money to be easier to borrow, the central bankers are hoping that the function of borrowing and spending will spur the economy and help move it forward.

FACT

It is said that, after the quantitative easing that followed the 2008 banking crisis, there was more than four times the amount of money brought into the system than the years previously. This brought about concerns of widespread inflation and caused ramped up speculation in the commodities markets.

If a currency pair is priced at one interest rate, and there is an announcement of a change in one of the ends of the pair's interest rates, then the pricing of the currency pair will change. It usually works that the lower interest rate will move lower and the higher interest rate will move higher. The net effect is a change in the price of the currency pair.

Economic Announcements

There are other announcements that are related to interest-rate changes but these announcements are a whole other concept. One example that has been in the news lately is what is often referred to as quantitative easing. Quantitative easing is a way of altering a country's money supply by purchasing large quantities of that same government's bills, notes, or bonds on the open market. When a treasury or central bank purchases massive quantities of its own debt on the open market, the purchase has the effect of pumping huge amounts of fresh money into the system.

The way this works is simple. If there is a $1,000 bond outstanding and held by a bank, the home country's central bank or treasury will step in and buy the bond from the bank. Now the bond is on the balance sheet of the treasury and the bank has $1,000 in cash. Since the bank is in business to make money, this $1,000 will be lent out to its customers who are looking for loans. The borrowed money is spent by the consumer, and the merchant puts the $1,000 in his (the merchant's) bank. Due to the fractional-reserve banking system, only part of the money needs to stay in the bank while the rest can leave again in the form of a loan. For the second time, money is lent out, spent, and deposited in a bank. The fractional-reserve system means only part of that money needs to remain in the bank, and again, the rest leaves in the form of another loan. The system repeats itself over and over again.

Quantitative Easing in 2008–2009 and 2011

It is quite impressive how an all-out quantitative easing campaign can work. It was done in full force after the 2008–2009 banking crisis. Most of the major economies of the world engaged in some form of quantitative easing. Naturally, the largest players in the world bought the most debt. This means that Great Britain, Japan, Europe, and the United States were the most active in the process of buying their own debt and thereby putting the most money in the system.

There has been some confusion as to whether quantitative easing has worked for these countries. Even after the second round of easing in the Unites States, which was known as QE2, the economy remained sluggish. In addition to this, the perceived value of the U.S. dollar went down considerably.

In this case, there were concerns of added money supply as well as added debt problems. In the summer of 2011, the Unites States had its debt downgraded from an AAA status to an AA status. While the effects of this new development have yet to be determined, the currency markets pummeled the U.S. dollar before, during, and after the news.

FACT

The Rothschild Group is a family bank that goes back to the beginning of the 1800s. It is often considered one of the most influential and powerful banks of all time. The bank made a habit of buying into the debt and currency of countries that were going through tough times, only to sell the debt later at huge profits.

Always Plan Carefully

There is quite a bit of economic news that can come out that is not related to the usual scheduled economic numbers. The key is to be on the lookout for developing news and to plan for the worst when you see it coming. At the same time, once the bad news passes over, there is a very good chance that the currency will rebound. With this in mind, you should always ask yourself if you should buy into the beaten down currency, only to sell out at a later date, and at a big profit!

Geopolitical News

Other factors that can affect the price of currency pairs include geopolitical news. This is the type of news that has effects that go beyond money and currencies. It includes developing storm conditions, hurricanes, earthquakes, floods, etc. It is the type of news that comes fast and sudden, and with devastating results. Other factors include invasions, wars, hostage crises, etc. You will know when these current events develop. It might be in your home country that the bad news is taking place, or it might be in a country or part of the world that you care deeply about.

During these times, the world's currency markets can be in total, illogical upheaval, and the conditions can last until the end of the crises. It is not recommended that you trade during these times, as currency pair directions are very unpredictable at best, and there is the chance of the old valuation models being thrown out completely.

If you have overnight trades and you wake up to very bad news, then most likely you have either won big or lost big. If you have won big, take the time to close out your trades and walk away from trading for a while. You got lucky. These things can't be predicted, and for every winner there is a loser. Wait until the bad situation works its way out, and then re-evaluate the prices of the currencies. They might be permanently changed.

ESSENTIAL

Part of learning how to trade currencies is learning how to close out losing trades. If you are tied up in a trade that has gone bad, you will have to decide if it is worth waiting for the trade to turn around, or just taking your losses and walking away, to trade another day.

If you have long-term trades and you are now in a losing situation, take a look at your broker's reports before closing out and realizing the loss. If your brokerage is good, it will most likely have very good advice for you as what to do with your positions. It might be that brokerage analysts are recommending adding to the position as they see the new price change as short-term and temporary. Either way, proceed with caution!

What to Do When the Market Crashes

When the market risk appetite jumps for whatever reason, there will be a typical reaction in the FX markets. The best thing to do is to first know beforehand what currency pairs react strongly to this increase in market risk appetite. Second, you need to know when the risk appetite has changed, or is about to change.

Consider Your Positions

If the risk appetite of traders has changed for whatever reason, then you will need to re-evaluate your positions. If you are long the AUD/USD and short the EUR/SEK and the markets suddenly take a turn for the worse, then most likely you will be in a loss situation. If you have been building your positions over time and with a smaller amount of your available margin, then a downturn in the market should in no way wipe you out. With a bit of care and risk management, you should be able to keep the account liquid enough to withstand even very drastic downturns in the market.

If you are in the risk trades such as the AUD/USD and EUR/SEK, and the market goes against you in a very dramatic way, you might want to consider putting more money in the account to buy more into those currency pairs that have lost so much. In any case, some of the pairs will be paying very good interest. If your average cost of the AUD/USD is 102 and all of a sudden bad news comes out and it falls to 97.75, then you have a wonderful opportunity to buy into an excellent interest-paying pair at a lower price. Depending upon how much you can add to your account, you can double or triple your exposure to the long AUD/USD or the short EUR/SEK in such a way as to add to your bottom line significantly when the market decides that it has had enough and it reverses due to the bargain hunting and bottom-feeding of so many of the market participants. Remember, markets always come back! If the market is very, very beat down and an interest-bearing currency pair such as the Canadian/USD or the AUD/USD or the New Zealand/USD falls to the point of being grossly undervalued, then by all means, buy into as much of the pair as you can!

This is a situation of "beep-beep, back up the truck!" Do whatever you have to do to get as much as you can off the beaten down currency. This is an awesome opportunity to get into a currency pair that can turn into big profits. In the meantime, when you are waiting for the markets to turn around, you will earn the interest on the account. If you have a 50:1 margin, and you commit one-third or two-fifths of your account to the trade, then you will earn 70 to 90 percent interest in your account on a yearly basis (not including any gains in the currency pair!).

This is an excellent example of what to do if the market's fortune and your account's fortune changes for the worse. If you have built it properly, your positions will be able to withstand quite a beating. If this happens, stick it out, add to the position, and change direction for a while by going into carry-trade mode.

FACT

Keeping your head and wits about you in bad times can add to your bottom line. Many Forex traders take advantage of the worst of times. You, too, can use bad markets to your advantage by using carry trades, adding to your positions, or being a contrarian trader by going long on risk-loving currency pairs.

Consider Closing Losing Trades

Of course, if you have other trades on the books, and they are also losers, then you might consider closing out some of your losing trades in order to redeploy the cash into a more attractive trade. For example, if you are in a long AUD/USD, a long GBP/USD, and a short EUR/SEK, and they are all down due to extreme risk aversion, then you might want to consider closing out some of your better losers such as a closing out your GBP/USD and the EUR/SEK in order to go all out long in the AUD/USD, and secondly to free up some much-needed margin if you are close to a margin call. A few bucks lost are worth it if you are going to use the margin in a way that will gather returns very quickly when the markets return in the future.

Additionally, the market might be much skewed in its analysis of its conditions at the time. When this is the case, the money will flow back into the classics first. These would be the trades that take the least amount of speculation to determine if they will recover. If the AUD/USD has performed well over the years, then it will most likely perform well in the future. It is a classic trade, and you should be thinking of the classic, uncomplicated trades in bad times. Most of the other traders will be doing the same, and you will be able to capture the profits then.

The Herd Instinct and FX

When everyone is pushing the market and it has been riding high for a several days or weeks, then there is a good chance that there will be a slowing or even a reversal of the markets. The currency markets are tied to the idea of growth in economies, plain and simple. If one region is experiencing rapid growth and another is experiencing slow or slowing growth, this has the makeup of a good currency pair to invest in and trade.

This pairing is true because economies that are slowing are most likely to keep their interest rates on hold, and economies that are growing are most likely to raise their interest rates to keep the home economy from overheating. This is the key to finding good currency pairs in FX.

Consequently, if there is an idea of a growing economy, the world's stock markets will go up in value. The up and down motion of the world's stock indexes, such as the German stock index (DAX), French stock index (CAC)40, London stock exchange (FTSE)100, and the Dow Jones industrial average (DOW) 30, serves as a sort of proxy for how well the investors and traders think the world economies are doing. Since most investors and traders look at the same charts and have access to basically the same level of information, they will react to this information and these charts pretty much the same. Remember, it takes quite a bit of force for the world's stock markets to fall (or rise, for that matter) by a significant amount. It takes a large number of sellers of the options of the indexes and stock in those indexes to sell off and make the price levels fall 2, 3, 4 percent or more.

If you sense through your readings and studying of the charts and news that the markets will soon perceive that the economy is slowing, plan accordingly. You can set some long-term trades that act as feelers of the market. You can set up some long EUR/SEK, or short AUD/USD, or even some long USD/EUR, all trades that would benefit from a shrinking in the price levels of the world stock markets.

ESSENTIAL

If the world's stock markets have been beaten up for a while, and you sense a comeback in the markets, then you can be a contrarian investor and place some trades that will react strongly to positive news when it comes. You have learned some of the best trades for this type of market environment: go long on risk currencies.

In order to learn to pick your own pairs you will need to look to go long in a higher-than average-growth economy and go long that currency. Then you will need to pick a slower-than-average growth economy and short that currency. This is the basic reasoning behind currency trading. It really does come down to growth rates and the interest rates that are related to them. Everyone in FX is reading the ticker, and looking for what is the next thing to happen to the interest rates of those economies that have currencies that are traded. The only difference with one pair and another is popularity, which in turn can add fuel to the fire of a carry trade or shorter-term trade.

For example, if two trades have good growth and slow growth parts to the trade, the most popular one will most likely move higher and perform with more reliability, which in turn makes it that much more popular, and then more and more reliable, etc.

If the same thing can be accomplished with a short USD and long South African rand as can be done with a short USD and long Australian dollar, the AUD/USD trade will be the best one to get into because there will be that many more other traders getting into the trade at the same level, and seeing the same patterns as you.

Small Positions, Big Time Frames, Long-Haul Strategies

You might sense that the market has been going up (or down) for quite some time. You might wonder how you can place some longer-term trades in order to capture market-price movement to the downside without exposing yourself too much to any more up movement.

Give Yourself Plenty of Margin

You might want to try some longer time frame-type trades for this purpose. The best way to do this is to have smaller positions with plenty of available margin just in case the market does not move in your favor quickly. Better yet, plenty of margin will allow you to add to your positions even after the market has moved against you, but you are sure that a correction is coming.

If the market has moved up (or down, just reverse long for short) for many days and the run seems to be getting a bit long, then by all means clear out all of your trades and go on a spree of selling risk short. You have learned the currency pairs with which this approach works best. You have also learned the one-third margin rule. In order to capture the downward movement when it comes, you will need to divide your margins even further beyond the one-third that you would use for a shorter-term trade.

QUESTION

How can you tell it is time for the markets to turn after a big run?
The best way to know if a currency pair (or the stock markets) is ready for a reversal is looking at both fundamental and technical indicators. Additionally, you might want to tune into CNBC, as this station will be in a state of euphoria when the market is overbought and just ready for a crash.

The smaller amount of margin that you use with each addition to the position, the safer your overall account will be. If you use only one-twentieth of your account for each bite into the currency pair, then you will be very safe indeed. You can pace yourself to buy into the currency pair of your choice at small, measured paces in order to insure the liquidity of your account if there is any movement against your position. Remember, it is okay to have movement against you in your currency account. The best defense is to have ample margin to take the blow. It basically works as follows: As your account gains in profit you will be adding to your available margin; as you lose in your account, the losses will be taken out of your available margin. Once a certain level is breeched, then you will get a margin call, and you will be forced out of your positions at that price (a loss) and you would have blown up your account. This can be really easy to do if you are not careful and have too much product on your books and not enough margin to handle any downturn.

On the other hand, if you ease into the position, you will be protected. In the best-case scenario, you will be protected from the downside. In the worst case, you will limit the amount of your gains to how much of the currency pair you have on the books when the market does finally reverse and take a dive. So, you will be protected, yes, and you will win in your trades, (even if only by a small amount.)

Build Up Your Positions at Slower Rates

The key is to find ways to protect your account and at the same time, build up the positions at a slower rate. This slower rate will give yourself time to build the position and insulate you from any market movements against you. This will be done in a kind of dollar cost averaging. For example, you could start with 100 units in the morning, and then check your smart phone for the status of your trades. The position could be down; if it is, add more units in proportion to how much it is down. If it is down a lot, add 100 more units. If it is down just a bit, add only 25 units. The idea is that you will be adding when you are down in a method of buying on the dips. This buying on the dips can go a long, long way in keeping your trade profitable once the market does turn around. Just think, if you have made ten or fifteen buy-ins over a three or four day period and then the market does fall, you have prevented yourself from blowing up your account at the first sign that the trade is moving against you. At the same time you will be adding more and more of a trade that you have a strong idea will work. In this case you would never want to overexpose yourself. The maximum trade exposure would be two-fifths of your total available margin. If, after three days, things haven't happened, but the market has slowed down, then you too take a breather. This would be a good time to walk away from the market and enjoy one of your other hobbies, whether it be collecting coins or playing sports. In times like these, you have to remember, the trades are good. You know you will be worried. You know you will keep checking. Try to take it easy and go for the medium- to long-term and wait for the trades to turn. If you want, you can enter in some take-profit points to alleviate any pressure that you might miss the trade. Most people find that the adding of a take-profit point to a longer-term trade adds to the problems of checking. The best thing is to let the trade ride and come back to it when you have cooled off a bit. Look at it with a fresh eye, and wait for the trade to turn around. Remember, it's a good trade, you've thought about it. Let the trade work for you.

CHAPTER 12

Putting It Together, Putting in an Order

Now that you've got your currency account open and you've done the fundamental and technical research that goes into deciding what currency pair to trade, the next thing to do is to learn exactly how to trade. In this chapter you will learn the idea of having different buckets of money to trade with: some for ultrashort-term trades, some for overnight trades, and some for very long-term carry trades. You will also learn how to hedge and make profitable FX trades in risk adverse markets.

Currency Trading with Buckets of Money

When trading in with a Forex account it is most likely that you will have your margin broken up into different buckets. The first bucket would be the main part of your cash account. Since you will most likely be trading with relatively huge margins compared to a regular stock or mutual fund account (50:1 as opposed to 1.5:1) you will absolutely have to keep around 60 percent to 70 percent of your account in cash at all times. This is for safety purposes: you should keep this amount in cash to prevent the chance that a position goes against you quickly.

Careful Trading with Your Cash Account

It is still possible to earn a good living or make a good profit from an account where you are actually trading only a 25 percent of your available cash at any time. If you have a smaller account of $2,000, you will still be able to trade $500 at one time; at 50:1 margin you will be trading $25,000 worth of currency at any one time. You can easily earn $500–$1,000 per week with this amount by trading a very conservative trading style.

ESSENTIAL

Set a goal for how much you would like to make out of your currency trading on a weekly basis. If you set yourself a goal that is easy to reach, you will feel very happy with yourself when that amount of profit is reached. Conservative profit goals are a good way to keep you from overtrading your FX account.

Ultrashort-Term Scalping Trades

The second bucket would consist of a large portion of that one-quarter of your account to be committed to trading in ultrashort-term scalping trades of fewer than ten minutes. These types of trades can earn you big money. The problem with these trades is that most currency pairs move very little in a ten-minute window. In order to earn a decent amount with this type of trading you need to commit upwards of 25 percent of your account to each and every trade. With this large amount of capital committed to each trade, you will amplify the small percentage of the FX pair movement to yield a larger return from each trade.

Overnight Trades

The third bucket of money should be committed to trades that are overnight in length. Overnight trades require no more than 10 percent of your total margin available; in fact a more conservative amount would be around 9–10 percent of your total margin. The reason a smaller amount is needed is because with overnight trades, a wider take-profit stop should be programmed into your trading software. With this longer time frame of overnight, you can ask a higher percentage in your FX pair movement. Since most currencies move up and down (if even just a bit) over the course of the night, you can enter in a stop that will earn you a good profit from this small amount of capital committed.

Carry Trades

The fourth and final bucket of capital committed is a carry trade, or one that is intended to last many weeks and perhaps months. With this type of trade the profits come slowly and gradually. Since you are committing to a long time in the trade, a very small amount of your capital can be committed, around 3–5 percent would be sufficient. At 50:1 margin, huge gains can be made as a FX pair moves over the weeks and months.

Quick Trades, Quick Profit

The risk you undertake in your trading account can be directly tied to the amount of time you are actually in a trade. If you are in a trade for a very short time of a few minutes, you will be effectively reducing your exposure to risk and limiting the chance of a trade going bad. It is also true that FX pairs usually move less in shorter-time length trades. In order to compensate for this you will have to commit a greater amount of your capital to the trade. Additionally if you are performing short-time frame trades it would be best to commit to one or two trades at a time.

A good way to think of it is to think of short and ultrashort-time length trades as a power lifter would think of lifting a weight above his head. When an Olympic athlete lifts 400-plus pounds over his head, he does it in a clean, quick, jerking motion. Once the weight is over his head, he lets it go as quickly as possible. This type of lift is called a squat; your ultrashort-term trades can also be called squat trading. You can pile on the money in your account to one big trade and in less than five minutes be out of the trade, with the profits going into your account. This would be similar to a power lifter piling on the weight to the barbell, quickly lifting it, and then letting the weight drop.

FACT

The amount of money you have at risk can be reduced by just keeping out of the market! If you are only in the currency market for five or ten minutes at a time, you are limiting your downside risk, as a currency pair usually takes hours to move a significant amount.

This can actually be a really good way to rack up profits at a quick, relatively risk-free rate. In order to do this you would need to concentrate on only one or two currency pairs. The best ones are the AUD/USD, the NZD/USD and the EUR/CHF. This type of squat trading works best in the slower hours of the trading day, which is about the time that the late night movies are showing on TV. It is quite possible to put the kids to bed, watch the 10:00 P.M. show, and spend a few hours entering into and exiting out of trades on your laptop computer. Trading in this ultrashort-term fashion can be a kind of recreation, much like playing video chess while spending the night watching reruns of *Matlock* and laughing with your significant other.

If this sounds like a fun way to spend an otherwise dull weekday night, then you must absolutely incorporate late-night, short, quick trading into your overall FX trading program. Keep in mind that you should use a quarter to a third of your overall available margin with each trade, and have only one trade on your books at any one time. Also, it works best if you ignore the long-term direction of the FX pairs. It would be better to keep your focus on a five-minute or even a one- minute chart. With these short-term charts you can almost see each and every trade as it comes into the session: the bar chart will gently move up and down.

More on Scalping

At this point, open up your place order window and enter in the appropriate size of the trade, and place your mouse over the "Place Trade" button. The best results are when you just sit there, and watch your movie and wait for a sudden move up or down. Often you will be able to capture this sudden and rapid price movement and exit out of the trade when it is done moving and at a new level.

An example of this process would to get the kids down to bed, turn on a light-hearted movie, turn on your laptop, and make yourself a cup of hot chocolate. As you sit there and sip the sweet, warm cocoa, get your computer screen to show the FX pair of your choice. You are going to look at the AUD/USD pair in this example. Switching to back and forth between a five- and one-minute chart, you begin to get a feel of what is happening in the market this early morning in Tokyo and Sydney.

ALERT

Don't allow yourself to get too caught up in looking at any one time-length chart. It would be best to keep switching back and forth among long, medium, and short time-length charts in an effort to get a grip on what direction that currency pair is moving.

The chart will show very little movement, and at first glance you wonder if the FX market is actually closed. The bar chart will begin to move, up and down with each and every one minute that goes by. Nothing much is happening.

Time gently ticks by. You have a good feel for the trading platform, the AUD/USD pair, and you are now ready to trade. You open up the "Place Trade" window, get your calculator out and figure that you will commit a fourth of your account to the next trade. You enter this amount in the trade-size section, place your mouse over the "Place Trade" button, and wait.

Be Patient

You are waiting for the perfect time to get into the trade. This time will come when there has been a movement (up or down) in the chart. Usually what happens at this time of the day is that the movement will happen, and then for a few minutes (one or two) there will be no movement at all. You will know that the perfect time is coming when you see an up or down on the chart and then the chart goes completely horizontal (no price movement) for two or three periods. The longer the periods (use a fifteen-second or five-second chart) go without a change in price, the greater the movement will be once it finally does come. You will almost be able to hear the FX traders of the world thinking of how to place the next trades. It is almost like they are all waiting for the next guy to make the first move. You are waiting too: You are ready to trade; you are set up, just waiting for the break, and then jumping in for the ride!

Make Your Move

After the FX community waits to see what direction to go, the chart will begin to move. You should wait until it moves faster and more dramatically in one direction. At that point get into the trade. Once you are in the trade and going in the same direction as the rapid price movement, hurry and get your "Close Order" screen up; get ready to close out the order completely. You should wait for either the movement to stop or slow dramatically, or for your profit from the trade to bring a smile to your face. When the movement stops, then definitely close out of the trade. On the other hand, if your trade-profit indicator is making you giggle just a bit, and you're happy with what you just made, then by all means close out and take the profit. Remember, keep it fun: You are enjoying the time and making money to boot!

Overnight Trades

During the trading hours most of your money will be in cash. You will have your other three buckets of investable cash. One of the most exciting forms of using this investable cash is engaging in what is called overnight trading. Overnight trading is when you look for the developments at the Asian markets in the early evening in order to get a good idea as to the direction of your bets. Once you have decided in what direction to place long or short, an entry point would either be made or programmed into your trading platform. The activity in the markets in the middle of the night will trigger your trades and hopefully allow you to exit the trade at a preplanned and preprogrammed profit point.

The key to successfully placing and profiting from overnight trades is asking yourself if it is the right time to get into the trade at all. Once that question has been answered, then choose whether long or short of a few currency pairs should do the trick. This will allow you to wake up early to a nice profit in your account.

QUESTION

Why is it that the world's markets seem to go up and down every few days?

The world's stock markets, precious metals markets, and currency markets usually go up for only so much before fortunes reverse. This is because many of the world's traders will engage in profit taking and sell their positions after a few days of gains in the markets.

One of the best times to get into an overnight trade is if the world's markets have been doing well for the past few sessions, and the Asian markets begin to fall on the second or third day. It is then a good idea is to short the EUR/CHF, go long the EUR/SEK, and short the AUD/USD. These three trades spread in 9 percent of your portfolio will go a long way in capturing any price movement that is risk adverse. FX markets usually go risk for a few days and then reverse and go risk averse for a few days. The idea is to set up two or three overnight trades to capture when the world's FX traders are going to set their trades in a less risky fashion.

The short EUR/CHF, short AUD/USD, and long EUR/SEK is a good hedge that the world's risky assets will decrease in value. As you will notice, there is only one long USD position. This is because a USD trade is a bit more difficult to predict against the EUR and other currencies. Since the USD has the position of being the most widely traded currency, it can sometimes move illogically and therefore be difficult to predict. With overnight trades, the euro proxies and the carry trades can be very easy to predict.

For one, a carry trade is considered a risky position, and if there is any indication that European and U.S. markets are beginning to go down (as predicted by the lower Asian markets in Hong Kong and Tokyo) then most of the world's currency traders will sell out of their long AUD and other carry trades such as NZD, Mexican peso (MXN), and South African rand (ZAR), etc., which are more risky in nature and go long the corresponding safer counter currencies such as the USD.

The other suggested trades involve a long Swiss franc position against the euro and a short Swedish krona position against the euro. In this case, the Swiss franc will gain against the euro since the Swiss franc is considered a safe-haven currency. Conversely, the Swedish krona is considered a risky asset when compared to the euro, as the Swedish krona closely follows the U.S. stock market. This combination will offer you a slight hedge if there is any rise in the price of the euro against the Swiss franc.

More on Setting Up an Overnight Trade

You will most likely get an indication as to the direction of the world's stock markets a few hours before midnight Sunday through Thursday nights. After making an evaluation whether it is a good time to place an overnight trade, you must then decide if it is going to be a risk trade or a risk-averse trade. To determine this, you must be a bit of a contrarian investor. Contrarian investing is a fancy word for going against the wave.

If you have been watching the world's stock markets along with your FX positions and you notice that there has been a strong direction in the past two or three days (whether up or down), then this movement should put you on alert to keep watch for the next reversal of fortunes in the Asian markets. If the Asian markets such as the Hang Seng or the Tokyo markets are leading in a different position of 0.65–1 percent, then this is a perfect time to set up an overnight trade.

If all things look good for the setup of an overnight trade, then get your calculator out and determine the size of each trade. You can use a bit of ratio to help you get a feel of how much of the 9–10 percent should be in each trade. If there has been a really big run-up in the markets in the past two or three days, and it looks as though the Asian markets will be down by 0.75–1 percent, then it would be safe to assume that the AUD/USD will fall further in percentage than the Swiss franc will gain against the EUR. The SEK will also fall a great deal against the EUR, as the SEK very closely follows the good fortunes of the European and U.S. stock markets. It is safe to say that if the U.S. stock market is going down, then there is a really good chance that a short SEK will make you money.

With this in mind, it would be good to put 4 percent in a short AUD/USD, 4 percent in a long EUR/SEK and only 2 percent in a short EUR/CHF. This will give you a good chance of gaining when the USD goes up. You will also be 200 percent covered if the EUR gains. To figure out your hedge, think of it this way: You will make two dollars for every EUR that goes up (long EUR/SEK is 4 percent) and possibly lose one dollar for every EUR that goes down (short EUR/CHF is 2 percent). If the world's traders can't figure out what to do with the EUR/USD, then you will be effectively hedged on both directions of the euro and the U.S. dollar. This is a good example of a partial hedge for the very unpredictable EUR/USD currency pair.

ESSENTIAL

Part of the fun of trading the currency markets is just getting your calculator out and planning out trades and hedges for those trades. Planning an effective, active hedge can be a challenge within itself. Three-sided trades can work especially well as an actively managed currency-trade hedging system.

The next thing would be to figure out ahead of the trade your take-profit points. You can think of a 0.5 percent gain for each pair and then triple that for a stop loss of 1.5 percent. In this case you will exit out of the trade with a profit three times as often, as you are forced to close out of the trade due to a loss. Remember, winning is what counts in currency trading. The more wins you can score, the stronger your account will be, the more confident you will become, and the more money you will make!

Carry Trades

The last bucket of traceable money that you should allocate is the money that is set aside for carry trades. A carry trade is a longer-term trade that is set to collect continuously compounding interest over the weeks and months that you are in the trade. Carry trades are placed by selling a lower-yielding currency and buying a higher-yielding currency; the JPY, USD, and CHF have historically been used to fund long exposures into the fairly secure, high-yielding currencies such as the AUD and NZD.

This type of trade will make money as you pay the interest on the charge of borrowing low and investing at a comparatively very high rate of return. The difference may be upward near 5–6 percent on a nonleveraged basis, and 250–300 percent at a 50:1 set leverage.

It is best to get into these trades after a correction in the stock market. It is at this time that currencies such as the AUD will fall the most as compared to the USD because risky assets such as AUD, NZD, MXN, and ZAR will fall considerably when the world's stock markets get even the tiniest bit deflated or corrected. A few percentages to the downside of a currency pair can really go a long way in keeping your carry trade in the profit point.

When you read in your broker's statements that a correction is coming in the AUD/USD or other classic carry trade, get your calculator out and commit 3–5 percent of your total capital to this type of trade. The trade should be long AUD/USD and it should be set up to fire at a preset entry point. If your broker is recommending or you have noticed that the AUD is fading against the USD, then put in an order for entry into the trade at about a 3 percent correction of the price. It might take a bit of calculation, and the price might seem far away from where it is currently. The idea is to have your order filled when there is a big correction in risk assets. It is then a good time to get into the carry trade.

FACT

Some carry trades can last for years and years. A classic example is the carry trade that went on between the JPY and the AUD and NZD from 2005 to late 2008. Carry traders all over the world quickly reversed these positions during the 2008–2009 banking crisis, causing the carry trade to collapse very quickly.

Once in the carry trade, do not set a take-profit point to exit the trade. In fact, the best thing to do is to walk away from that trade mentally. Bury that trade deep in your mind, and only look at it every week or so. It will accumulate interest and grow in price over time as the trade gets back up to the level it was before the correction. Carry trades sometimes go on for quite a while.

Just to keep things conservative, if (in this example) the AUD/USD pair gets back up into the range that it was before the 3–4 percent correction, then it is safe to close out the position and take your profits off the table. Remember you are trading at 50:1, and a 4 percent gain would equal a 200 percent gain. If you had a $10,000 portfolio, and you committed 5 percent to the trade, you would have made $1,000 on the trade ($10,000 × .05 × 50 × .04 = $1,000).

Of course, a true carry trade can go on for several months and even up to a year. If the carry trade is set up properly and things go well, it is possible to earn 8–10 percent on a carry trade within six months, not including the interest that is being earned minute by minute! This can equate to a $2,500 return on a $500 investment six months earlier.

You should keep different mental buckets in your account for different types of trades. From the ultrashort, lower-percentage gain scalping trade, to the automated overnight trade, to the long-term, high-percentage gain carry trade, each has its own merits and each has its own place in your currency trading system.

CHAPTER 13

Building an FX Account for Your Style

You have the ability to build your currency account to match your trading style. After considering your risk tolerance, your overall investable assets, and the amount of time you would like to spend trading in the currency markets, you then need to build your FX trading system to match your goals. Whether you are a high risk/reward trader or a low risk/reward trader, you can find and build the FX system that works for you.

The Elements of FX Risk

The basic principle behind investing is that a portfolio that is fully insulated from risk will by definition have a zero yield. To put it another way, in order to have the potential for gain, you must assume some risk.

If you think of yourself like an investment bank, hedge fund, or even an FX trading house, what you will then naturally do is think more professionally. You will enter into risk and then at a later date exit out of that risk. You will also expect compensation for undertaking that risk.

FACT

Taking cash, exchanging it for a currency pair, and holding it for a length of time before exiting the trade and going back to cash is a form of banking. This process is one of the basic functions of financial intermediaries. It is called asset transformation.

This transformation is also the basis of the risk-return relationship in currency trading. While it is true that you must assume risk in order to have the chance of a return, there are limits to the return that can be made for the risk that you assume in your FX portfolio. In addition to this, there is an idea that you should not go about investing in risky or very risky assets expecting returns, all while not monitoring the quality of the risk. Rather than putting your money in high-risk assets and expecting high rewards, there is a way to get the most for your risk. The idea should be to get the maximum return for each unit of risk that you are undertaking.

This principle of seeking out the most return for the least amount of risk undertaken can be measured. An investment's **Sharpe ratio** is the method of comparing how good an investment (or investment portfolio) is performing compared to others. The Sharpe ratio is calculated using an investment's daily up-and-down movement versus its overall return. The higher the Sharpe ratio, the better and more efficient the investment is comparatively.

This more return for less risk is the driving force behind most investment systems. More return for less risk can be the idea behind your currency-trading system also. If you know where the risk comes from in trading currencies, then you can take steps to limit this risk and effectively get more for your money. Additionally there are ways to tweak your FX investments to make your currency portfolio detuned for a lower, slower, more manageable trading account. Conversely, you can amp up your FX investments and turn your portfolio into a hands-on, high-return account.

Determining Your Risk Tolerance

Determining your risk tolerance can go a long way in helping you decide what type of currency trading you would like to try, and what type of currency trading system you need to set up to keep you in the FX game. It would not be right to become tame and dormant with your trades if you would like to make a living at currency trading. It would also not be right to have a trading system that takes hours each day in order for it to work effectively if you are seeking a slow and steady return.

Ask yourself what you would like to gain out of currency trading, and then ask yourself what you are and are not willing to give up in order to achieve those investing goals. If you do this questioning, you will be on the path of starting to develop a currency-trading system that works for you.

ALERT

Look at your past history when thinking about your risk tolerance. If your past investments have been in commodities, options, or futures, then you are definitely more risk tolerant. On the other hand, if you normally only invest in government bond mutual funds, then you are likely more risk averse.

You can read this and every book in the stores about currencies, trading, and analysis, but until you are comfortable with what you are expecting out of your FX trading endeavors you will never actually get into trading. So, the best thing to do is to look at yourself and ask, "What do I want from Forex?" The answer can be anything, from treating it like a competitive sport with your friends, to earning enough in profit to make the payments on a new car, to adding return to an otherwise ultraconservative (and low-yielding) bond portfolio, to a making it your full-time business and relying on currency trading for your weekly salary.

Ask yourself the tough questions. It is okay, whatever your goals are! Once you have a good idea of what you would like to try to gain from trading currencies, then you will begin to see what your overall picture is and where FX fits into those plans. It is safe to say that if you want to make enough money to make the payments on a new SUV, then a smaller account with a more conservative trading style would be a good trading system. You can consider yourself lower risk tolerant. If you are looking to supplement the returns to an otherwise low-yielding AA- and AAA-rated bond portfolio, you, too, can consider yourself as having a very low-risk appetite, and can be very conservative in your currency trading.

On the other hand, if you are looking to make the mortgage, or even live off your earnings and draw a weekly paycheck, then you can say that you will have to be much more risk tolerant with your trading system. Whatever your goals are, look to see how much you actually need to make a month to meet those needs. If it is a big number, you will need to build yourself a more risk-oriented portfolio in order to squeeze out those returns. If you only need coffee money, well then, a microaccount and an hour of trading a night will yield you enough for a latte in the morning.

Overall Investable Assets

A good place to start when looking at what you expect to gain by your currency trading is to look at your overall investable assets. Contrary to what you may think, you should not look just at how much money you would like to make or how much money you need to make. In other words, if you are in a bit of a money crunch and are looking for Forex trading to fill in some of the gaps in your income, you are kind of going about it the wrong way. This is because with this sort of mindset you are looking at the dollar amount of profit you need to make, and not considering the risk level you will have to expose yourself and your FX account to in order to achieve this amount of profit.

To explain further, if you are a student, and you have very little money (like most students), then you should first look at how much you can afford to put into an FX account to trade with. If you are a mother of three and you would like to earn extra money setting up trades while the kids are in school, then you need first to determine how much you can put into your

FX account. The same goes for high net-worth millionaires who have most of their wealth in a low-yielding and 100 percent safe bond portfolio: First you need to ask, "How much to put into the account?"

In order to do this you must first determine your overall investable assets. It would not be wise to take all of your life savings, put them into a currency-trading account and risk the entire amount in order to get the big house on the hill. A smaller amount would be best, and if you are the mother of three (and have responsibilities) or are just starting out with Forex trading, then the whole learning curve will be a lot more pleasant if you just put in your extra money. In this case you are allowed to really have fun with FX; you can learn to trade and make money at it while not going into a panic attack every time something doesn't go exactly as planned!

ESSENTIAL

One of the best ways to keep currency trading fun and stress free is to trade only with money you are 100 percent willing to lose. If you have already written off your trading money mentally—that is, it is already gone—then you can fully enjoy taking trading risks with your Forex account.

The next thing you need to do is to look at your list and ask yourself: "How risk averse am I?" If you see that you wanted to earn enough money in your account to make the payments on a new car, then you are conservative and risk averse. If you had the idea that you wanted to make the payments on your mortgage, then you are risk tolerant. After determining what levels of risk you are willing to assume, look at the size of your Forex account. If you decided that your online currency trading account would be $500 or $1,000 and you are risk tolerant, then you are not going to be able to make enough money to make the payments on the mortgage! Your predetermined account size simply can't handle the dollar gains you would have to squeeze out of it in order to come up with a consistent amount to pay a mortgage! With a $500 or $1,000 account and a risk-tolerant trading system, you have a good chance of making the payments on a new car, though.

As you can see, it is not only your goals that determine how much you can earn in your currency- trading endeavors. You must also factor in the overall size of your investable assets and the size of your account. Then you can determine what is a realistic goal to expect from your type of trading system: risk averse or risk tolerant.

FX and Investment Portfolios

One of the ways to consider how much money to invest in a currency-trading account is to look at your overall investable assets. If your investment portfolio, whether a retail account, 401(k) or IRA, is invested in more traditional assets such as bonds, stocks, and mutual funds you can view an actively managed Forex account as a kind of alternative investment. While most of your assets are in the more traditional investments, you can allocate a certain amount to be in your FX account, and this will act as a hedge against your overall portfolio's returns.

You might ask, "Why does FX trading act as a hedge against the typical traditional portfolio?" The answer is that while your bonds and stock move up and down, the returns in an FX account can be completely uncorrelated to the overall performance of the stock and bond markets. Currencies are always moving up and down; you can go long or short a currency pair. You can also earn interest in a trade and have short- and long-term time frames.

FACT

If your overall portfolio is invested heavily in stocks, then you can build your currency portfolio to act as a directional hedge against your large equity exposure. You could have the entire goal of your currency portfolio to act as a hedge against any downward movement of the equities in your overall portfolio.

With this in mind, it can be a really good idea to have 10–20 percent of your overall investable assets in an actively managed currency-trading account. This is the amount that full-service, wealth management firms such as Merrill Lynch and UBS recommend as a percentage of overall assets that should be in alternative assets.

Currencies are an asset that is uncorrelated to stocks and bonds, and therefore the returns on currency trading are not tied to that of the overall market. With this said, you can consider a good currency strategy as a form of alternative strategy, and the FX pairs as alternative assets. Other alternative strategies can be to have a position in precious metals such as gold and silver, and commodities such as oil. You might consider that gold, silver, and oil are priced and traded worldwide in dollars, and therefore these investments act much like a currency themselves. An investment portfolio that has a 10–20 percent position in currencies, precious metals, and oil can be very well diversified with the inclusion of those alternative strategies.

In 1952 Harry Markowitz wrote a paper called "Portfolio Selection." Since then, it has been an undertaking of most every professional money manager to follow modern **portfolio theory**. Modern portfolio theory is the attempt to produce the most portfolio returns for the least risk by maximizing return and limiting risk by diversifying an investment portfolio to include assets that have uncorrelated returns with the other assets in the overall portfolio. You can achieve uncorrelated assets by including both stocks and bonds in your investments. Further, you can achieve diversification by the inclusion of an alternative asset such as a Forex account, precious metals, and oil. The old adage of "don't put all of your eggs in one basket" holds true here. Currency trading can be the key to your overall investment's reaching high returns with uncorrected assets, with the total effect of making your investment portfolio safer and less a victim to the whims of the markets.

Good Intentions, Expected Results

You should go into your trading career each trading day with good intentions to get to the dollar amount of profit you need. If you know that you would like to generate $550 a month to pay for your Mercedes E350, then get the calculator out and see just how much a day or week that really is. If you consider that there is an average of twenty trading days in a month, then you need to earn about $27 a day or $135 a week to get to your goal.

When you look at it this way, the monthly payment on your Mercedes can seem easier to achieve. Your $550 a month in profit equates to a $1,000 account, traded at 10 percent of its value, using a 50:1 margin and making two 0.5 percent trades a day. Keeping these numbers in mind to get to your Mercedes goal, you could easily trade only two hours a day to build up enough profits to make your monthly withdrawal to your bank account, and then make the car payment.

If your only goal is to pay for the Mercedes, then you should trade in a manner that reflects this intent. In this way, you are trading with a goal: You can get into trades that will yield you the 0.5 percent that you need, and you can walk away from the ones that offer less of a yield. You can also walk away from the trades that promise more, but are offering that return at considerably more risk. Remember, your goal is that $550 a month. If you are risking the principal in your account to earn an additional $550 by taking on big gambles, then you are not investing with good intentions and you are not going to get your expected results.

ESSENTIAL

Many people currency trade every now and then, with no real goal in mind. If you are this type of FX trader, that is okay! You are most likely a recreational trader who enjoys the thrill of trading without the stress of making your nut or even having a daily minimum profit goal.

It should not be a goal to earn as much as possible in your currency account. This is *not* a goal! Think about it: Where is the governance in such a plan? What would you use to gauge if a trade were too risky to take? When would you have the knowledge to walk away from your trading desk following a series of good trades? The answer is that making the most money is not a goal, and in fact, it is an unachievable goal. A goal such as this will lead you to take on more and more unnecessary risk, and will lead you to blow up and whittle your account away to nothing by overtrading your account and chasing too high returns. Steer clear of such a goal for your FX trading.

Professional money managers know that people will only give them cash to invest if there is a long history of slow, steady returns. Sure, everyone likes to romanticize about the mutual fund manager that made 70 percent last year. The real test is if that fund manager can do it again, without risking the principal in the account. CNBC is always interviewing the senior fund manager who consistently earns 10 percent per year, year in year out, in good times and bad. These are the fund managers that you should emulate.

While 10 percent per year might seem paltry in an FX account, making the payment on a Mercedes E350 for the next sixty months is definitely something to use as a benchmark goal for your trading profits.

FX Trading: Profit or Income

There are two basic goals in currency trading, profit and income. You can use both goals in your trading system, and both will add to your overall end-of-the-year returns. Profit is the process of buying at one price, and then selling at a later date (from several minutes to several months) when the price of the currency pair has changed in price. These profits are called capital gains. Most likely you can easily understand the concept of capital gains in FX trading: it is similar to the buy low, sell high idea in most other trading.

When you are currency trading, the bulk of the money will be made from buying and selling at different prices. Since you can trade ten to fifty times per trading session, it is easy to see that this can be the bulk of your gains while you engage in FX trading.

The other type of gain is called income. When you engage in what are called carry trades, you will be going short a low-yielding currency and going long a high-yielding currency. It works out that you basically convert your USD cash balance to the low-yielding currency. You borrow the low-yielding currency, and then take the proceeds and invest them in a higher-yielding currency. You will then be paying interest on your low-yielding currency loan and earning interest on the investment.

Your income is the net difference between the two currencies. If you borrow USD at 0.05 percent and invest in the New Zealand dollar at 6 percent, you will earn 5.5 percent, which is the net difference amount. At 50:1 this equates to 275 percent per year.

FACT

When currency traders consider carry trades, they look for the difference between the high interest rate and the low interest rate. Another big factor that traders look at is the quality and price stability of the high-yielding currency: All high-yielding currencies are not created equal!

With this rate of return you can set up an income-generating certificate of deposit. While CDs are 100 percent safe, some people use these and bond mutual funds as a source of income at times in their lives when income is more important than growth. If you are looking for a source of income, are more conservative in nature, and are not interested in trading in your currency brokerage account for capital gains, then an income strategy can be for you.

Using currencies as an income strategy is basically a very long-term carry trade strategy. Most bond mutual funds require a $1,000 minimum investment. Bond mutual funds that are set up for income are usually called high-yield funds and can pay anywhere from 5–9 percent annually, plus growth. In this example, if you took the same $1,000 and invested 20 percent in a carry trade such as a long NZD/USD or long AUD/USD, you would earn the net interest difference.

This net interest difference at 50:1 margin would net you a yield of anywhere from $400 to $650 a year on your FX investment. This equates to a dividend of $33 to $54 per month on your $1,000 deposit. Compare to a monthly dividend of $4 to little more than $7.00 per month with the high-yield bond fund! Granted, the bond fund is safer than the FX investment, but with a little bit of planning you can build an income portfolio of both high-yield bonds and income-oriented carry trades to increase the overall monthly yield of your income bond portfolio.

CHAPTER 14

High Risk/Return Traders

If you decide that you would like to build your currency account to be high risk/high reward, then you will have to consider if you have a few key elements first. In order to give yourself the go-ahead to trade more aggressively, you will need a certain level of assets, available time to spend on FX, and a high tolerance for the added stress that trading large amounts of highly leveraged cash can bring.

Larger Overall Assets

If you decide that you are the type of person who is willing to accept a higher risk in his currency portfolio in exchange for a higher return, you will first need to see if this type of account is actually possible. The main requirement for a high risk/high return currency portfolio is that you have a large amount of investable assets. If you have a large amount of investable assets, then a currency account that is amped up and tuned for high performance should be no problem. This is because your main assets, such as your stock and bond portfolio, will be holding their own and providing a slow, steady, and reliable return.

Since this is the case, the money you put into an FX account can be heavily traded and risked often enough to squeeze out more returns than a more conservative portfolio. If you have a large base of secure investments, you can set aside an amount for an FX portfolio. This currency portfolio can consist of 20–25 percent of your overall portfolio. This 25 percent can be used to press hard, take risks, and earn returns.

Many financial advisors who work at firms that specialize in high net-worth clients recommend having some money set aside for risk taking. This money is often put into a separate account, and is used to trade aggressively. If you desire, you can turn this portion of your overall investable assets into a currency account.

FACT

Many people put money in an account to play with and to trade at will. This money is often used to trade penny stocks, startup companies, and other forms of very risky stock that have a chance of earning high returns, but also a chance of becoming a loss. This at-will trading prevents clients from touching their secure investment accounts.

You can use your currency account to trade aggressively and win big. Of course, in order to trade aggressively, you will need to take more risks in proportion to the size of the account. A larger account size will also allow you to sustain larger swings into and out of profit range. Since not all of your trades will work out all of the time, a larger account will allow you to have a greater percentage of your account that will be sitting in cash.

You can then trade aggressively with only 10 percent or 15 percent of the account assets. This would leave 85–90 percent of the account available to soak up any reversals of fortune with your FX trades without causing a margin call. If you have 85 percent of your account in cash, this leaves a lot of room for a trade to move into negative territory without the need for you to close out the trade. If you have the cash in margin, you can allow time to work for you and wait in the trade for the price of the pair to reverse. Once it reverses, you can then get out of the trade at a profit, or at the very least, a breakeven.

Higher FX to Traditional Investments Ratio

If you would like to build an aggressively managed, high risk/high reward currency account, you will need to allocate a higher percentage of your total investments to Forex. While a traditional currency account would amount to about 10 percent of your total investable assets, a high risk/high reward portfolio would be around 20–25 percent of your investments. If you put 20–25 percent of your assets in your FX account, you will have the dollars available to take on multiple currency pairs at one time. You will also be able to use advanced hedging such as three-sided trades. Lastly, you will be able to pyramid into your currency positions.

A larger account can allow you to have enough dollars to take big bites into trades when the opportunity presents itself. When the Asian stock markets crash and in turn the European and U.S. markets follow suit, the currency-risk trades will also fall. Sometimes they will fall dramatically. The SEK will fall against the USD, the EUR will fall against the Swiss franc, and the Australian dollar will fall against the U.S. dollar. These are the times that a currency trader loves! These are the setups that you should be looking for, and with a larger account, you can buy large amounts of Swedish kronor, euros, and Australian dollars.

With a higher percentage of your assets in a currency account, you can buy proportionally larger amounts of these risky currencies relative to your assets. You can also buy larger amounts of these directional trades (meaning they are profitable only when the markets start doing well again) and still build in enough cash margin to cushion the blow if the market continues to fall before rebounding.

Essentially, a larger percentage of your investable assets equates to giving yourself time to withstand a continued fall in the market after your first buy into the long side of a risk trade. You would buy into the long side of a risk trade after the market has gone down. This type of trade will earn you a profit when the market goes up and the world's traders are once again looking to increase risk assets in their portfolios.

A high balance in your account will also give you the opportunity to add to your currency positions at a lower price. This can add to your earnings if the currency pair continues to move against you once you are in the trade. If you have a large balance you can engage in a more risky procedure of buying more of the currency pair at lower and lower prices. For example, if the risk appetite of the world's traders goes down and the AUD/USD falls from 108 to 105, then you might decide that it is a good time to go long the AUD/USD and buy some Australian dollars. If on the next day the U.S. and European stock markets continue to go down, the AUD/USD might fall from 105 to 103 or even 102. If you have a large account and cash margin to spare (think of your cash margin as wiggle room) you can double or even triple the amount of AUD you now have in your account. Doubling or tripling the size of an already cheap trade can boost the gains on the long AUD/USD trade. Such an increase in your position is adding to your risk, but once the risk appetite comes back to the market you will be looking at enough gains to take the rest of the week (or two) off!

Higher Pressure Tolerance

High risk/high reward trading not only ads to your profit, but it also ads to your pressure. You must have a high pressure tolerance in order to trade aggressively. In order to get the maximum out of your FX account you will need to buckle up and really be in your seat during each trading session. If you are scalping and using a system of getting into and out of trades many times during the trading day, the tension and pressure can build quite dramatically and very quickly.

If you have a large account, this creates an added mental burden: You have more to lose and more to gain by your efforts in currency trading. Also, if you are trading aggressively for hours at a time (even just half a day at a time) day after day, you amplify the chances of putting your money into a bad trade mistakenly. Remember, every time you are in a trade, that money (and your cash margin) is at risk.

ESSENTIAL

> If you are trading three scalping positions an hour for a six- to eight-hour trading day, you are risking a quarter to a third of your account eighteen to twenty-four times a day! That can generate quite a bit of pressure, but it can also generate quite a bit of excitement!

If your Forex trading account is 20 percent of your total assets and you are putting a third of that account into each scalping trade, then you are really risking upward near 7 percent of your total investable assets in each trade. If you had a $50,000 overall portfolio, and you invested 20 percent in FX, your FX account would be $10,000. If you took a third of this account in each trade and traded three scalps per hour, for eight hours a day, you would be trading nearly $4 million in currency a day! This can be shown by:

$10,000 × .333 = $3,333 account used,
$3,333 × 50 = $166,650 margin used,
$166,500 × 3 = $499,950 amount of margin used per hour,
$499,950 × 8 = $3,999,600 amount of margin used per eight-hour day.

Another way to look at it is by asking yourself "How much money am I used to handling?" If you have built up a $50,000 account with investable assets, then you most likely know how to handle calling up your broker to place stock, bond, and mutual fund trades that fit in a $50,000 account. You might even have an online brokerage account and are very used to trading on margin. Even if this is the case, in this example you would have been placing trades of $5,000 or even $10,000 at a time with each individual order. Even if you day traded in your inexpensive online broker account you would have to wait for each trade to settle (usually three days) before the money could be used again for another trade.

As you can imagine, trading a $50,000 account at a brokerage firm is much different from trading nearly $4,000,000 a day in a fast-moving currency account. Since this is the case, nerves of steel are a basic requirement of a FX trading system that is all-out, high risk/high return. If you can master your emotions and nerves, and you have the knowledge on how to look for setups and then scalp and trade, your Forex account can get very profitable, very fast.

More Stress

Scalping and trading a third of your currency account, day in and day out, can lead to some very stressful situations. If you aren't showing a profit for a few days or if you have a trade that goes bad for a time, and you are stuck with a loss—these are the situations that can creep up on you and make you wonder if you should continue trading in an aggressive manner, or if you should just take your money out of the FX market altogether and put it into a money market account. If this happens to you, don't worry! If you need to cool off from currency trading, go ahead and walk away for a time. You might need the rest of the week off, or you might need a whole season off. If you have the feeling that you don't have the knack for it, what you most likely need is a break. Forex trading full on is hard to do, and it takes its toll on you mentally and physically. The tension can begin to build up in your shoulders and neck. Pretty soon your knees ache because you have been sitting tense at your computer desk for days on end. You might get easily frustrated at your loved ones when they ask the smallest thing from you. It might be your turn to make dinner, and you find yourself resenting the time it takes to cook, let alone the time it takes to eat with your family.

ALERT

> Because high risk/high reward trading can bring so much pressure, many professional currency traders are avid athletes. Whether they swim, jog, or kickbox, professional currency traders find ways to exercise away the muscle tension and stress that day in, day out FX trading brings with it, good days and bad!

These are the warning signs that you are overtrading your account. You will know something is wrong: Forex trading used to be fun. What happened? If you are showing these signs, or your family and friends are giving you signals that you are acting differently, then you have to shut down your account for a while.

Forex trading can be very profitable, and therefore very fun. If it begins to be not fun for any reason, for any length of time, it is causing you too much stress. If you are under too much stress then you are running the risk of making a mistake with a trade. You might be so stressed out with your trading that you secretly want to lose big so you are forced to close out your account and stop trading. This reasoning is more common than you think. This is why so many people seem to fail at currency trading when, in fact, it is not that hard to make a profit at all.

You might be expecting too much profit. More likely you are not used to managing a large margin account. It might seem an easy thing to do to place a trade for $25,000, $50,000, or even $100,000 worth of currency at one time. The fact is, that is quite a lot of money, and you most likely will get just a tad bit conservative in nature when trading. Questions like, "What if I lose?" are the most common. If this is the case, give yourself time to cool off.

A good way to do this is to shut down your account for a while. Take all but $50 out of the account and have it sent back to you in a check or wired to your bank account. Take the money and use it on a vacation or weekend trip with your family. Maybe spend some money on a special holiday or dinner party for the extended family. If you are single, spend the money on a set of skis or a new road bike. Go on a trip with your friends and exercise off that tension. This getting away will give yourself time to think about what is wrong with your FX trading system, because something is definitely wrong with it if you are not enjoying it!

More Time to Spend on Trading

After deciding that you have the assets to invest into trading currencies, the next thing to ask is if you have the time to currency trade. If you are going to build an account that is larger in dollar size, and you plan on trading in an aggressive, high risk/high reward way, then it follows logic that you will have to spend more time on trading. It might be that you are an evening scalper, and that you plan on placing only six or seven large bets over the course of watching the late movie before going to sleep. You might have an idea of getting up in the early morning and trading from 4:00 A.M. to 6:00 P.M. before you go to work, or before the kids wake up. Whatever your plan, you will need to spend a proportionally greater amount of time on currency trading.

Your actual trading time might only be two or three two-hour sessions a week. This limited amount of actual trading time is a good plan: It would keep you fresh and excited about currency trading. With this type of plan, you can lead a pretty normal life. You can have a regular job, you can raise kids, and you can have free time. It is possible to lead a relaxed life and still trade your FX account in an aggressive nature.

In order to do this effectively, you need to spend the time you are not actually trading reading, studying, and looking for setups. You could build this into your normal day. You could take the kids to the park, let them play on the swings, break out your iPad, and read the currency news websites. You could go to the coffee shop a few minutes before you are going to meet your friends, pull out your laptop, and read a report that your broker sent out that morning.

ESSENTIAL

Work out a schedule for studying about the markets and doing research. If the kids go down for a two o'clock nap, then this might be a good time. If you can read at your desk during lunch, then maybe this is your best time. Find a good time and get into a routine of reading about FX every day.

Putting in the time to train in currency trading will go a long way toward getting you to the point that you can recognize when a good trade is about to happen. The more you know about the world's economies, the world's political climate, and the world's currencies, the more you will be able to buy into and out of trades during the hours that you are actually trading currency pairs. This knowledge will go a long way toward keeping you confident. This confidence will then keep you less stressed and then you will enjoy FX trading even more.

Once you are in the groove of reading, studying, and listening to the news, brokers' reports, and central bank websites, then it is really easy to sit down to a night of FX trading that is stress-free. You would be surprised how fast you can build up knowledge of currencies and economies. This knowledge will help you place well-thought out trades, trades that earn you profit.

Whether you are planning to trade a little or a lot, you still need to put in the time to learn the markets and stay up on the news. Aggressive trading with a large sum of money can be stressful. You can combat this stress by being well-informed and well-schooled in your chosen subject of currency trading. It pays to put in the time.

Less Expectancy of Overall Profit

When you are aggressively trading your account and you have it set up for high risk/high return, you will naturally be entering into a greater number of trades per trading session. Additionally, you will be trying to capture a greater percentage movement in each trade. You will also be taking advantage of many more trading opportunities than you would if you set your FX trading system to be more conservative in style.

These elements will combine to have an effect of actually increasing the chance that you will have a greater number of trades that do not work out. It is a bit counterintuitive, but since you are trading more with an aggressive risk/reward account, you have to have an acceptance of a greater number of trades that just aren't profitable. Most likely the percentage amount of trades that are profitable will be the same as a regular low-risk account, but the sheer number of trades will mean a higher number that is not profitable.

QUESTION

How often should I have winning trades?
Making money in currency trading is a matter of numbers. If you consistently win one trade a day more than you lose, then your currency trading is profitable. Some professional currency traders are happily profitable by winning only 1 percent of their overall daily positions!

This higher number of trades that you are making is directly tied to your trading plan. It is just a function of math that you will be stuck with a higher number of trades that only break even or worse, are losers. If you are trading for six or eight hours a day, in and out of currency pairs, and you are getting into and out of five, six or more trades per hour, then the number of losers can be discouraging.

The percentage of winners to losers is most likely the same. Since you have a large account, the dollar amount of the losses can be quite large, and this, above all things, can lead you to discouragement. When you are looking at your losses, you should remember to compare them to the dollar amount of your gains. Most likely you are winning big too, and most likely you are still having a net gain in your account when you take the winnings and subtract the losses. If you are creeping ahead, that is fine! A few days or even a few weeks of slow growth are normal. Sometimes the FX markets are very dormant and there are very few good trades to be made. As long as your winners beat your losers, then you are okay.

It is sometimes psychologically daunting to overcome a loss that involves a big dollar amount and therefore looks really bad. At these times you must realize that you are probably trading very often, and with a lot of money in each trade. This is the reason the losses look so bad. This is also the reason that the winnings are so wonderful. An aggressive risk/reward profile and loads of margin in your account can lead to sometimes hurtful losses. It can also lead to big money when the FX trades are on your side.

CHAPTER 15

Amp Up the Risk/Return Ratio

There are several methods to increasing the return in your currency portfolio. While each one of them can bring added risk, they will bring an added reward to your normal trading ideas. You can use concentrated positions to increase the upward movement in your profit and loss statement. You can also diversify these concentrated positions across geography and industry in an effort to hedge out as much risk as possible. Lastly, you can use automated trading to double dip, in order to capture rapid swings in FX pairs.

Concentrated Positions

There are several methods to getting more out of your trading account. Once you decide that you would like to amp up the risk-return ratio of your FX portfolio, you can use these methods to get maximum results from your account. Most currency traders will have four, five, or even six different currency pair positions on their books at any one time. When you follow this practice and have many different positions open (both long and short), you can hedge away some of the risk in your currency account.

This hedging comes from using different pairs to create positions that are both risky and risk adverse in nature. You can go long commodity currencies, long the currencies that do well when the U.S. stock market does well, and go long the safe-haven currencies.

ESSENTIAL

Widely diversified currency trades have the effect of alleviating the problem of guessing what direction the markets will move in the next trading session. Make sure that you have three to five currency pairs on your books if you are unsure of the direction of the next few days' risk sentiment.

With many trades on the books, you can capture the gains on up, down, or sideways market movements. The overall effect is a bit of loss, and a bit of gain. With this you will gain, but by smaller amounts.

If you are setting up your trading system to be a high performance account, you need to go against the diversification strategy. The strategy that works best for getting the most out of your accounts is one of concentrated positions. Instead of five different currency pairs, you would get into two or three currency pairs.

Additionally, you would have these three currency pairs be the same direction. If the three pairs are the same direction, they are not hedged, and all will move in the same direction according to the risk sentiment of the markets. For example, if you have two positions and both are risk trades, they will both win or lose as the markets accept or reject added risk to their portfolios.

If you have two long commodity-currency trades on the books, even though they are different countries' currencies, or even from different parts of the world, they will move up when the traders of the world are feeling good about the economy. If you have an AUD/USD and a USD/NOK on the books, they will both move in the same direction when there are reports that the world economies are chugging ahead and everything is going fine.

Concentrated positions in the same direction will give your account an added return when the currency market and the stock markets move in your favor. Even if you have risk-averse trades on the books, if you are long the USD, the JPY, and the Swiss francs, you are still concentrating your positions in directional trades. All of these currencies will move up when the economy is feeling sick. If the world's stock markets have been run up for a while, even if for three or four days, you could buy and go long USD, Japanese yen, and Swiss francs.

More on Concentrated Positions

Even though these are three currencies from three major parts of the world, they will all react in the same way when the stock markets correct themselves. Stock markets correct themselves after a three or four day run-up because the professional traders of the world like to take money off of the table and sell out of some of their positions to lock in their gains from the markets. Once the stock markets go down, risk assets all over the world will also fall, and the safe havens will gain. This means your long USD, JPY, and CHF will gain also.

FACT

> One of the main reasons that the stock markets of the world rise and fall every two or three days is that the professional traders all see the same buy and sell indicators on the technical charts. This reading of the market makes most traders add money and then take money out of the market at the same time.

Since your three positions will gain in this situation, what you essentially have is a directional trade. Even though you have three currencies, they are all risk averse, and therefore act as a concentrated position. The three FX pairs on your books actually act as one FX pair. Granted they are diversified in geography and in counter currency, but they are concentrated in direction. If these are the trades on your books, you will win big when the world's traders decide that they would like to take some money out of the market and reverse their positions. Stock markets go up and down all the time. One, two, or three pairs in the same direction will make you capture very good profits when the time comes.

Since the three trades on your books are actually a concentrated position, it is best to diversify these three positions in proportion to each one's potential movement. In order to do this you should first have an idea as to what currency pairs to buy into for this type of setup.

In this example, you are looking to get into three unidirectional trades that are diversified as much as possible. Since the stock market has run up in the past several days, it is safe to assume that the U.S. and world stock markets will fall due to profit taking by traders. While planning for this to happen, you decide that you are going to use a total of 12 percent of your margin for the entire risk-averse position.

You then decide that in order to have risk-averse trades, you will short a commodities currency, a growth currency, and go long a safe-haven currency. With this in mind you consult your broker's reports and your trading journal. You can choose to short the New Zealand dollar and the Swedish krona, and go long the safe-haven currency, the Swiss franc. All of these currencies are sensitive to the risk sentiment of the markets, but they are diversified somewhat.

The Anatomy of a Hedged Directional Trade

The short NZD/JPY trade will capture profits in two ways. The first will be when the high yielding NZD falls out of favor. New Zealand is usually considered a high-growth economy. If the market senses any form of slowing growth, high-growth economies such as New Zealand will be one of the first to suffer. The market will react to the idea of slower growth by beginning to think that the Reserve Bank of New Zealand (*http://www.rbnz.govt.nz*) will not raise rates in the future, or worse, will cut rates.

This will cause the currency traders of the world to desire to have a low-yielding currency such as the Japanese yen more than the NZD, the currency of the possibly slower-growing New Zealand. The JPY will look more attractive because it is already low yielding, and the thought is that it is so because the economy has already slowed in Japan. If an economy is already slow, that central bank can lower rates only so much more. Therefore, there is a bit of a built-in safety net in owning lower-yielding currencies.

You will also achieve a diversified position by shorting the SEK and going long the USD. The Swedish krona is sensitive to the risk sentiment and is considered a growth currency. This is because Sweden's economy is small and tightly focused on banking and industry. Sweden's banks historically have had a large customer base in the Baltic nations. These Baltic nations are economically stable, but derive much of their prosperity from heavy industry. Additionally, Sweden is home to both Volvo and SAAB-Scandia. Both are car, truck, and heavy machinery manufacturers.

With this in mind, if the world's stock traders and economists think the world's economies are doing well, and they are willing to continue to push up the price of stocks because they have a strong risk appetite, then the SEK will do well also. The reverse is also true. A bad stock market leads traders to think a bad economy, which leads traders to think: sell the Swedish krona. With a long USD/SEK, you will also be capturing the upward movement of the dollar, because money flocks to the USD in bad times. The USD is considered one of the safest currencies to own, and many people want to hold dollars when the world's risk sentiment increases, like after the stock market falls.

QUESTION

What trades would I place if the market was expected to go down?
Most of the examples in this book are to set up a trade that would earn money if the stock market were to go up. If you would like to capture gains when the markets go down, just short the growth currency and go long the low-yielding, safe-haven currency.

The third and final diversifying position is a short EUR/CHF position. In this case you would capture the increase of the Swiss franc over the price of the EUR. Since the euro is the main currency of Europe and is frequently traded against the USD, the play between the euro and the Swiss franc can be very easy to predict. In this example, money will flow out of the euro and into the Swiss franc as the world's traders take risk off the table and move their assets into the ultrasafe franc. Even though you could short the euro against the U.S. dollar, a more predictable gain would be to short the euro against the Swiss franc.

While all of these three positions will capture gains in a falling market, they will all do so for different economic reasons. It is true that you are managing your currency account aggressively. You have concentrated your positions and have designed the trades to be one big directional trade. Even though this has caused added risk, you have used diversification within your concentrated position to hedge away some of that risk. The position is hedged across geographic and economic influences. You are now ready for the markets to fall and for you to reap the profits. This is a good example of an active hedge within a directional trade.

Double-Trading Volatile Currency Pairs

Double-trading volatile currency pairs is an additional method of aggressively capturing FX gains. In order to do this effectively, you would need to trade a pair that is very risk sensitive such as the AUD/USD or the USD/SEK. Both of these pairs move in an up-and-down fashion that follows the movement of the U.S. stock markets. The idea is to enter a market order at the beginning of a strong upward or downward movement. You will know the direction to take by looking at the news going into the weekend. If the news reports are stating that it will be volatile or a bumpy ride the next week, then this is the best time for this type of trade.

For example, the previous Friday the government might have issued a negative economic report regarding jobs or durable goods orders. The indication is that there will be a slowing of the economy. Over the weekend you look at your USD/SEK three-hour chart and you notice that the USD and the SEK have been like a yo-yo for months, and seem to be range bound between two points. You also notice from the chart that the USD has started to move up against the SEK and, in the last trading session on Friday, it moved up considerably.

You do your research and you notice that the Riksbank, (*www.riksbank.com*), is not planning to have a rate meeting in the next few weeks. In fact, you gather from your reading that the management of the Riksbank believes that growth and inflation is on target. This information leads you to think that there will not be an interest rate hike for the next several months.

Switching to your trading platform on Sunday afternoon, you place a long USD/SEK order. This long USD/SEK order will capture profit as the U.S. and European markets open after a weekend of contemplating the bad news out of the United States. Most likely the trend of the strengthening USD against the SEK will continue. You know that this trend line will continue until the risk sentiment in traders' minds rises; i.e., when the traders of the world reverse their tastes and decide to add more risk to their portfolios.

ALERT

Some currency-trading software will only let you close out the first trade of a series of trades in the same currency before allowing you to close out the second and third. This closing out in order or entry means that you might have winning trades in which you are unable to realize the gains.

After placing the long USD/SEK trade, you then open up the "Modify Order" screen. You should then observe the peak of the trading range. Remember, the SEK has been moving up and down against the USD in a consistent up-and-down pattern that is range bound. If you program the computer to take profit at just below the range-bound peak, you will ride the trade into the profit, all while the U.S. and European markets are in turmoil.

In order to maximize your automatic trading and automatic profit taking, you would then enter in a short USD/SEK order that is set to fill just above the point that the long order is closing out. The momentum of the markets will allow you to have a trade that is long USD and capture profits during the bad market conditions. This trade will then automatically close out at the range-bound historical turning point. At this point your automated trading platform will fill a short USD/SEK order, allowing you to capture the price movement of the then strengthening Swedish krona. This trade will be held until the cycle will repeat itself.

Using Naked Trades to Trade Aggressively

You can also trade aggressively by trading naked. Trading naked is a method of going into trades without any stop losses or take profits pre-programmed into the trade. In order to do this you must first wait for the best time of the day: 6:00–7:00 P.M. eastern. At this time of day the trading will be very light to nonexistent. Because of this, the limited orders of any size will greatly affect the market. This is due to the fact that there are so few players at this time of the day: the New York traders have gone home, and the Hong Kong traders are just getting to their desks. A little trading can go a long way here. You can use your skills and margin to capture some wonderful profits. You can use a combination of scalping and overnight trading to really get into some powerful price movements.

Again, the time to do this type of trading is when the markets are in a major reversal. Look for the Asian markets to be way down, and the S&P 500 futures following suit. If the Asian markets are down anywhere over 1 percent and the S&P 500 futures are down the same, then clear your trades to get fully freed up on your margin and get ready!

The best way to begin is to get a calculator out and divide your margin into tenths. You will be placing four trades over the next two hours that will total 40 percent of your margin. These trades will be at the market, meaning you will get the prevailing price at that time. As the two hours pass, the markets will begin to heat up. The traders in Hong Kong, Tokyo, and Sydney will begin to realize that they do not want to be in risk-oriented trades. The same idea will be thought by early risers in Europe, as well as the traders who, like you, are in the United States and are trading after dinner.

The best trade for this type of scenario is one of shorting a tried-and-true carry trade. One of the best examples of a currency pair that will capture a contraction in the stock markets is the AUD/USD. This currency pair has become the favorite of traders who want to capture big, predictable profits in a market downturn.

Make your first one-tenth margin trade, and then sit back and wait. In the next twenty to thirty minutes the pair will move and you will be in the profit point. Enter another sell order at this point, and again wait a half hour to enter the next trade. By this time there should be some direction to the market, and it should be easy to see by switching to a five-minute chart. When you are on a five-minute chart, you will see the entry points clearly marked. You will also see the chart move down and down, allowing you to capture more and more profit. You should have the last of your four trades in by 8:00 P.M. eastern.

FACT

> There are many ways in which you can amp up the risk and return of your FX brokerage account. Naked trading is one of the most aggressive methods. Naked trades usually have no stop losses and no take-profit points. This type of trading can yield huge gains, but can also bring big losses.

These trades are considered naked because there will be no hedge, and no take profit entered into the trading system. You will be assuming the full force of the risk; you will also be able to take all of the profit. The reason that there should not be a take-profit point is that you are not sure how far down the markets will go, and for how many days. There are times when the market is set for a fall. When this happens, the trade described here can go for days, allowing you to capture big profits.

It is important to walk away from your computer at this time. You should have some activity lined up that will keep your mind off of trading for the rest of the night. Perhaps going out to dinner, or going to a movie with friends; whatever you do, do not close out the orders on your computer. When the time is right, you will close them out. It is best not to check your trading platform in the morning. This type of trading works best when you monitor it remotely and you can do this best by following the Australian dollar currency ETF, FXA. You can program your smart phone or iPad to follow FXA, and by doing so you will be able to get an idea of how poorly the AUD is doing.

You can watch the AUD fall in percentage terms from the day before with this ETF. You can then return to your trading platform when you see a sizable fall in the value of the Australian dollar in the FXA ETF.

Once you notice a good amount of movement to the downside of AUD, only then return to your trading platform to take a peek of how well your positions have done. This would be a good time to close them out, take your profits, and take the rest of the week off.

Trade Ahead of the News

Another very aggressive trading technique is to trade ahead of the news. In this way, you will have to use every bit of your market knowledge as well as have the best fundamental analysis and technical analysis skills. If there is a day that there is a lot of upcoming news scheduled, then on these days most traders will be out of the markets completely. At best, they will hold on to the positions that they hold already. They might even enter into a few hedging strategies.

If you are trading aggressively, then you can take advantage of these opportunities to build up your FX positions. If the market performed horribly the day before, and the S&P 500 futures are down significantly (by more than 2.5 percent) then you have to stop and consider if the market has already priced-in the risk-averse sentiment into FX prices.

ESSENTIAL

Charts can help you determine if risk trades are properly priced, allowing you to trade ahead of the news. Technical charts will tell you if each pair is at the bottom or top of its price cycle and if it is a good time to enter a trade that would allow you to capture any rebound in the next session.

This can be a difficult task, and it takes a bit of observation and predictive skills to see if the AUD/USD or the EUR/CHF will move further down before an anticipated extremely bad day in the market. When determining if you should get into a trade before the news, you must remember that the aftermarkets in Europe have been open after a day of very bad numbers, and many traders will enter the market as bargain hunters. This action of buying at this time will help form a bottom of the market, and will set the stage to begin the inevitable climb of the markets.

Additionally, if the European markets have done poorly, and the U.S. S&P 500 futures are set to show that the market will open lower, there is a strong possibly that most of the FX trading has taken place by 6:00 A.M. eastern, which is an hour before the US New York markets open. This is true because the heaviest time of the FX trading day is when the U.S. and the European markets overlap. If you consider that most of the new pricing of the currency pairs will have taken place in anticipation of the U.S. markets' opening lower, then you could conclude that you could actually take some long positions of some of the currency pairs that reacted the most to the anticipated bad day in the markets.

This is an example of trading ahead of the news. Most of the time you can get into trades and have a good idea of what direction the FX pair will take in the next few days. The problem arises when there is very bad news. During these times you should take added precaution with your Forex trades. With a bit of foresight and long risky positions, you can capture strong rebounds in the market.

CHAPTER 16

High Risk/Return Strategies

If you would like to trade your FX account in an aggressive manner you'll need to have some good ideas of what to look for in high risk/return strategies. You could set up your account to trade the market's risk appetite. You could also trade exotic currencies that are from countries that are experiencing rapid growth. Lastly, you could trade the quasi currencies such as gold, silver, and oil. Any way you look at it, you will need to know where to look for trading strategies that attain higher returns.

Trading the Market's Risk Appetite

You can trade the market's risk appetite by capturing the gains of currencies that are considered low risk and selling short currencies that are considered high risk. When the world has a lower-risk tolerance, it will sell off risk assets. These risk assets include the selling off of the world's stock markets and higher-yielding currencies. The world's traders will then move into bonds and safe-haven currencies. One of the reasons that these sell-offs occur is that most traders will be looking at the same information, and they will come to the same conclusions. They will all want to protect their money, and will all do so in the same way.

ESSENTIAL

The markets can move with stampede-like force once a large number of traders start selling off securities at the end of a big run-up in the markets. The U.S. markets have been becoming more and more volatile in the last few years. This rapid and forceful up and down spells opportunity to currency traders worldwide.

This happens during times of unrest and upheaval, but on the opposite side of the spectrum it happens every other three or four days after a strong run-up in the market. If the U.S. and European stock market has run up 3–5 percent in the past three or four days, people will begin to feel like they have had enough success for a while, and will sell off their winning securities in an effort to lock in the profits they have won.

You can use your observations and trading journal to get an idea of when the U.S., European, and Asian markets have moved up over the past few days, and when they are getting ready to make a reversal due to profit taking. If the market has done well and has gone up 3–5 percent in the past few days, then this might be a time for a turnaround. Another major indicator that it is time for a turnaround is if the U.S. stock market's gains have been heavily in the news. If the stock markets make the news for how much they have moved up, then this is a surefire way of knowing that it is time to book some currency trades that will make money when the market corrects. This is because by the time the stock markets make the general news (such as the regular afternoon and 10:00 P.M. local news), it is already old news, and the market is stale.

If the stock markets are making the news on stations such as WLS-ABC Channel 7 Chicago, KNXV-ABC 15 in Phoenix, or similar local news stations, then you should be getting ready to make a few trades in your currency account. These trades should make money when the world's stock traders have had their fill of risk assets: when they are selling short the DOW 30, The CAC40, and the Hang Seng. If you have shorted risk, and you have bought safety, you will make money. At the same time, if the market has been down for four days or even a week, and it makes the news, then this is a good time (for the same, but opposite reasons) to go long risk and sell short the less risky assets.

Selling Risk Short with Currency Trading

If the DAX, the S&P 500, and the FTSE100 have all gone through a sudden good fortune and have risen for the past several days, then you could start to look around for ways to capture the risk aversion that will inevitably come. It is human nature to think that the stock markets will go up forever; in fact, professional traders secretly hope that the average investor will push the world's stock indexes higher after they have begun to rise. The world's professional traders, both equity, index-futures, and stock-options traders know when it is time to take their profits and run. They will have no problem in reversing their positions and taking the cash out of the long-risk trades. The same should be true for you. You can learn when the market is going to change direction, and trade accordingly. With this strategy, you will essentially be trading risk. You will be buying and selling the attitude of the equity traders of the world. With the right directional trade you can capture the heightened risk aversion that happens after a big run-up in the markets. The values of currencies are very closely related to the growth of home economies. If there is a perception that there is slowing growth—or worse, stagnation—then the risky, growth oriented currencies will fall relative to safety currencies.

One of the best ways to capture this safety and growth relationship is the shorting of the Swedish krona against the EUR and the USD. The Swedish krona is considered a growth currency and is tied very much to the successes of the U.S. and European stock markets. This is true because Sweden, while an independent currency, is heavily reliant on the export of its industrial and consumer goods to Europe. It is safe to say that long USD/SEK and EUR/SEK positions will gain when stock markets fall.

FACT

While most Forex brokers allow you to trade upward near fifty currency pairs, this book only covers the basics. These basic currency pairs are used to teach you the inner workings of setting up winning trades. It also helps that these basic trades offer more than basic returns!

Traders will unwind SEK positions, and this will force the upward movement of the USD and the EUR. Also, money will flow into the USD naturally as the USD is considered a safe-haven currency during times of economic uncertainty. This is a second factor to sway you to go long a USD/SEK position.

The second pair that will most likely move dramatically is the EUR/CHF, if you short the EUR into the Swiss franc. The EUR/CHF pair is a favorite of professional currency traders worldwide: it has a predictable movement when times are (or seem) to be getting worse. Money will flow from the euro and into the Swiss franc at even the slightest perception that times are getting worse in Europe. This is because the Swiss economy is considered naturally stronger than that of neighboring Belgium, Luxembourg, and France, which are countries that use the euro. Additionally, the Swiss National Bank (*www.snb.ch*) is considered to be very well managed, and historically has done a fine job of being conservative, which, in turn, is good for the Swiss franc.

This short EUR/CHF will allow you to capture the rush of risk assets (EUR) into the risk averse asset (CHF). The combination of going long the USD and the Swiss franc and shorting the EUR and the Swedish krona will go a long way in keeping your account protected and profitable during times of economic uncertainty such as when the world's stock markets fall.

Developing Countries/Exotic Currencies

Once you have traded risk sentiment by going long and short the safe-haven currencies, then you can take some of your margin and move on to exotic currencies. The currencies of developing economies can be profitable, as they usually offer a high rate of interest and can therefore act as a carry trade. Additionally, their return can be independent of traditional money centers, and therefore can act independently of the good or bad fortunes of the United States, the United Kingdom, Germany, and Japan. Exotic currency trades can allow you to capture the sometimes phenomenal growth of countries such as Brazil, Turkey, Hungary, and Poland. These are relatively stable countries that are in a pattern of growth that is independent of the growth rates of the more mature economies such as Japan and the United States.

You can capture the growth-rate differential between the United States and Brazil much like you can capture the interest rate differential between AUD and USD. In fact, you could capture a huge interest differential, as you could borrow USD at 0.5 percent and use it to buy Brazil reals earning 10-plus percent. This type of trade would allow you to capture simultaneously the growth and the carry trade of the currencies. If Brazil were to heat up economically still more, then you would benefit from additional rate hikes, which would boost the difference of the USD/BLR even further, giving you added gains.

QUESTION

Where do I look for exotic currency trading ideas?
You can find out what currency pairs your Forex broker offers and look up the symbols on the Internet. Once you see what pairs are available, then perform research on those countries' central bank websites to search out trading ideas. Of course brokers' reports can certainly help you know what currency pairs are likely to work out well.

Another good trade is to use euros to buy the Polish zloty. Poland is a strong industrial and agricultural economy and trades primarily with the euro-bloc countries. The PLN has grown over 20 percent against the euro in the past three years. Poland would like to become a European Union member, and it continues to be a favorite of the currency brokers in relation to other developing economies. The PLN offers a good compromise between currency trades, stability, and economic growth. Its desire to enter the euro bloc is an added bonus.

A third and safe trade would to go long the Czech koruna, CZK against the euro. The Czech National Bank has historically done a good job of keeping its inflation target around 2 percent, and has done so by raising interest rates. Secondly, there is an expectation by some of the larger currency brokers that a normalization of monetary policy (after the 2008–2009 banking crisis) will take place; and thirdly, the Czech Republic is entering a deficit-reduction regime. All three of these factors add up to make a short EUR/long CZK trade to be very promising in the future.

If you are considering entering into long positions in any one of the developing nation's currencies, it would be best to consult your broker's reports for an indication as to price levels for entry. Developing nation FX trades tend to be longer term in nature, therefore waiting until the proper price point for a long exposure should not be a problem, as you should be in no rush to build a CZK position.

Gold and Silver and Your Currency Portfolio

You should also consider adding some gold and silver to your high risk/reward portfolio. Gold and silver are priced in USD and are traded in uniform amounts all over the world. Additionally, most FX brokerage accounts allow you to go long and short for spot gold and silver on the same platform and with the same software as normal Forex trades. If you are considering trading gold and silver, then electronic-spot trading can bridge the gap between futures and physical metal.

The lots that are traded are usually 100 ounces for gold and 1,000 ounces for silver. With these size lots, the profit from trading gold and silver like a currency can be huge. Gold can go up nearly 1 to 3 percent per day against the USD, and it is common for silver to go up 3–5 percent against the USD on the days gold moves up. If you add to your overall FX portfolio a long or short Gold/USD and long or short Silver/USD exposure, you can open yourself up to very large price movements.

For example, it is possible to go long 20 percent of your available portfolio in a long Silver/USD position and triple the size of your account during a strong run on the white metal. It is quite common for silver to go up over 100 percent in a year. This would equate to a 5,000 percent return on the actual dollars you have invested in a silver trade at 50:1! If you had a $10,000 account, and you set your leverage to 50:1, and you put 20 percent of that margin in a Silver/USD trade, you would have over $200,000 in your account at the end of the year. This can be shown by:

$10,000 × 20% = $2,000 × 50 = $100,000 × 2 (100% growth) = $200,000

ALERT

Some currency brokers offer gold and silver spot trading, but your leverage is set at 20:1 or 50:1; it will automatically switch to a 1:1 leverage when you enter into a long or short, gold or silver spot trade. Check with your FX broker before you enter into these trades as they will skew your profit calculations!

A long Gold/USD position can act the same way as a long AUD/USD position. It can capture the movement of a strong AUD, but at the same time a long gold position can act as a safe-haven play right along with a long Swiss franc and a short Swedish krona play. In fact, a long gold position has become one of the most sought-after hedges in the currency markets as gold has taken a front seat in traders and investors' eyes.

This front seat for gold has been due to several reasons, one of them being added risk aversion and added money supply in the United States and Europe. Only time will tell if gold and silver continue to have a glitter and a gilt, and only time will tell if they continue to have record price levels and record returns. In the meantime, a long Gold/USD and long Silver/USD position can be treated like an FX trade in your currency-brokerage account. This is for a reason! Gold and silver are currently being reconsidered as alternatives to the paper-based **fiat** currencies of the world. Central banks from around the world including Russia, Europe, and the United States hold gold in their vaults as a hedge against their paper-backed currency holdings.

Look on some of the central bank websites for an indication as to how much gold they own, and at what percentage.

One of the world's best managed central banks is the Swiss National Bank (*www.snb.ch*). A search through its website will reveal that it has CHF 270 billion in assets; nearly CHF 50 billion of this is in gold reserves while CHF 200 billion is in foreign exchange reserves, a 1:5 ratio. In mid-2011 South Korea increased its gold reserves by 25 tons, worth about USD 1.25 billion. The purchase represented a nearly 1,700 percent increase in its gold holdings. These facts can serve as the basis of a plan to keep gold and silver in mind when considering an actively managed, aggressive high risk/reward currency portfolio

Building Up Confidence

When you are just starting out with your trading, you might wean yourself off looking at the FX markets from a distance onto trading in a demonstration account. After you feel comfortable with trading in the demonstration account, you will most likely begin trading in a live account. Once you get to trading in a live account, you will begin to feel an altogether different emotion than when you were trading in the practice account.

FACT

There is nothing like having a few bucks in your account and getting down to some real FX trading. Having real money to trade with can make you feel alive inside. You might find yourself even walking around with a spring in your step as you know that you are matching wits with the Forex traders of the world.

In order to work in the style of a high risk/reward trader, you will need to develop the confidence required to engage in risky trades. Since dealing with actual money, as opposed the play money of a practice account, is the best way to develop confidence, your real nerve will develop after you have traded with actual real cash.

While it is true that you have to trade with actual real cash, it is not required that you trade with large amounts of actual money to learn how to handle the process of entering in the trades required for winning big in currency trading. In fact, you can learn some of the trading systems described here with a very low account balance. For example, you can enjoy and experience the emotion of setting up a successful hedged directional FX trade with as little as $30 in your account. Some Forex brokerage firms such as OANDA allow low balances and odd lot sizes that allow you to develop your skills without risking huge amounts of your hard-earned capital.

The money you would be putting in these accounts would still be at a much greater risk than the money that would be invested and traded in the more conservative style that is also described in this book. This money would be working very hard, and you would still be trading it in a hard, quick fashion that would allow it to gain as much *percentage wise* as it would with a much larger account. You can trade a $30 dollar balance with the same principles and ideas as the ones presented in the high risk/high reward chapters, and still get great results.

You can experiment with double-trading volatile currency pairs, trading risk sentiment, and trading exotic currencies. The secret to doing this is to watch the percentage gain of your trades. If you transfer in $20 from your VISA debit card to your Forex currency account and you spend the early evening getting out the calculator and placing some well-thought out trades, then you will learn very fast the skills and technique it takes to make it trading currencies in an aggressive way. By the time you switch on your computer in the morning, and your trades have worked all night long, you might be up seventy-five cents. This seventy-five cents might seem small to some, but it is actually a gain of 3.75 percent overnight, which if done every night for the next year equates to over 900.00 percent returns, *not including compounding!*

As you can see, you can build up the skills and experience required for trading Forex aggressively by first learning how to trade very, very small sums. If you would like to try your hand at learning how to earn big gains in the currency market, then this might be a good starting point for you. Remember, if you try to learn with smaller amounts, look at your percentage gains, and do not get too caught up in the actual money that you are earning. The big money will come later, after you have earned your stripes with aggressive FX trading.

The Pitfalls of Too Much Confidence

There is something that happens to everyone who gains early successes at any endeavor. Whether you are beginning a sport for the first time, are starting your own business, or learning how to trade, you will suffer from hubris. Hubris just a fancy word for what is also called the winner's curse. It might happen to you when things have gone good for a while and you've earned a few dollars in the currency market. It could happen to you after a few months of being very successful at paper trading in your demo account. It could happen after you correctly predict the direction of an interest rate hike by one of the major central banks. Either way, it could happen to any trader at a time when she is the most confident and at the top of her game.

It usually starts by taking more and more risk and ending up with better and better results. Pretty soon, you might think that you know that your trades are all good. It is at this point that you must stop trading and take cover! Most currency accounts blow up and experience the heaviest of losses during these times. Historically, FX traders have a series of early successes, and then, a huge loss. The idea is to know yourself so well, that you can tell when you are getting overconfident.

If you begin to feel these feelings, if you begin to feel overexuberant in your trading style, then this is a sign that you are not respecting currency trading enough. The FX markets demand to be respected! If you hold what they tell you in high regard, if you listen to the markets and look at the charts, if you're trying your hardest to not get yourself into trades that are potential disasters, then you will be rewarded. The reward might not come in big, prideful gains. The reward may, on the other hand, come in a way that keeps you away from your trading desk when the markets are sour, or when your confidence is too big for the market itself. You might be rewarded by being allowed to keep your currency trading account until the next trading day.

CHAPTER 17

Low Risk/Return Traders

You might want to run your currency trading in a lower risk/reward style. In order to do this you will need to know the basics of setting your FX trading account to operate in an easy going way, including how to use the right-sized accounts in relation to your overall assets. You will also learn the ins and outs of getting to know how to trade in a low-pressure style, including how much time you should expect to spend as well as establishing reasonable expectations of profits.

Proportionate-Sized Accounts

The first element to trading currency in a low risk/low return style is to limit the amount of money you are actually trading. The facts are that you will only be able to lose the amount that you have in your account. To explain it further, in a worst-case scenario, your losses will never exceed your account balance. It is quite possible to make a good profit on an account that has a balance of as little as $250. If you need to or want to you can start with a balance with a smaller amount of $100, and still enjoy the thrills and excitement of currency trading.

A $250 or $100 account can be very fun indeed! For the price of a fancy dinner you can have a profitable and productive FX-trading account. You can spend your evenings scalping or setting up overnight trades just like the bigger currency accounts, and you can make money to boot! It is quite possible (and very common) to earn an average of $10 per day in a $250 account with very gentle trading. In fact, this amount can be earned with three or four trades a night.

ALERT

Don't let the size of your account limit the fun you can have from currency trading. Not only that, don't let a small-sized account let you begin on the path of not respecting the markets. If you don't take care you could still lose money in the account; in fact you could wipe out your small fledging account quickly. Take care with whatever size account you have!

There are tales of college students spending the wee hours of the night trading in the currency markets with very little money in their accounts. These ultrasmall account holders use PayPal to put money into their accounts in the evening, and then spend the night currency trading. They set up trades while studying and otherwise spending the night in front of the TV. When the morning comes, they again use PayPal to move their earnings out of their accounts. They go on to use this money for their morning coffee at the local hangouts and snack shops.

Clearly this is an extreme case of the small account FX trader. You will not have to trade all night for your lunch money. You can, however, fully enjoy your weekly and monthly earnings with whatever size account you have. Some people find currency trading with a small account *more* enjoyable than if they had big money on the line. You can take the approach that winnings are winnings, and find the comfort in risking smaller amounts that are more to your taste. There is no rule of how large or small your account should be; it is the percentage of your gains that will bring a smile to your face. If you think about it, that's precisely the reason some Forex brokerage firms will allow your account balance to be as low as $1!

Smaller FX/Traditional Asset Ratio

Another requirement of a lower-risk, currency-trading system is to invest money in your FX-trading account at a smaller ratio to traditional assets than an aggressive account. For example, while an aggressive currency account will be 20 percent or even 25 percent of your overall investment portfolio, you would deposit 5 percent or less of your overall investable assets into an actively managed low risk/low reward FX account.

Depending upon the size of your stock, bond, and mutual fund assets, you might be investing a very tiny percentage of your money in an FX-trading account. Smaller amounts will enable you to take advantage of currency pair swings and earn you a high percentage gain in proportion to your more mainstream investments. A 2.5 percent investment of $25,000 can still earn you a return of $3,000 per year, which equates to an increase of 12 percent of your overall investment portfolio. This number can be achieved with an average of ten trading days a month, and four to six trades a day or night. Again, this is a conservative number, and would be obtained from some of the most basic trades, including overnight carry trades and well-diversified, short-length position trading.

A proportionally smaller amount also means that your overall portfolio can remain invested in safer assets. Smaller proportions will enable you to rest easy at night, knowing that your money is not going through wild swings in the currency market with excessively large chance of misfortune and the possibility of economic pain. You can use the small percentage you have chosen to invest in FX as a form of "vent." It just might be that your overall portfolio is invested very conservatively, and you have an itch and craving to experiment at a new form of investing. Perhaps you are exchanging having some money to play with in the currency markets for having your money tied up in something that is well structured to deliver solid, but boring returns.

ESSENTIAL

Most part-time FX traders only trade when the time is right. If you have time one night and the market is making good setups, then spend a few hours trading. If on the other hand, if you can't trade for a while, then by all means put your trading computer away and wait for a better time to come along.

You can trade very conservatively in currencies and still earn much more than you would trading stock. You might also decide that currency trading is more exciting than trading other forms of high-return financial products such as options. In order to trade options, you need a larger account balance and a more involved knowledge of how to set up trades that are profitable. The acceptance of smaller account size and the knowledge of a few different trading scenarios can get you up and running very quickly into the world of fun and profitable currency trading.

Lower Pressure

Trading in a less aggressive manner will also reduce the overall pressure associated with currency trading. With a more casual and easy going approach to FX trading, you will be able to experience all of the profits and fun of currency trading without some of the fear and upset that can come with a high risk/high reward trading program. A low risk/low reward trading program will yield you the involvement in the world's currency markets and all of the action that such involvement brings.

If you have a live account, no matter how small it is, you will be able to enjoy the emotions that all Forex traders enjoy. You will be able to experience the excitement of going to the world's central bank websites and reading their committee reports. You can then use this as well as other fundamental knowledge to place winning trades. No matter what your Forex account size, you will undoubtedly have a certain level of pride after a winning trade is made. You can experience reading all of the brokers' reports, you can get the currency market updates on your smart phone throughout the day, and you can read the technical charts; you can still profit from becoming an expert at the currency markets and at currency trading. The only difference would be that with a low risk/low reward trading style you will be foregoing some of the high pressure situations that can inevitably occur if you would be trading in an aggressive manner.

ESSENTIAL

You will be doing much to reduce your overall mental burden by taking on a less-pressured trading style. You will be reducing the amount of time spent trading, you will be reducing the money at risk, and you will be reducing overall the chance of losing in your trades by a great amount.

You can change a high-stakes game of currency trading into a gentle sport. By reducing an otherwise very risky endeavor into something that is less risky, the enjoyment level of currency trading can be brought up to that of a hobby.

If this type of low risk, casual, hobby-like trading is for you, then keep in your mind that you will only trade when you feel good, and when the trading is fun. If at any time the FX trading becomes a mental burden, take some time off from currency trading; the Forex market will still be there! Also, if you find that you are straining with trying to set up a trade in a difficult trading environment, by all means, *close out your positions and stop trading!* Wait for the bad times to blow over. Part of an easy-going trading style is that it is supposed to be easy-going!

Less Stress and a Safer Currency Account

If you are thinking of trading in a lower risk/low reward fashion, then you will undoubtedly enjoy a reduced stress brought about by very tame trading sessions. These tame trading sessions can follow the same basic course as the more aggressive trading, but the lower dollar amount and the lower number of trades will work to alleviate any excessive pressure that might otherwise come about from currency trading. You can work to lighten the load of FX trading and still make money. The money you make might be smaller in percentage to a more aggressively managed Forex account: This is the price that security charges.

It is a common misconception in the investing world that security should be free. Everyone expects that if they put their money in a secure stock that they will earn a return. They also expect a return on money that is considered safely tucked away in a FDIC-insured CD or savings account. The opposite is actually true. In order for an investment to be truly safe, there must be a cost associated with its safekeeping.

To extend this theory further, if you are trading your Forex account in a safer (safer than an aggressive manner) then you should expect to bear a cost for this safety. The overall effect is that you are willing to accept a lower daily and yearly yield on your Forex trading than you would if you were trading aggressively. This lower yield is the cost associated with the safekeeping of your valuables.

FACT

Some business schools spend time going through the mathematics behind the safekeeping of valuables. The mathematically based experiment involves the cost associated with the safe keeping of gold coins in a bank sometime back in early history. The experiment is worked through to show that there is actually a cost associated with safekeeping of valuables.

With this in mind, if you are trading in a low risk/low reward manner, then you will naturally be Forex trading in a tame, pleasant fashion. This might include gently moving into and out of long AUD/USD positions after dinner to capture the upward trend in risk sentiment in the Asian markets. The basic trading ideas for low-risk trading are the same as high-risk trading. The only difference is there is a use of hedging and smaller proportion position sizes, etc., all coupled with a slower, more casual pace. The overall effect is low-yielding, more comfortable trading sessions. The secondary effect is a higher chance of keeping your account profitable and therefore a higher chance of keeping you in the currency trading game. Just the thought of having a higher chance of keeping your Forex account 100 percent intact can be enough to help you decide what type of trading system you would like to try for yourself.

Keep in mind it is possible to switch between an aggressive trading style and a tame trading style in the manner of minutes. In order to do this you would get out your mental calculator and wall off a section of your account, leaving you with a self-imposed limit as to how much of your margin you can use on each trade, as well as change the type of risk management used in limiting risk. This switching between trading styles is often done by professional traders in times of market upset. It is also done at the end of the month, when the heaviest trading and most profit has already been made for the trader's accounts. These traders feel that their money has been made for the month, and they do not wish to take any unnecessary risks with their Forex accounts, choosing instead to trade in a low-risk style.

Less Time Spent Trading

If you have decided that a low risk/low return Forex trading system is the way for you, then you will rest assured that you will not have to spend a lot of time trading in order to meet your profit goals. You can get very good results and earn enough to make yourself proud by trading just a few hours a day in early morning or early evening only a few days a week. You can even design a trading program in which you trade only when the best setups are available, giving you the strongest possibility for a gain on the trades. In fact you could spend much more time just keeping up on the news than by actually getting in front of your trading platform and having to decide whether to go long or short a currency pair

In this type of currency trading system, you could live your normal life at your day job or with your family and check in on the markets once a day. You could set up a routine of getting up in the morning, getting the kids off to school, and then scanning over the stock market news that developed during the night. If there is nothing of importance, you could then call it quits for the day, and not trade at all that trading session.

On the other hand, if you got up in the morning and you noticed that the Asian and European stock markets were doing especially well and were up over 1 percent, then you could just as easily turn on your computer and enter into some long AUD/USD and short USD/SEK positions before the New York stock markets opened at 7:30 A.M. You could set up your trades to buy in at the market level, and then enter in a tight take-profit point. This would allow you to continue to get ready for your day while the computer did the watching of the account for you.

Taking the safety one step further, you could check on your profit and losses at half hour intervals. Once your position is showing a profit of any amount at all, click on the "Close All Positions" screen and proceed to close out all open positions. When you check your account every half hour, you are giving the market just enough time to move in a direction that will win or lose; this amount will usually not be by much either way. The secret to the whole process is to click on the "Close All Positions" with a profit as often as you can.

ESSENTIAL

When you are about to close out all of your positions, it will be natural for you ask, "Did I make enough at this trade?" The answer is always, "Yes!" You will never lose by closing out your positions when you are showing an overall profit on your trades, no matter how many trades you have open at the time.

If you have three, four, or five trades open, and only three (or fewer!) are currently profitable, but your trading blotter states that your positions are net profitable then you are in profit, period. This is the time to click on "Close All Open Positions," and book your profits.

In the situation that you have several trades open but only a few are gains, but your overall value is profit, you have built a hedge, and the hedge has worked. In essence, you have lost some, you have won some, but overall you are a winner. Checking whether to close out your positions every half hour gives you a kind of internal clock to gauge when to close out. If you did not have an internal timer, then your early morning or late afternoon trading hours would spill out into the rest of the day. If this were to happen, you could find yourself in a position of not getting away from your trading, being late for work, staying up to the wee hours, etc. The half-hour system keeps you on track, and forces you to close out your positions at the first sign of profit. Do not worry that there is not enough profit in each trade: the profits will add up over the month.

Higher Expectancy of Overall Profit

When you are trading your account in a more conservative way and have it set up with a lower risk/low reward profile, then you will most likely be trading less in your Forex account. If you are trading less in your Forex account, then you will naturally be limiting the chances of placing a bad trade and walking away with a loss. In essence, your will be expecting a higher percentage of winning trades for the number of trades you will enter. Granted, the percentage gain on each winning trade might be smaller than if you were trading aggressively. In any case, the percentage of wins to losses, no matter how small the percentage, will add up to having your account be profitable in the long haul. The key to this type of low-risk trading is just that: Only enter into trades that are low risk, and offer a great chance of success, even if that success is only 1 percent or 2 percent gains. A 1 percent or 2 percent gain that is repeated consistently for months on end can add up to a huge return on your money. It is very easy to be in a small one pair trade in the early afternoon, and close out of it by dinnertime. It is easy to gain 1 percent or 2 percent with a bit of certainty and safety. Compare this 1 percent or 2 percent daily gain to the 7–10 percent that can be gained in the stock market in a *year.* If your goal is to gain safely, then consider placing your currency trades in a way that will allow you to gain slowly and steadily.

FACT

Set yourself income goals for each session of around 1–3 percent per night or morning. When you make your goal, get out of the trading platform for the day (or night). Think about it as a part-time job; it takes time to do a bit of work, make your money, and then go on and live your life.

This system can be more easily performed if you enter into each trade with a more conservative stance. This conservative stance will then help you make a higher proportion of wins to losses. Do not be too concerned with the fact that the wins are small. They are wins; it is money, and you are developing skills that might make you want to trade with larger and larger amounts.

Either way, your higher expected win/loss ratio can be satisfied by smaller trades, diversification, shorter time in the trade, and the use of very tight, automated take-profit points. Additional measures of expecting a higher number of winning trades is to check your net position profit every half hour. If you are at a profit point, then close out all of your trades, including the losers. The result will be a house cleaning of your account twice per hour. If the position looks good, close it out and book the profits. You would be surprised at how fast your money, skill, and talent will accumulate when you follow this procedure. Remember, a win is a win. And it doesn't take one big win to do well in currency trading; it takes a lot of little wins that add up to big profits in your Forex account.

Smaller Bets Relative to Account Size

One of the best ways to de-tune a Forex account is to divide your available margin into thirds. From this, divide into thirds again. The number you end up with should be the maximum amount of margin that you should invest at any one time. If you are trading in a nondiversified, unidirectional manner, then three entries of the same currency pair is the best way of diversifying your cost basis in the currency pair.

For example, if you are trading into a commodities currency in order to capture the added risk sentiment of the world's traders, then you might choose to go long the New Zealand dollar against the U.S. dollar. This type of position would allow you to gain if there are signs of added risk sentiment across the markets of the world. It might be that Europe has had a satisfactory development in a sovereign debt issue. It also might be that China's growth numbers have just come out, and they show a year over year increase in the industrial growth of this manufacturing nation.

Either way, if you sense a growth signal, you have the all clear to place some trades that will capture the growth orientation of the world's traders. The same would be true for a long Swedish krona versus the USD or EUR as well as other classic currency pairs including a long NOK and long AUD versus the USD or even the EUR. Depending upon the technical and fundamental analysis, you can achieve your goal of capturing the movement in the currency markets by trading a number of currency pairs.

In the case of a long NZD/USD (or other risk-loving pair) you would build your position by three equally measured bites at the pair. If the news developed overnight, and you are building a position after the news, then the three buy ins can be done every half hour to forty-five minutes. On the other hand, if the news has taken place in the morning, and the U.S. markets have already reacted to it, but you were not able to place your bets into the FX market until the afternoon New York time, then your three trades can be placed every ten minutes. This shorter time frame is due to the fact that there is very little movement in the currency markets between 3:00 P.M. and 6:00 P.M. New York time. If you are trading at this time, then there will be very little difference in the prices of the currency pair with each third. Since the markets will undoubtedly be getting ready for a second day of upward movement, then it is best to get your positions in well before 7:00 P.M. New York time, which is just about when the Sydney, Hong Kong, and Tokyo traders get to work in the morning.

Whether you are trading in the morning, at mid-day, or in the evening, your Forex account's risk level can be greatly reduced by trading only one-third of your margin at any one time. Of this one-third, three equally measured trades will get you into your position with a form of dollar cost averaging. This dollar cost averaging is a method of buying more or less as the market moves up and down. If the FX pair is cheaper, you will buy more units for the fixed amount of margin. As the FX pair gets more expensive, you will naturally buy fewer units for the fixed amount of margin, as each unit will cost more. In this way, you are getting more at a cheaper cost basis and less at a higher cost basis. This is a method of building a position that is recommended by mutual fund managers to buy into shares over time. The same principle holds true; in this case, the "over time" part will be anywhere from one hour to three hours, instead of months and years as in mutual fund purchases.

CHAPTER 18

De-Tune the Risk/Reward Ratio

There are several ways to de-tune your currency trading portfolio to allow it to run with a low-risk profile. Some of the ways to de-tune your account include knowing how to diversify your positions, knowing when to unwind profitable trades, and knowing when to roll over your winnings into a completely different currency pair direction. Building up the profits in your FX account can be the key to getting some real money out of your account on a daily and weekly basis.

Diversification Is Key

Another key factor to consider when you are de-tuning your FX account is to use the proper amount of diversification within your one-third of margin that is being used at any one time. For example, you could build a position in your account that uses one-third of your available margin divided into three different currency pairs.

In this example showing actual trading results, you can begin the middle of the trading week with a zero balance in your trading account. You could then go through the "Add Funds" screens of your currency account to add $225. This $225 is a smaller amount, but with three well-placed trades, you can capture enough movement to make a large percentage gain, learn the ins and outs of currency trading, and get used to closing trades by using a smart phone or iPad.

After you have added the funds to your account, they will most likely be ready to trade with. You scan the news and discover that there has been major news coming out of Europe that has sent the risk sentiment of the European currencies and others to the downside. Further investigation of your daily brokerage reports informs you that not only has the risk sentiment lowered, but the world's traders have begun to sell their stock holdings to get into bonds. This has caused a downward pressure on the U.S. and European stock markets.

Sensing that it might be a good time to be a bottom feeder and a bargain hunter, you proceed to divide your account into thirds. Using only one-third of your total margin, you enter in three equally placed trades that are diversified. While the overall goal of all the trades will be to capture the inevitable rebound in the markets, the trades will be diversified across industries.

The first pair that you enter into is a sell order for 133 units of EUR/SEK @ 9.22618. You know that while the EUR has been underperforming against the USD during this latest bit of bad news, you also know that the SEK is very sensitive to risk appetite and will most likely go up against the EUR when good news comes about.

The second trade you put in is for a sell at the market of 133 units of USD/NOK @ 5.67152. You know that while the NOK is considered to be a very well-run currency, Norway's fortunes are tied to the price of its main export, which is crude oil. Taking your observations further, you know that the price of crude oil has been tied to risk sentiment lately. You know this is due to the world's traders linking the growth of the world's economies to the demand of oil.

> **FACT**
>
> Many of the best trades in the Forex markets are involving currencies that are tied to the value of commodities. These currencies are in traders' minds even more because of the correlation of commodity consumption and growing economies. Growing economies consume and use commodities; this in turn drives up the price of commodity-producing countries' currencies.

If there is a feeling that the world's economies will slow down, then the price of oil will go down proportionately. Hence, the reasoning behind your long NOK exposure. The trade would allow you to capture any anticipated increase in the price of crude oil.

The third and final trade is a market order to buy into the AUD by selling the USD. You know and have read that the AUD/USD pair has been hurt lately due to the sour feeling in the markets. Your order is for 100 units long AUD/USD @ 1.02359.

These three trades add up to approximately one-third of your available margin. By leaving two-thirds of your margin free, you are insuring that your account will be able to withstand any downturns in the market. Having two-thirds of your margin free allows you to breathe easy, and not worry about any margin calls until the FX pairs turn in your favor. After reviewing and recording your trades and observations in your trading journal, you shut down your computer and take the rest of the night off.

Dismantling a Profitable Trade

After you have set up three trades that are of equal size and total one-third of your available margin, you spend the rest of the night with your family or friends. The morning follows the usual routine, with getting the kids off to school and then going to the gym for spin class. Just before you go into locker room, you stop by to look at the markets as reported by CNBC in the gym's lounge. The market is up for the morning, not a lot, but enough for your trades to play out.

A few days before, you downloaded an app onto your iPad that lets you navigate your trading platform with buy and sell commands. The app does not allow you to see all of the technical indicators, only candlestick charts and a few other charts. No matter, as you only need to check your balance to see that the net for your trades is up $42.10 for the night. That is approximately an 18 percent return on your $225.00 balance, a good profit for the day.

Navigating your iPod or smart phone to the "Close Order" page, you close out each of the three trades and book your profit. The USD/NOK trade closes out @ 5.5881, the EUR/SEK closes out at 9.1627 and the AUD/USD closes at 1.0320. Your new tradable balance is $262.10. Knowing it is best to walk away after a good day in the markets, you continue on to your classes at the gym.

After the gym, you stop by the coffee shop with your laptop. You enjoy a double-shot espresso while analyzing your trades. One of the questions you might ask is, what caused the NOK and SEK to move so much when the obvious choice of long AUD/USD did not have that much of a strong upward movement? Switching to your broker's statements for the day, you read that China's growth numbers came in overnight (while you were sleeping) and they showed a slightly slower anticipated growth for that consumer of raw materials. Since Australia provides much of the raw materials to China, this implies a slower growth of Australia's raw materials exports.

ALERT

> Trading with a smart phone or iPad can allow you to get out of your office once in a while. Don't fall into the trap of thinking that you can use a handheld device as your only form of managing your trades. You will still need to monitor your account from the full-featured trading software every now and then.

Knowing that this is the answer, you make a mental note to closely monitor the AUD/USD pair. Your broker has recommended accumulating any amount of AUD/USD at prices near parity, or near 1/1. The broker's report also states that the pair will most likely have a hard time getting above 1.045. Overall, for the short term you will be looking to get into AUD at these levels. The trade is still a good carry trade, and the pair continues to react well to positive news. It is just that this overnight's news put a slight damper on its upward movement.

Continuing Trading/Rolling Over the Profits

After you have read through your notes, news, and brokers' reports, the next thing you need to do is to decide if you would like to roll over your profits. Since most of the action in the U.S., European, and Asian stock markets has worked its way through the system, you feel as though that you should look elsewhere to make some money in the afternoon and into the next morning.

Scanning through your broker's reports for new ideas, you notice that a report was issued last weekend that discussed the GBP/USD. The report discussed the heightening inflation situation in the island nation, and it recommended building long GBP/USD positions at anything under 1.600.

You switch to your technical line chart with a one-hour time frame. You notice that the GBP did not benefit from the run-ups in the market to the extent that the SEK, NOK, and AUD did. With further checking you notice that the GBP/USD pair is at 1.587. You decide to buy into the pair at this level.

Dividing your account into thirds, you decide to build your position by taking three bites at the pair. You decide that you will buy in three equal parts with the first at this price level, 1.587. You go ahead and place your first trade of 1,500 units of GBP/USD. The best thing to do now is to close out of your trading screen and continue on with going about your business for the day. You check in forty-five minutes later to see how your pair has been doing. You notice that it has gone down just a bit, and your position is down $3.

Since it is in the middle of the afternoon New York time, you know that there will most likely not be any big price moves in either direction. With this knowledge, you buy in your next third at this price level.

Knowing that you will be busy for the rest of the afternoon and into the night, you enter in a limit order that will purchase the final third at a preset price. You know that this limit order will only be filled if that price level is met, and your trading platform will then automatically fill the order. You make the price to be the same distance from the second order as the second order was from the first. Before you submit the limit order, you place your take profit for all three trades at 1.63. This rate is intended for you to make good money, even if the trade takes a bit of time to finish with a profit. The last thing you do before you quit trading for the rest of the week is put your trading app on your iPad on "Audible Order Reporting." Only then do you pack up your computer, put your iPad in its slip case, and forget about trading for the rest of day.

You go about with the usual drama of your life, fully forgetting about trading completely. You are getting ready for work the next morning when you hear your iPad sound a chime in the next room. At this point you have totally forgotten about your currency trading endeavors. You have been busy running your household, going to work, etc. While you have been going through your routine, your FX trading platform has been tracking the markets and has been waiting for the price of the GBP/USD to reach a point in which your preset limit order can be filled. You check the message on your iPad. It states that your order has been filled, at what price, and how many units were in the order.

Your entire long GBP/USD order has been filled. Not only has it been filled, you have mathematically placed them at well-spaced points. You smile to yourself: You have rolled over the gains in your currency account, and you invested in a pair that was recommended by your broker at the price the broker liked. You're set!

Managing Expectations

In this example you have done very well. You have placed three evenly sized diversified trades that turned a profit overnight. You closed out the three trades and booked the gains. You even walked away from your computer for a few hours to give yourself time to cool off after an 18 percent overnight gain. Lastly, you took a calculated risk and placed three trades in one currency pair that was recommended by your broker.

Knowing that you needed to take the rest of the week off from trading, you have set automated take-profit points for the three long GBP/USD trades. Your mind begins to wander toward your currency trading endeavors every evening near dinnertime. This is a good time to check the balance in your account, as the FX market is usually very slow at this time of the day. Even though you have set up a take profit point at 1.63, you know that you would be happy with a profit sometime before the end of the week. If this were to happen, then you would close out all of your positions and go into the weekend in 100 percent cash.

ESSENTIAL

The best way to get to know how to use automated take-profit points and automated stop losses is to practice on your demo account. The automation can take some getting used to and it can take time to learn how to estimate the approximate range of a currency pair. Automatic trading also takes some practice to program it effectively!

Sadly, the week has not shown any real movement in any direction of the currency pair that you are in. You have to make a decision at this point. The weekend is coming, and you need to decide if you should carry the trade over the weekend, or if you should close out and go into 100 percent cash. In this instance, you should make an effort to find out why there has been very little movement in the GBP/USD pair. It could be that there has been very little action in the FX markets (and the world's stock markets) because of an upcoming economic report that is due to be released out of the United States next week. It could be that there has been a run-up or losing streak in the stock markets and traders are taking a breather going into a long weekend. Whatever the reason, you will have to decide if you should close out or keep your long positions.

If you run into this scenario, then the best thing to do is to look over your original trading plan. If the idea of getting into the long GBP/USD pair was a good one from the beginning, then there is a very good chance that the original trading plan still is good. Just because nothing has happened in the currency markets yet doesn't mean that the trade will not work out in the end. In this case you know that the GBP/USD pair frequently makes it up to 1.63, so you know that your take-profit point is within reach of the normal price range.

Reviewing the quality of your trades as a method of deciding if you should let the positions ride or if you should close them out can make for good business. Reminding yourself of the reasoning behind a trade is also a form of quality control that will ensure the keeping of good trades when you are thinking of doing the opposite.

In this case it would be best to wait for the long GBP/USD trade to come around and make a profit. While it might be tempting to close out a trade that seems to be flat, the reviewing of your notes can lead you to stay in the trade and wait for the 1.63 price level to come your way. If you have the patience to wait for a well-placed and well-thought out trade to work out, you can be rewarded, sometimes with very substantial gains. Gains from well-thought out trades will go a long way in keeping your currency account profitable, and keep you in the currency trading game!

Buying into Long-Term Trends

If you are trading your currency account for low risk/low return results, then you should be looking for longer-term trends for your trading ideas. Long-term trends can mean slower currency-price movements, which can equate to a chance to build up your positions over a length of time. In addition to building up your position over several weeks, you can use much smaller bites at the currency pair.

A good example of this would be if your broker recommended that you build up long positions in GBP/USD at any price below 1.60 as was presented earlier. The situation might be that the GBP/USD might not move in any direction for a several weeks or even a few months. In this example, you could go about an accumulation of the pair by a two-pronged method.

The first way would be to begin with your current margin balance and divide by thirds. The idea is that you will limit the total exposure of your long GBP/USD account to no more than one-third of your total margin. While it is usually recommended that you divide this third into three equal entry points of the FX pair, you should now divide this one-third into six equal parts. These six parts are intended for you to enter into the trade over the coming weeks.

Although it is normal to buy into a currency pair with full force within a few hours or days, you will be buying into the trade only every two or three days. This will spread your entry point across two or three weeks, which will, by nature, give you a smoothly averaged cost basis. This means that the average price of your long GBP/USD will be divided over a longer time frame, which in turn will give you a greater variance in price. This greater variance in price will give you the greatest chance of buying more on the dips, as the currency pair's price will move along a wider range in proportion to the length of time covered.

ALERT

> It is quite common for a currency broker to issue a buy recommendation of a currency pair only to turn the buy recommendation into a sell recommendation within days. If they have an idea that their original idea was not correct, brokers will not hesitate to admit that they called it wrong, and ask you to reverse your stance.

The second prong to your long-term building of your long GBP/USD position is to add new money to your account over the weeks and months. It is natural to feel a bit squeamish about trading with too big a balance in your FX account. A method to ease into a position is to build it up over the weeks using the six parts of one-third method and at the same time slowly transferring in additional money to add to your tradable margin. You might decide to add a preset amount to your FX account every week. You might start out with a $250 balance and add $25 every Friday afternoon, just before the market closes.

After you have added the additional monies each week, you would once again divide your margin balance by thirds. This new calculated balance would become your new target number to have invested in the GBP/USD over the long haul. This building up of your position every two to three days coupled with small capital injections to your FX account will combine to form a kind of moving target that you will continually try to build up by additional purchases of the GBP/USD pair. This process can go over a six- to eight-week period, which is a good amount of time to slowly build up your long GBP/USD position. Granted, your account would be diversified, but you would be hedging your exposure by buying into the pair over time at an upward sliding scale.

Playing the Interest Rate Differentials

Another trading idea that works well in a low risk account is called "playing the carry trade." When you play the carry trade you essentially are trading for the long, long term. If you are willing to be in a trade for six months up to several years, then this type of trade is for you. In order to set up and execute this carry trade properly, you would need to find a funding currency and an interest-earning currency. The idea behind choosing a good funding currency is shorting a very low-yielding currency such as the Swiss franc, USD, or the Japanese yen. These currencies have historically been used as funding currencies because they have had low interest rates.

Once you decide upon a low-yielding funding currency, you would go long a currency that is paying a high interest rate. Classic examples can be found by looking toward the commodity currencies such as the Australian, New Zealand, and Canadian dollars. Other classic currencies include the high-yielding South African rand and the Norwegian krone.

The idea is that you would short the low-yielding currency and go long the high-yielding currency. Behind the scenes you would be paying interest on the shorted currency (as it is a loan), and you would be earning interest on the higher interest-bearing long currency (as it is an investment). This is the basic method of how all currency pairs are funded, the only difference is that you usually do not notice the interest earned because currency trades usually have a length of only a few minutes, hours, or days.

ESSENTIAL

Even if you are in an FX trade as a carry trade, you should have no hesitation to close out the trade when the pair gets profitable. Forex pairs that are used as carry trades can go up in price rapidly. You might find your carry trade turns out to be a capital gain that becomes too tempting to pass up.

On the other hand, when you are getting into a currency pair with the intent of a carry trade, then the interest you will be earning will be compounded over weeks, months, seasons, and even years. While the currency pair goes up and down, you will earn the difference between the interest of the low-yielding currency and the high-yielding currency. Not only will you earn the difference, you will earn that interest second by second, with payouts once a day. This continuous compounding can add up very quickly.

Carry trades are considered very low risk, and if timed properly can go on for a long time. The interest earned can be up to 5 percent or higher. If you are trading one-third of your account at 50:1, the interest that you would earn would be over 80 percent of your total account balance. In other words, if you have a $1,000 balance, you would earn over $800 in interest per year (if the interest difference was 5 percent).

This type of ultralong-term trading also known as a carry trade can be used to go a long way in building your account to earn a very high rate of return over months and even years. If you would like to try to get into this type of trading, then spread your buy ins at properly timed points. This means waiting for the world's stock markets to fall or otherwise experience a bit of bad times. Waiting for these market conditions will ensure that you are buying into the commodity or other high-yielding currencies at the lowest prices.

Waiting It Out for a Correction

If you have spent time building up a well-thought out position that looks good technically and fundamentally, then the next thing you have to do is to wait for the trade to play out and earn you a good profit. Even though it feels satisfying to be in and out of a trade in a matter of minutes, most of the big money is made by extending your time horizon, sticking to your plan, and allowing the trade to work for you.

ESSENTIAL

> If you find a charting system, ratio, or indicator too complicated, too difficult, or too hard to understand, feel free to switch to a chart system or indicator you feel comfortable with. Currency trading can be hard enough, and you shouldn't feel obligated to complicate it further.

If your well-planned trade is taking a bit of time to work out, the best thing to do is to go easy, and give the trade a chance to work. Sometimes it seems that all of the currency traders of the world are heavily focused upon the same currency pair, and that currency pair is not yours. Sometimes it seems that everything in the market is moving except the FX pair in which you have taken money and time to build a position. Sometimes the currency market is totally flat, such as between seasons, and before and after major holidays. Either way, when these times happen you should not get nervous about your trading ideas. During these times it is best to go over your trading diary and review the logic of your trades.

Once you have reassured yourself that your ideas were and still are good, then you would be best served by setting a take-profit point that is one-third the distance of your stop-loss point. If you have your stops set up in this manner, then you will be able to ride out three times as many downward swings as upward swings. In other words, if you have your program automated to win one-third as much as your loses will trigger, the law of averages will mean that you will close out at a win three times as often as you will close out at a loss.

ESSENTIAL

The best way to stick to a trading plan is to be interested in something other than currency trading. You might find yourself so wrapped up in the markets and Forex trading that everything seems very important. Find other ways to enjoy your time while you are waiting for your well-thought-out FX trades to play out.

This suggestion might seem to go against logic, as it would seem to be that you would want to set your wins to be three times your losses. If you were to follow this plan, it would take three times the movement to finally close out the trade with a win in your pocket. At the same time you would be booking losses three times as often as you would be booking wins. You must remember that a win is not truly a win until it is realized. In other words, a win is not truly yours until the trade closes out and the profit posts to your account. On the other hand, a loss is only a loss when the trade is actually closed out and the loss posts to your account.

If you find yourself in the situation that your trade is standing still—or worse yet, losing—then you have to make the decision to close out the trade or wait until it corrects. Since currency pairs have a pattern of moving back and forth, it could quite possibly be true that your stagnant or losing trade will soon rotate to a winning trade. Often this happens when you are not looking at your account, or otherwise not monitoring your position. With the use of properly placed take-profit and stop-loss points, you can build your trade to withstand downturns and still be ready to capture the gains when the time comes that your Forex trade turns around.

CHAPTER 19

More Trading Ideas/ Putting It Together

There are several ways to set up trades that limit the amount of risk in your Forex account. This chapter will give you some ideas about the use of trading as an income enhancer and the use of currency trading in place of options in a well-run 90/10 portfolio. You will also learn how to use currency ETFs as a proxy to trading currencies for a very conservative trading plan. Lastly, you will learn about the endgame: putting it all together and running your currency trading endeavors like a business.

Using FX as an Income Enhancer

While most people plan on trading currencies for the express purpose of gaining as much as possible in their accounts, there is an alternate trading goal that is more conservative in nature. With this system you would focus on having the primary goal of your Forex account as being a savings account earning interest. The secondary function would be capital gains, which would help in the overall gains in the account. This combining of earned interest and capital gains is called investing for total return.

You can use your FX account as a total return account. In order to do this, you would allow your currency account balance to sit in cash for 80 percent of the time and trade only 20 percent of the time. The 10 percent of the time you were trading you would be looking for the best trades only. You would trade to pick up as many capital gains as you could using the usual one-third of your total margin and breaking up the trades into three tranches of buy ins into your favorite currency pairs.

With this method you would close out each and every trade at the bare minimum of gains. When you trade in this type of total return investing you would exit out of the trade as soon as your profit and loss chart would be in the green. Trades of this type can be closed out with only a few tenths of a percent of gains. The logic behind getting out of the trades in a short time frame and as soon as there is a profit is that your trading is actually acting as an income enhancer to the regular interest that is accruing in the account.

FACT

The longer the length of time you are in a trade, the higher the risk. If you have a trade that goes overnight, or worse, over a weekend, you are assuming much more risk than if you are closing out the trade as soon as it makes even the smallest returns.

Since Forex accounts pay continuously compounding interest calculated every second, your account will be earning a better rate of return than you would have if the money was in a regular savings account. The gains from your trading, no matter how small, will go a long way in adding to the returns in your account.

If you are looking for maximum safety and have returns as the secondary goal, then this total return investing would work out well for you. If you keep your money in your Forex cash balance as much as possible, and trade only to capture enough gains to add to the interest earned, you can easily earn 5–10 percent combined interest and gains over the course of a year. In order to reach this 5–10 percent goal, you would have to trade the absolute minimum. It could be reached with only a few trading days a month, with only one or two hours of trading at each session.

The secret to getting the safest yet highest gains is to close out of the positions as soon as the gain is made. Further safety could be provided by using only one-tenth of your margin at each trade instead of the usual one-third. This would limit your exposure even further and force the chance of possible loss to be very small indeed. Again, this type of trading takes a certain level of hands-on monitoring, more than the automated-type trading that is done with more aggressive trading systems. A good time to accomplish your total return gains is in the early afternoon when the markets are very slow. This would give you time to react to any trade, up or down in price. Overall, if you would like to try this type of trading, be ultraconservative, and use the shortest time frame charts such as thirty- and fifteen-second charts to time your open and closing of the trades.

The One-Tenth Solution and T-Bill Investing

If you are like most conservative investors, you will most likely have part of your overall portfolio invested in bonds, CDs or cash. You might even have your money invested in a bond mutual fund, which is one of the most popular investments for European investors. Either way, if you are looking for a good solution to investing between the stability of bonds and the return of stock, then a mixture of one-tenth currencies and nine-tenths T-bills would be perfect for you.

This mix of risk and risk-free is the one of the methods that is recommended by high net-worth financial advisors to their big clients. The logic behind it is that there is very low risk to AA-rated T-bills spread out in a laddered fashion. Since most of your portfolio will be in these relatively risk-free bills, you will virtually be insuring that 90 percent of your portfolio will never be at risk. This 90 percent invested in T-bills will earn 0.01 percent–0.2 percent depending upon market conditions.

FACT

Even though the credit rating of the United States has been downgraded from AAA to AA, T-bills still reign supreme as the safest investments available. While some government bonds are rated higher, these are usually issued in the foreign currency. Therefore they are not as desirable as dollar-denominated U.S. government debt.

You will then invest the remaining 10 percent in your FX account. You will use this money to trade in a conservative fashion of both capital gains and interest-earning carry trades to form an accent to the total return of your bond portfolio.

With conservative investing you can still trade to capture the risk sentiment of the world's stock markets and capture its gains; you would, however, be capturing these gains through proxy, or risk trades.

You can set up your portfolio to be in 90 percent T-bills or CDs while the remaining 10 percent is in the FX market earning you solid returns. In this way you have the ability to earn gains much like if the FX portion were invested in S&P 500 index options. This is precisely what you will be shooting for with your FX positions: you will be attempting to duplicate the effect on a portfolio of investing 10 percent of your assets in index options. With the Forex proxy to options, you can forego the large account balance and complicated trading that usually goes with options trading. Additionally, you will benefit from the fact that Forex trades do *not* expire, and can be carried on for months and years. This is not the case for options: these instruments usually expire within a few months at best. Lastly, there is the benefit of capturing worldwide market gains with properly placed currency trades. This includes the long AUD/USD and short EUR/SEK, among others. Finally there is the diversification benefit that you can achieve by investing and trading in three, four, or five (or more!) currency pairs at the same time.

You might try to capture any big gains in the U.S. and European markets by going long AUD/USD, short EUR/SEK, and short USD/NOK. You could finally mix it up a bit and go long a developing economy nation such as

Poland zloty (PLN), or the Czech koruna (CZK), against the euro. These currency pairs carry a bit of security with them as well as growth potential. The reason is that each of the countries behind these currencies is making an effort to run the countries' fortunes in a conservative or otherwise well-run manner. Some are making efforts to pay down debt; others are running surpluses. Still others have stronger economies than their counter currencies. All of these reasons add up to make these currency-pair plays really smart and also well diversified. If you are looking to capture any upward gain in the world's stock markets, then these four trades are for you.

Just 10 percent of your portfolio is enough to capture big gains and add to the otherwise low return of your T-bill investment. You could get creative in adding safety to your trades by limiting your exposure to only 25 percent of your available margin as opposed to the usual 33 percent of available margin. You could go one step further and divide that quarter into fourths, with each pair getting equal exposure of one fourth. You can get creative at this point and add more to the basic trades such as more long AUD/USD and more short EUR/SEK while putting less into your short USD/NOK and even less so into your short EUR/CZK. By this time you should be getting a feel for what works in the market. Perhaps the short EUR/CZK is a bit of a long shot and you would divide that small part in half, putting half again into a short EUR/PLN position. This way you would be very well diversified across five currencies, each with different reasons for doing well, and each with different movement rates.

Research, and use your practice account to learn how different currency pairs work together to capture gains in the stock markets. You can soon discover that the one-tenth solution is perfect for accenting the returns of your T-bill portfolio.

Currency ETFs: Monitoring, Tracking, Trading

One of the safest, if not the easiest way, of investing in the currency market is by investing in currency exchange-traded funds (ETFs). ETFs are built like mutual funds on the inside, but trade during the day like a stock. ETFs have become very popular in the past five years, and more and more have popped up over time. Some of the more successful ones have become stock day trader's favorites, and some have been used by large fund managers to build positions easily in otherwise difficult to obtain markets.

Currency ETFs have all of these good features and more. Inside they are usually invested in money-market cash accounts in the home country of the currency. In this way, they follow the price of the currency as their value, and often pay as nice a dividend as the interest rates allow. Their interest is paid once a month, and is usually not reinvested into the ETF.

Some of the best currency ETFs are managed by CurrencyShares (*www.currencyshares.com/home/CurrencyShares.rails*). This company offers many FX alternatives, including ETFs for the euro, Swedish krona, Russian ruble, Swiss franc, Australian dollar, and others.

If you are looking to get into currency trading for diversification purposes and to capture gains in currencies against the USD but are wary of highly leveraged accounts, then perhaps investing in currency ETFs are for you. You can buy these in a normal full-service or discount brokerage firm just the same way you would purchase a stock. You can enter limit orders, stop losses, and take profit orders just the same way that you would be able to on a stock, and very similar to how it would be done in a regular Forex account.

ESSENTIAL

You can build your portfolio to include a variety of hedges using ETFs. You could build a hedge against your long AUD, SEK, and CZK positions by buying a volatility index future ETF such as VXX. With this ETF you can gain upside return when the markets are in turmoil and your FX trades are falling in value.

You can even use leverage to buy these products, but your leverage would be limited just as it would be when buying as stock.

This is actually a good alternative for many investors who are just getting into watching Forex pairs and getting to know the FX market. In order to invest properly you will still need to read your broker's reports, go to central banking websites, etc. You might find that FX investing with currency ETFs is perfect for you. If you like it, then work it into your overall investment plan and reap the rewards that FX investing can bring.

Get Up to Speed with a Demo Account

Whether you are new to currency trading or you are an old hand ready to try out new ideas, you should get familiar with your FX broker's demo accounts. Demonstration accounts are usually offered by currency brokerage firms as a way for people to try their hand at currency trading without getting into using real money or even opening an account.

You can do your research to help you determine which Forex broker to use and then sign up to use their free demo accounts. Most of them are set up to allow you to download their free trading platforms. This is usually very easy and done by following the prompts on the website.

Once this is done, you will have to choose your starting balance, usually $100,000 to $1 million. It is best that you start with a number that is closest to what you expect your actual opening balance to be in order for you to get used to placing orders, trading, and earning profits in this size account. As you can imagine, it would do little good to get used to trading a $1 million account when you are planning to put $2,500 in the account once you are ready to trade with real money. If you don't set your opening balance close to your actual expected balance, then your experiences will be tainted. You will be getting used to buying larger amounts, and getting used to earning bigger money when in actuality, this amount of money might be difficult to gain without taking undue risks and overtrading your account.

The second thing you will have to do is to set your margin. This is a key factor. Once you set your margin and begin trading, you will quickly get used to the speed at which things happen in your FX account. Gains and losses happen much quicker with a margin set at 50:1 then at 20:1 or even 10:1. You will be asking for a disaster if you have been trading at 10:1 in your practice demo account for the past three months and all of a sudden you switch your margin ratio to 50:1. You will be so used to trading at the lower margin ration that you will most likely blow up your account in no time, and you will not even know what has happened. You will have the most difficult time setting up trades and having a reasonable expectation of what to expect in the movement of the trades. You will most likely place orders that are too big; once the FX pair begins to move it will do five times as fast as in a 10:1 account! *Bam!* A blow out and a margin call.

The only way to prevent this is to set your margin at the beginning of your currency trading career and leave it at that. Don't change it once you have started with a particular ratio.

ALERT

Most of this book has been written with the assumption that you will be trading at 50:1 margin ratio. Even though this is ratio is five times as high as a more conservative ratio of 10:1, you can build the size of your overall used margin amount to be a very conservative number, therefore limiting your risk.

Using a lesser ratio means you will have to commit greater amounts of margin to a trade to gain the same amount. There is no winning at this, so your best bet is to learn on one ratio and stick with it. 50:1 is fine if that is what you get used to, and that is what you are learning to trade. A margin of 10:1 isn't any safer than one of 25:1 or 50:1 if you are not fully trained in its movements, both up and down.

Developing the FX-Trading Lifestyle

The FX-trading lifestyle is one to be admired. You can develop your own version of this lifestyle by bringing to it what you find important. If you would like to earn a bit of money by trading part-time, you could spend your free time reading reports and websites. You could look at your technical charts every time you have a chance, even if this chance is every three or four days when the kids are at the sitters. You could look for setups after dinner and wake to find fulfilled orders in the morning. You could check your profits and close out your trades via your smart phone or iPad while in the park, riding the train, or eating lunch at your desk at your day job.

The choice is yours; it is up to you to make currency trading work for you. If your lifestyle and money situation is such that you would rather spend time developing skill and technique, then open a demo account and trade away. There are stories of currency traders who had traded in the past, but decided to trade only in demo accounts for an entire year. This might work for them because of a preoccupation with another facet in their lives, lack of investable (or risk) funds or during times of extreme market unrest. Whatever the reason, these traders are still practicing their craft of FX trading. They are developing skills over time, and allowing the pressure to be off while they are learning. Perhaps they are following the markets very closely; they might check the currency prices several times a day. They might be visiting the Riksbank website, as well as following the Fed's economic reports.

If you find yourself in this situation, then this is your Forex-trading lifestyle. If things get to where you invest $100 or $1,000 and begin trading, then that is your Forex-trading lifestyle. You might already have a Forex account and months of experience and are reading this book in search of some tips on how to make your trading a bit more profitable. Maybe you didn't even realize what a currency-trading lifestyle is, but now you do, and you would like to go into FX trading full time. Whatever your starting point, you have a choice to build your FX-trading system to work for you. This system not only includes low risk/high risk plans, but the time spent learning, reading, and searching for good trades to come your way. It also means thinking about how much time and effort you would like to (or can) spend with your currency trading endeavors. Lastly, the amount of money you would like to make can make a difference in what your currency trading lifestyle turns out to be like.

How to Successfully Build Up Your Winnings

While it is natural to have some losses to go with your winnings, you will most likely find that currency trading is very profitable and that you win more than you lose. With skill, knowledge, planning, and luck, you can build your account to be a cash-generating machine. Once you have started to earn good money in your account you should move on to taking some of the money out and enjoying it.

Money upon money in any kind of brokerage account is never a good thing. Money should be used and enjoyed. If you keep compounding your winnings into bigger and bigger piles then there is a good chance that you will get into a situation where you'll make a mistake. This mistake could cause big losses in your account. Mistakes usually come from a feeling of glee that you get when you've won too many times in the market. It is common for traders to get the winner's curse (hubris) when they win too many times. If this happens to you, watch out!

The best way to prevent this is to get some value out of your currency trading beyond just the additional winnings. Set up a goal for yourself that you will take out of your account any amount over 20 percent gain on a weekly basis. This might seem to be contrary to logic; the usual approach would be to let your winnings grow. The sad fact is, if you do not enjoy your winnings somehow, you will be looking to enjoy your trading. Enjoying trading is good, but remember, you are trading for money, and that money is to buy things with, and to pay bills with. Piling up money just to play with more and more money is never good! On the other hand, having a big account or having a lot of money is fine indeed! The secret is to skim off your money every now and then and use it.

Give Yourself a Paycheck

The best way to do this is to give yourself a paycheck. Pull out a weekly amount that is over and above a preset account limit. For example, you could let a certain amount of your winnings stay in your account and take the rest of that week's money out to use. Wouldn't it be nice to take a vacation with your winnings, buy a new car, or pay off a credit card? Having a goal helps too.

ESSENTIAL

Giving yourself a paycheck that comes from your trading will set in your mind that you are trading as a business and therefore for profit. The best thing to do is have a set amount of money coming out of your account every week or two. This will keep you interested in currency trading and help you enjoy your winnings.

If you do not do this there is a good chance that you will lose interest in the very type of trading that has earned you such good money! You might even be so bored with winning every time and plain trading that you add to your risk level. This is how most accounts get destroyed! When you are just a tad bit gleeful of your winnings, take some money off of the table. If you don't want to buy anything, or use it in any other way, use the money to diversify your holdings. Use the money to buy into a well-run mutual fund or even a mutual fund that is unconstrained by any normal investment systems. These types of mutual funds are often called multistrategy funds and can be found by a Google search. One such example is UBS's Dynamic Alpha, market symbol BNACX. Dynamic Alpha is set up to be a mutual fund that acts and is managed like a hedge fund with long, short, and leveraged stock, bond, and derivative investments. The performance of these types of funds can add to the overall stability of your larger investment portfolio, as you can use them to further diversify risk. Multistrategy mutual funds do not follow a benchmark, and their performance is usually independent of the stock and bond markets.

Using Your Winnings

These are just a few examples of what to do with your winnings. When you start to win, use the money to build up your account. It can really help to take some money off the table every now and then to in order to take some of the heat out of the account. FX accounts can grow big very fast, and it might take you some time to learn how to manage these bigger and bigger amounts. In the meantime, pay yourself a salary at set levels and enjoy your winnings!

Tax and Business Considerations

Taxes can bring terror to even the most hardened of traders. The best solution to the tax time problem is to keep good records. And get a good accountant. You might open up a separate checking account for the purpose of buying all of the newspapers periodicals and cups of coffee that go into getting up to speed to buy and sell currencies.

If you keep it in your mind that you will be running your currency trading endeavors like a business, then you will have the right ideas when it comes to record keeping. Be aware that all of the income and interest that you make will probably be recorded and forwarded along to the IRS. In order to combat the effects of your winnings on taxes you will need to keep all of your receipts that relate to the running of your currency trading business.

This includes working out a plan with your accountant in regard to the number of deductions you can take for the costs associated with your home office (if you have one) as well as any portion of utilities you can attribute to FX trading. Other things to include are the costs of any computer hardware, smart phone, and iPad. You might also want to talk to your accountant about the possibility of expensing the cost of any coffee and meals out that you might have paid while working on your trading outside your office.

Of course the cost of trading school and even this book should be considered when you are getting together the costs of doing business.

Running your trading activities like a business means keeping track of income by periodically printing out screen shots of your accumulated profit and loss statements, and if possible, resetting them to zero at the first of the year. It also means that you will be trading for profit, as business only exists to produce a profit!

CHAPTER 20

Making It Work, Making It Pay

This chapter deals with getting out there and becoming successful with currency trading. It begins with the basics of picking an FX broker, and then moves on to some of the secrets to building up a good-sized currency trading account. You will then learn how to develop skills over time and also deal with some of the emotions that come with currency trading. Lastly, you will learn how currency trading can make you financially independent of the markets and economy in general.

Picking a Currency Broker

Picking an FX broker can be as easy as doing a Google search. It can also be as hard as buying a used car. Almost every FX broker offers the same thing: lower account minimums and access to high margin. There are differences though, and they become quite apparent when they are compared side by side.

Almost all FX brokerage firms will allow you to deposit money in many ways, from sending a check, to debit and credit cards, to a bank wire. Getting money into the account is not usually a problem. Getting your money out can be, though. If you have deposited money in your account a certain way, then there is a good chance that your FX brokerage firm will only refund you the money in that same way. This is a function of the anti-money laundering laws that came about several years ago.

Also, some brokerages strictly follow U.S. law (even though they might be based in Europe) and others follow the trading laws of the country in which they are based. For example, Windsor Brokers is a Forex firm that is based offshore in Cyprus. It allows margin trading on gold and silver as well as currency pairs. It is regulated by European Union authorities, which allow the use of up to 500:1 margin. On the other hand, OANDA, which operates under U.S. regulations, only allows up to 50:1 margin, and does not offer leverage on spot gold or silver trading (OANDA offers 1:1 margin on metals).

ESSENTIAL

Some currency brokers allow futures and options trading as well as access to international exchanges. You might want to consider looking into one of these if you are thinking of bundling all of your brokerage accounts into one account and trading them on one platform.

Most of the brokerages will offer very competitive pricing schedules. The main difference is the number of currency pairs that are offered to the account holder to trade. All firms will offer the basics, but only some offer all of the euro proxies such as the SEK and NOK, as well as the exotics such as the CZK, HUF, or PLN. This is key if you want to trade these currencies with some of the pairs that have been discussed in this book.

Additionally, most of the currency brokers will say they offer an easy-to-use trading platform. Usually, the opposite is true. You will have to try out several FX brokers to determine what trading platform or system is best for you. Some are very easy and intuitive to use; others are more complex. The Forex brokers that offer more complex trading platforms are usually intending for their customers to program automated trading programs right onto the software using C++ or another computer language. If you plan on getting into this type of currency trading, you should inquire if the broker you are looking into can accommodate you in the future.

Lastly, you will need to have some sort of reporting of your trades. It might be a simplified version of a profit and loss statement that can be carried forward throughout the year, or it can be a more complex record of each trade. Either way you will need to have a record of how much you make and lose over the months and years. Providing these records will greatly add to the value of your broker come tax time.

Build Up Your Account

Whether you are going to trade in a conservative manner or a more aggressive manner, you will eventually have to have enough money in your account to make it worth your while to spend the days and nights reading about the currency markets. Smaller accounts are good to start with, as they are much easier to stomach when a trade goes against you. Trades that go against you are a normal thing in currency trading. It takes some getting used to in order to learn how to build up trades and then learn how to figure out what to do with them once they are at a profit.

It takes a certain amount of skill to know how to work with money. It is best learned by starting with smaller amounts. In that way you can look at your wins and loses with an educational slant, somewhat free of the negative feelings such as fear, greed, and guilt. These feelings can run rampant when you have an FX account; the best way to deal with the feelings is to learn how to trade with small amounts and build up the size of your account at periodic intervals.

It might be best for you to add money into your account on twice a week, once a week, or once a month. The idea is that you will be gaining experience with the money level that you have, and you will have that account size mastered by the time you deposit more money into the account at a later date. This is the best way to learn how to work with money, a skill that includes learning how to deal with the emotions that come with bigger and bigger wins and the occasional, inevitable loss.

Learning how to handle money can be a quickly learned task. Once you are successful at currency trading you will undoubtedly want to add more and more to your account in order to reap the rewards of your currency trading skills. The best way to do this is to add funds regularly.

FACT

Adding funds to your account can seem like a daunting task when you first start. Like anything else, you will soon become used to putting your extra money in your Forex brokerage account and you will look forward to the weekly additions to your account. This is what it takes to build up a good-sized currency trading account.

Wanting to add money to your account in order to trade with larger and larger amounts is the easy part. Finding the money to add to your account can be the hard part. In order to do this you will have to have access to more and more amounts of cash. If you are already fully invested, then the next thing that you can do is to set up some sort of budget in order to free up cash from your everyday expenses to use to trade with. You can look to free up cash in the most low-impact ways as possible. This way you will not notice the difference in your lifestyle too much and you will not feel as though you are giving up anything that would strengthen your financial picture.

For example, you would not want to sell off your great-granddad's collection of rare gold coins in order to fund your FX-trading account, and you wouldn't want to fund your account with a credit card (even though some brokerage firms allow you to do this). You should still look at the FX world as an accent to your overall investing *even if it earns you a majority of the returns!* It takes only a small account to earn big in currency trading. Building up your account should be as worry-free and painless as possible. Look for free money that is actually free, and you will not go wrong.

You can look at it this way: If you normally order a Danish and a double low-fat, low-foam latte each morning, and you switch to breakfast at home and just a plain brewed coffee, then you are freeing up nearly $4 a day. If you go to the coffee shop every day, that's $120 a month that you can put into your account each month. At a 50:1 margin this equates to a potential of investing in $6,000 worth of currency! If you invest in a carry trade earning 4.5 percent net interest and you follow this program for a year . . . well, you can guess how much better off you will be for giving up the Danish and the latte each day!

Skill Building Over Time

You will most likely want to get into currency trading and be good at it right away. It takes time to develop the skills required to read the central bank websites, analyze the brokers' reports, look at technical charts, and make good trades. It also takes time to learn how to manage your margin, use stops and take-profits points, etc. The best way to do this is to read as much as possible on the subject. Don't let this be the last book you read on currencies, trading, or technical analysis. Keep reading all and any information you can get your hands on to develop the skills it takes to have a well-run FX trading account.

It takes time to get into currency trading in a way that will allow you to win as often as you would like. Just as it takes time to learn a new career or gain the skill to be good at a new job, it will take the same amount of time to get to the point that you can trade currencies with enough skill to draw a paycheck and therefore call it your job (even if it is your part-time job).

It also takes time for the world's stock markets and the world's FX markets to work through situations and cycles, and sometimes the best lessons are learned by watching stories and conditions develop over time. It might take several months for a condition to work its way through the FX markets. It might take several months for you to notice a trend. When this happens you will step back and tell yourself, "Oh, now I see how that worked out."

The best way to trade is to trade over time. You might be a scalper, and only want to be in each trade for less than an hour, or you could be a carry trader and have a goal of being in a trade for several months or even a year or two. Either way, you will learn best by sticking with the program and putting in the time. Even if you trade for a while and then take time off while learning new skills in a demo account, you should make it your desire to learn and keep trading. Continuing to trade and watch the developments of the Forex markets can go a long way in keeping you and your skills growing and developing, which in turn will go a long way in keeping your account profitable and you in the FX trading business.

ALERT

The best learning is done over time. Your mind will pick up the secrets to currency trading by working at it little by little every day. If you try to spend too much time trading at first you will not be giving yourself the time you need to see the Forex trades and patterns develop.

You will soon feel confident and able to call out a trade when you see it. You will know when it is the best time to get into a trade in a big way in order to capture the gains it will produce when the trade moves. You will master the feelings of greed and fear that prevent good trading, and you will be able to use these skills to close out profitable trades (without waiting for more gain) and you will learn how to stay out of horrible market-trading days. You will also know when to walk away from your trading desk when the day was good, and how to blow off steam and enjoy your winnings. Getting up the skills to do this takes time, study, and placing trades.

The Emotions of Trading

Earning money in the currency markets through trading (capital gains) can be a wonderful, thrilling experience. You have outwitted the markets and outsmarted them, and have made a financial gain to prove your smarts! When you feel the power that comes from winning in the markets for yourself, you will know how professional traders feel when they make gains in the market.

There are a lot of emotions that are generated from trading in the FX markets: the ups, the downs, the winning and the losing. Couple this with working early in the morning to set up a trade, or getting up at 2 A.M. to see if your order has been filled—you can see that it takes a lot to keep going at currency trading. Hopefully you will find that the winnings are enough to keep you in the game, keep you interested, and keep you trading.

Losses happen, and your emotions can be low after a bad trade. This is precisely why you should use some of the risk management techniques described in this book, and why you should build up your account slowly. Even though you are using huge amounts of margin, you should never get yourself in a situation in which you are getting a margin call. You should also have enough extra margin to double down and dollar cost average into a trade that has worked against you. Another thing you can do it to switch into a longer-term perspective, and wait for the trade to turn around.

It might be that the market is really suffering, and you can get into an AUD/USD trade at eight cents cheaper than it was at the beginning of the month. If the interest differential is the same, why not take advantage of a long-term carry trade while you wait for the markets to recover (even if this takes several months or years)?

On the other hand, you should have your accounts set up in such a way that you can leave your Forex trading for any reason. If the markets are not that good, and you do not feel like risking your assets and margin on trading, take the money out of the account. Have the Forex broker send you a check and use the money on something of value. These are the facts: if Forex trading is not adding to your life and bringing you enough value for the time and money that it takes, then take a break and use the money for a something that is of value.

FACT

You can set up your Forex-trading endeavors to be much like a business. In this way, you can set yourself trading hours, lunch hours, and even days off. You are in control of how your business operates. Keep in mind: Forex trading should work for you, not the other way around.

If you need to take a break, don't worry! The currency markets will be around when you get back to them, and the Forex dealer will happily arrange for you to add more money back into the account. If your 1984 Volvo 240 just died after 478,000 miles, and you need to take out most of your hobby or trading money to buy a new (to you) used 2000 Volvo XC70, then by all means, do so! Rest assured that in the future you will once again have enough money to put into your Forex account and trade evermore!

Being Financially Independent of the Markets

There will undoubtedly be times when the market is reacting in illogical ways. For example, there might be every indication that there is a big chance of inflation in the future, and you might have a few long gold and silver trades on your books. There are times of extreme volatility in the markets and these times could cause your logical trades such as the gold and silver to behave in very illogical ways, such as free-falling into losses. It might be that there is so much upset in the stock markets that traders and big funds are selling their positions in secure positions (gold and silver) in order to raise cash for the margin calls in their other trades in the markets.

It is quite possible that the emotions of the market have gone bad in a very fast way, and that there are too many sellers for the market to handle. It might be that the whole of the trading world is upset, and your currency trades are caught in the middle. This situation, in turn, can get you very worried about your FX trading and even the world in general. When there is talk of the world falling apart or how it's really bad out there, you have to make a definite decision of how you will handle the turmoil.

You have a choice. You can see yourself as a victim of the markets and subject to its each and every hiccup and stumble. Or you can see yourself as an independent person who is operating her own currency trading fund. If you take the latter approach, you will be prepared for downturns and extreme upset. You can do this by staying informed, using only limited amounts of your capital, and keeping a healthy portion of your money in very liquid assets outside of the stock market, the currency market, and other assets that have a tendency to react to bad news. You have to think of insulating yourself; at this point you are the manager of the fund and you are also your own customer.

If you had money in the market during the downturn of the 2008–2009 banking crisis, then you know how fast bad news can travel. Stock values, gold values, house values, and even the banks themselves can be under pressure. The markets' emotions do not have to be your emotions. In fact, you could build yourself and your financial situation in such a way that you are as insulated from problems just as if you lived on a financial island. Part of achieving this goal is to be independent minded when it comes to your investments. Thinking of yourself as a currency fund manager can go a long way in keeping your positions liquid and as riskless as possible during ugly times.

ESSENTIAL

Being and acting in a manner that makes you financially independent of the markets can seem to be a difficult task. In reality, it is very easy. All it takes is an attitude of independence and financial self-reliance. You will never fully live on an island, but you don't have to be subject to the ills of the markets.

The key to survival during these times is not set in stone. It might be the case that you are semi-retired and working part-time as a handyman while building up your bank balance and your trading account. It might be that you have enough skills and a big enough balance in your account to allow your FX trading to really, truly add to your income each month. Any way you choose to pursue it, being financially independent is not that hard of a goal to achieve. It might mean that you are insulated from the stock markets, job markets, and housing markets. It might mean that you have the foresight to short the market at its top and go long carry trades after the currency market has gone into full risk-aversion mode.

If the times in which you are trading are bad in the outside world, they do not have to be bad in your personal economy. Decoupling your fortunes and well-being from that of the rest of the world's economies can sometimes be a very rewarding goal to pursue. You will have to analyze how currency trading can help you lead a more financially independent life away from the trials and turmoil that economies have been facing after the banking crisis, housing collapse, and sovereign debt woes of 2008, 2009, 2010, 2011 . . .

Building Your Own Trading System

Whatever your initial thoughts on currency trading, hopefully the reading of this book has helped you navigate your way through the charts, websites, and the hard work of looking for setups in the market. You have learned how to look at fundamental and technical indicators and place trades. You now know how to build a trading system that is geared to your needs, whether aggressive or tame. You also know what to reasonably expect from Forex trading in terms of daily, weekly, monthly, and yearly returns. You most likely have gained a bit of understanding on how it feels to look a situation, get into a trade, close it out, and have a good idea of how it feels to call a good trade. Lastly, you now know how to use automation to help you build value into your trades by helping you close out at preset profit points.

Getting to the point that you can spot trends, read the central bank websites, and predict the direction of common currency pairs can be a daunting task. With a little time and practice, you will be able to turn your interest of currency trading into a full-fledged trading system that works for you. You might even get to the point that you have some goals for yourself and your trading. These goals might include getting to the point that you can go into Forex trading full-time, and reach the point that you are free from the economic worries of the world.

In order to do this you need to take your new knowledge and open up your first account. Whether you start small or large, high risk or low risk, you are now more prepared than ever to make a go at currency trading for fun and profit!

APPENDIX A

Glossary

2 percent rule

A method of building in stop-loss settings (automatic closing of a position) to limit the overall loss of a position to 2 percent of the cash balance of your total day trading account.

200-day moving average

A technical indicator that mathematically and statistically calculates the average of the currency pair on a 200-day rolling basis.

Automated take profit

The process of programming your trading software to close out a trade at a prespecified price; is often used to lock in gains automatically.

Bar chart

A technical chart that uses long and short lines to indicate the price movement of a currency pair within a set time frame. The length of the bar will show the range of movement of price within the time frame observed.

Base currency

The first currency listed in a currency pair quote. Also the currency that is divided by the second listed currency.

Big four

A term that refers to the largest in trading volume of the world's currencies: USD, EUR, GBP, JPY.

Blow up

When the losses in a trading account get to the point that the chances for rebuilding its balance through capital gains is unlikely.

Brokers' reports

Very helpful technical and fundamental reports of currency pairs and markets published by currency brokers and full-service firms for private client and institutional use.

Bubble

A market condition in which the price of an asset is inflated beyond its fundamental value.

Candlestick chart (Japanese candlestick chart)

A chart type that shows the range of movement that a currency pair has made during a set time frame. Also shows opening and closing prices as well as if the price finished higher of lower than the time frame directly before it.

Capital gains

When a currency is sold at a higher price than was paid for it during the course of a trade.

Capital preservation

A trading and investment goal of keeping assets safe; not seeking capital gains.

Carry trades

A Forex trade of selling a low-interest rate currency short and investing the proceeds in a high-interest rate currency. See interest rate differential.

Cash-flow statement

Cash-flow statements are comprised of the money generated from operations (trading) minus money expenses, plus money deposited in your account.

Central bank

A country's bank of banks; often considered the lender of last resort within that particular economic zone.

Central banking stance

The forward looking direction that a central bank will usually hint at in a press conference; the unofficial economic analysis of a central bank regarding its home economic conditions.

Commodity currency

A currency that is from a country that produces commodities as its main source of exports: NZD, AUD, CAD, and ZAR are some examples.

Consumer Price Index (CPI)

A periodic measurement of a predetermined basket of goods. The elements of the goods are measured against the prices at the prior term, and any differences are noted. The result is a gauge of how much more it costs for basic living expenses period to period.

Correction

When a market reverses its direction suddenly and quickly after a big run-up in value.

Counter currency

The second currency listing in a currency pair quote. The currency the base currency is divided into to get a trading price.

Currency crosses (or cross pairs)

Refers to pairs that are made up of either minor currencies or other infrequently traded groups—a currency pair that does not include the big four.

Currency trading

A form of trading where you buy and sell the money of the different countries of the world. The investment vehicles are digital money. (Also called FX trading and Forex trading.)

Dollarization

When a country uses a major trading partner's currency as their own. Usually done in small countries with close ties to one major trading partner.

Exotic pairs

Currencies that are from developing countries and have low trading volumes.

ETF

A basket of stock, bonds, or commercial paper that is traded intraday like a stock.

Euro proxies

The grouping of currencies that are closely related to the euro, but are managed by independent central banks: SEK, CHF, NOK.

Exotic currencies

The grouping of currencies that are low volume and generally related to developing economies.

Federal Reserve (the Fed)

The central bank of the United State of America. It independently sets the monetary policy of the United States.

Fiat

A currency system based upon credit and not upon a physical gold backing.

Fibonacci series

A system of using ratios to determine support and resistance lines in a Forex trading pair. Lines are drawn with technical analysis software on a bar chart from the lowest trading point of a time frame to the highest trading point of the same time frame.

Fiscal policy

The efforts of lawmakers to raise taxes and spend those funds in such a way as to spur growth of the economy.

Floating rate system

The currency method of allowing world currencies to rise and fall in value according to market supply and demand.

Forward-lag

If the Fed adjusts the money supply, the effects of the adjustment might not reach the average household for several months. This delay is called forward-lag.

Free-cash flow

When a trading account produces money above and beyond its cash additions and expenses.

Fundamental analysis

A method of predicting the price movement of a currency by looking at trading partners, future interest rates, and a country's balance sheet. Also uses the interpretation of a country's central bank website for hints of economic policies and any future economic policy changes.

Fundamentals

The economics of a currency, relating to growth and cash flows of a country. See technical analysis.

FX pairs

The method in which currencies are measured. A currency's value can be measured against the value of a second currency. Also the way to quote the price of two currencies in order to buy or sell.

Going long

A term used to state you have a trade that is set up to make money when the security or sector is moving upward.

Gold Standard

Pegging paper currency directly to the amount of gold in the vaults of a country's central banking vaults, thereby limiting the amount of money in circulation to the amount of gold owned by the country.

Grow organically

When a currency trading account gains in value from trades and interest income as opposed to adding more money from an external source such as a separate bank account.

Hedge fund

An investment vehicle that uses leverage to amplify the returns of its holdings.

Hedged-directional trade

A Forex trading method of being either long or short risky currency pairs, but using diversification of smaller groups of different pairs within the larger trade.

Interest

When money is earned for holding a currency for a period of time. Interest can vary among different currencies. Most Forex accounts accrue interest every second that the currency is held in a trade.

Interest differential

The net difference between the borrowing cost of a low-yielding currency and the investment yield of a higher-yielding currency.

Intervening in the markets

When a central bank buys or sells currency in the open market in order to force a change in the exchange rate of its home currency.

Investment grade bonds

Bonds that are issued from the highest quality lenders: used in a one-tenth solution portfolio. See one-tenth solution.

Lagging indicators

A fundamental economic indicator that is measured and reported to the public that monitors changes in the economy after the changes have already taken place (sometimes with a delay of up to three months or more).

Leading indicators

A fundamental economic indicator that can be used to determine the direction that an economy will be heading in the next several months. See lagging indicators.

Leverage ratio

The multiplier to determine the amount of currency you are able to trade with a given cash balance.

Liquidity

The ability to close out an asset quickly and go back into cash. Also when a central bank adds money supply into the economic system.

M1

The total of the cash, coins, checking account balances, and traveler's checks circulating in a particular economy.

M2

Everything included in the M1 plus savings account deposits, money market mutual funds held at brokerage firms, certificates of deposit, and U.S. dollars on deposit in foreign banks.

M3

The M3 consists of everything included in M1 and M2 plus the cash products that large banks and business have on deposit. It includes CDs and other structured time deposits in both domestic and eurodollars.

Macro fund

A hedge-fund trading idea that includes all forms of investments, including stock, options, futures, and Forex.

Major FX pair

A currency pair that has a big four currency on one of its ends of the trade. See big four.

Margin call

A forced closing of your positions when the losses of the account have reached a point of negative value.

Market risk appetite

The measure of how much traders and investors are adding stocks, commodities and other risky assets to their portfolios.

Melt value

The value of the pure gold content in gold coins that are less than 24 karat. Melt value is the value of the weight of the gold without the usual 5 percent to 20 percent markup charged by precious metals dealers.

Minor pairs

Currency pairs that are not the big four: GBP, USD, EUR or JPY.

Monetary policy

Efforts by a country's central bank to promote full employment, stabilize prices, and encourage long-run economic growth through controlling the money supply and interest rates. (In the United States, the Federal Reserve conducts monetary policy.)

Money

Anything that functions as a medium of exchange, store of value, or standard of value.

Money center

One of the main trading centers of the world: New York, London, Zurich, Frankfurt, Paris, and Tokyo are a few.

Money supply

A measure of all of the cash, coin, and electronic quantity of a currency that is in circulation and in accounts.

Mutual funds

An investment vehicle that is comprised of a basket of securities and offers the diversification benefits of an ETF, but has its price calculated only once a day, at the close of the markets.

Naked trades

A method of going into trades without any stop losses or take profits pre-programmed into the trade.

One-tenth solution

A method of investing 1/10th of your overall portfolio in a risky asset class and the remaining 9/10ths in a low-risk asset class.

Open market operations

The method that the Federal Reserve uses to buy and sell securities in an effort to regulate the amount of money in the economic system.

Options

A financial product that takes its value from the price of an underlying security (such as a stock).

Overnight trading

When you look for the developments at the Asian markets in the early evening in order to get a good idea as to the direction of your bets.

Pegging

A method of tying the price of a country's currency to that of its main trading partner.

Portfolio theory

The idea that numbers of investments are less risky than just one or two investments, all while producing the same return; diversification.

Pyramiding

Building and closing out a position in a single currency pair using a series of trades instead of one big trade in and one big trade out.

Quantitative easing

A term that refers to when a central bank adds liquidity and money supply to the economic system. See liquidity.

Quote

The way the price of a currency is listed on your trading platform.

Range bound

When an investment vehicle such as a Forex pair is stuck moving within the same price points.

Regression analysis

A method of using statistics to determine the factor that inputs have in an outcome. A good example is when it is used to determine what currency pairs affect the price of another currency pair.

Reserve portfolio

The savings account of a central bank.

Risk/Return ratio

The measure of how much risk is taken in a trading system.

Scalping

A method of trading a pair for minutes at a time.

Sharpe ratio

A measure of risk taken for reward gained.

Stop-loss setting

When you precalculate the maximum loss you would take in the trade before your trading platform places on automated closing out of the trade, thereby placing a limit on the percentage and dollar amount of the potential loss of the trade.

Strong economies

When a country has high employment and is operating at or near capacity. Strong economies run the risk of being too strong, this is why central banks will raise interest rates to try to limit inflation by limiting money supply and raising the cost of borrowing.

Technical analysis

Using charts, numbers, and statistics to come up with a trading plan.

Trading naked

A method of going into trades without any stop losses or take profits pre-programmed into the trade. In order to do this you must first wait for the best time of the day: 6:00–7:00 P.M. eastern.

VIX Index (CBOE Volatility Index)

An index that measures the upward and downward movement of the S&P 500 index options. The VIX can be used to gauge if a market is risk adverse or not.

Word on the street

The thoughts that are being written and spoken about on news sources such as CNBC and Bloomberg.

Value at Risk

A measure of how much of a portfolio is at risk at any given time: also known as VaR.

APPENDIX B

Additional Resources

Books

Archer, Michael D. *Getting Started in Currency Trading: Winning in Today's Forex Market.* (Hoboken, NJ: John Wiley & Sons, 2010).

Bernstein, Peter L. *Against the Gods: The Remarkable Story of Risk.* (New York, NY: John Wiley & Sons, 1996).

Bernstein, Peter L. *The Power of Gold: The History of an Obsession.* (New York: John Wiley & Sons, 2000).

Burgess, Gareth. *Trading and Investing in the Forex Markets Using Chart Techniques.* (Hoboken, NJ: John Wiley & Sons, 2009).

Downes, John, and Jordan Elliot Goodman. *Barron's Finance & Investment Handbook.* (Hauppauge, NY: Barron's Educational Series, 2007).

Ferguson, Niall. *The House of Rothschild: Volume 1: Money's Prophets: 1798–1848.* (New York, NY: Penguin, 1998).

Fraser, Jill Andresky. *The Business Owner's Guide to Personal Finance: When Your Business Is Your Paycheck.* (Princeton, NJ: Bloomberg Press, 2002).

Online News Sources

- **Barron's Online**
  http://online.barrons.com

- **ClearStation**
  http://clearstation.etrade.com

- **CNBC**
  www.cnbc.com

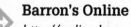

- **Dailystocks.com**
  www.dailystocks.com

- **The Economist**
  www.economist.com

- **Moody's Economy**
  www.economy.com

- **The Motley Fool**
  www.fool.com

- **MSN Money Central**
  http://moneycentral.msn.com/investor/home.asp

- **Yahoo! Finance**
  http://finance.yahoo.com

Research Websites for Fundamental Analysis

- **Bank of England**
  www.bankofengland.co.uk

- **Bank for International Settlements**
  www.bis.org

- **Central Bank Website Listings**
  www.bis.org/cbanks

- **Bank of Japan**
  www.boj.or.jp/en

- **CME Group**
  www.cmegroup.com

Deutche Bank USA
www.db.com/usa

European Central Bank
www.ecb.int

InvestorsEurope
www.investorseurope.com

Kitco Base Metals
www.kitcometals.com

Kitco Gold & Precious Metals
www.kitco.com

Kitco Silver
www.kitcosilver.com

The London Bullion Market Association
www.lbma.org.uk

London Metal Exchange
www.lme.com

Merrill Lynch International
www.ml.com

Monetary Authority of Singapore
www.mas.gov.sg

Norges Bank
www.norges-bank.no

OANDA fxTrade
http://fxtrade.oanda.com

- **Reserve Bank of Australia**
  www.rba.gov.au

- **Reserve Bank of New Zealand**
  www.rbnz.govt.nz

- **The Riksbank**
  www.riksbank.com

- **SW Consulting Directory of Swiss Banks**
  www.swconsult.ch/cgi-bin/banklist.pl

- **Stock, Futures, and Options**
  www.sfomag.com

- **The Swiss National Bank**
  www.snb.ch

- **UBS Global Homepage**
  www.ubs.com

- **U.S. Bureau of Economic Analysis**
  www.bea.gov

- **U.S. Department of the Treasury**
  www.ustreas.gov

- **U.S. Federal Reserve**
  www.federalreserve.gov

- **World Gold Council**
  www.gold.org

APPENDIX C

Financial Publications

There are dozens of publications that can be very helpful to investors and traders alike. These financially oriented newspapers, magazines, and newsletters offer valuable insights about the markets, including stock tips, mutual fund rankings, and in-depth articles with a more educational angle. Publications can be a good place to get investing and trading ideas, but you must still do your own research and analysis and make any investing or trading decisions.

The Wall Street Journal

Published by Dow Jones and Company, the *Wall Street Journal* is a leading global newspaper with a focus on business. Founded in 1889, the newspaper has grown to a worldwide daily circulation of more than 2 million readers. In 1994, Dow Jones introduced the *Wall Street Journal Special Editions*, special sections written in local languages that are featured in more than thirty leading national newspapers worldwide. The *Wall Street Journal Americas*, published in Spanish and Portuguese, is included in approximately twenty leading Latin American newspapers.

800-568-7625
www.wallstreetjournal.com

Barron's

Barron's is also known as the *Dow Jones Business* and *Financial Weekly*. With its first edition published in 1921, *Barron's* offers its readers news reports and analyses on financial markets worldwide. Investors will also find a wealth of tips regarding investment techniques.

800-975-8620
www.barrons.com

Investor's Business Daily

Founded in 1984, *Investor's Business Daily* is a newspaper focusing on business, financial, economic, and national news. The publication places a strong emphasis on offering its readers timely information on stock market and stock market–related issues. The front page of each issue provides a brief overview of the most important business news of the day. It's published five days a week, Monday through Friday.

800-459-6706
www.investors.com

Forbes

Forbes magazine is a biweekly business magazine for "those who run business today—or aspire to." Each issue contains stories on companies, management strategies, global trends, technology, taxes, law, capital markets, and investments.

800-888-9896
www.forbesmagazine.com

Money

Money is a monthly personal finance magazine from Time-Warner publications, covering such topics as family finances, investment careers, taxes, and insurance. Each issue includes tips, advice, and strategies for smart investing. The magazine also features other related matters like finding cheap flights, buying a home, and preparing for tax season. It also offers a substantive annual mutual fund guide.

800-633-9970
http://money.cnn.com

BusinessWeek

This weekly publication comes jam-packed with comprehensive coverage of both the U.S. and global business scene. From the economy to politics to how both impact stock prices, *BusinessWeek* provides in-depth market analysis and incisive investigative reporting.

888-878-5151
www.businessweek.com

Fortune

Every month, *Fortune* magazine, a Time-Warner publication, offers analysis of the business marketplace. The publication's annual ranking of the top 500 American companies is one of its most widely read features. *Fortune* has been covering business and business-related topics since its origins in 1930.

800-621-8000
www.fortune.com

Smart Money

Smart Money, a monthly personal finance magazine, offers readers ideas for investing, spending, and saving. The publication also covers automotive, technology, and lifestyle subjects, including upscale travel, footwear, fine wine, and music.

800-444-4204
www.smartmoney.com

Kiplinger's Personal Finance

One of the most respected names in financial publications, *Kiplinger's* offers investing ideas, updates on companies, insider interviews with top financial experts and fund managers, and very detailed listings of the best-performing mutual funds in a wide range of categories.

800-544-0155
www.kiplingers.com

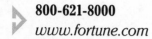

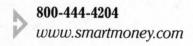

ValueLine Investment Survey

A weekly publication available at most libraries and through subscription, it offers ratings, reports, opinions, and analysis on about 130 stocks in seven or eight industries on a weekly basis. Approximately 1,700 stocks in about ninety-four industries are covered every thirteen weeks. CD-Rom subscribers can also purchase an expanded version containing reviews of 5,000 stocks.

800-634-3583
www.valueline.com

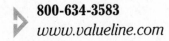

Index

D

E

F

Q

R

S

FOLLOW THAT FOOD CHAIN

AN AUSTRALIAN OUTBACK Food Chain

A WHO-EATS-WHAT Adventure

Rebecca Hogue Wojahn Donald Wojahn

Lerner Publications Company
Minneapolis

For Eli and Cal. We hope this answers some of your questions.

There are many links in the chain that created this series. Thanks to Ann Kerns, Carol Hinz, Kitty Creswell, Danielle Carnito, Sarah Olmanson, Paul Rodeen, the staff of the L. E. Phillips Memorial Public Library and, finally, Katherine Hogue

Lerner Publications Company
A division of Lerner Publishing Group, Inc.
241 First Avenue North
Minneapolis, MN 55401 U.S.A.

Website address: www.lernerbooks.com

Library of Congress Cataloging-in-Publication Data

Wojahn, Rebecca Hogue.
an Australian outback food chain : a who-eats-what adventure / by Rebecca Hogue Wojahn and Donald Wojahn.
p. cm. — (Follow that food chain)
Includes bibliographical references and index.
ISBN 978-0-8225-7499-6 (lib. bdg. : alk. paper)
1. Food chains (Ecology)—Australia—Juvenile literature. I. Wojahn, Donald. II. Title.
QH197.W64 2009
577.540994—dc22 2008021117

Manufactured in the United States of America
1 2 3 4 5 6 - BP - 14 13 12 11 10 09

FOLLOW THAT FOOD CHAIN

Contents

Introduction
WELCOME TO THE OUTBACK

Your small plane flies over the Outback just as morning breaks. Out the window, you see huge expanses of red earth. Nothing else as far as you can see! The Outback is the inner region of the country of Australia. It is one of the flattest and driest places on Earth.

Your plane dips down for a landing. You begin to see clumpy grass, pokey bushes, and scraggly trees. Termite mounds taller than your head poke out of the red dirt. It's a strange landscape.

But you won't just be exploring the red desert at the center of the Outback. The Outback is a big place with many different parts. On this Outback adventure, you'll see sand dunes, muddy creek beds, sheer rocky cliffs, towers of stones, and spreading trees too.

In much of the Outback, the air shimmers with intense heat during the day. Then, twelve hours later, animals shiver with cold at night. Everyone thirsts for water. The land can go months, even years, without rain. The heat and the dryness often cause huge fires across the Outback.

Australia is an island continent. It is separate from the rest of the world. Many of its creatures are unlike anything you'll see anywhere else. Here in the Outback, you'll find some of the most strange and unique animals on the planet. Frogs in cocoons, plagues of rabbits, not-so-cuddly koalas, spiky duck-billed echidnas, and bounding kangaroos all live in the Outback's different **habitats**. Come and meet just a few of them in this book.

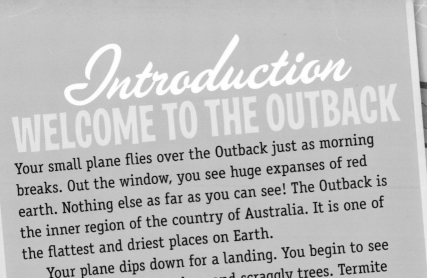

Arafura Sea
Coral Sea
Indian Ocean
South Pacific Ocean
N
The Outback
AUSTRALIA
Tasmania

Choose a TERTIARY CONSUMER

All the living things in the Outback are necessary for its health and survival. From the kangaroo bounding across the red earth to the crickets chirping under the eucalyptus leaves, all living things are connected. Animals and other organisms feed on and transfer energy to one another. This is called a **food chain** or a **food web.**

In food chains, the strongest **predators** are called **tertiary consumers**. They hunt other animals for food and have few natural enemies. Some of the animals they eat are called **secondary consumers.** Secondary consumers are also predators. They hunt plant-eating animals. Plant eaters are **primary consumers.**

Plants are **producers.** Using energy from the sun, they produce their own food. Plants take in nutrients from the soil. They also provide nutrients to the animals that eat them.

Decomposers are insects or **bacteria** that break down dead plants and animals. Decomposers change them into the nutrients found in the soil.

The plants and animals in a food chain depend on one another. Sometimes there's a break in the chain, such as one type of animal dying out. This loss ripples through the rest of the habitat.

Begin your journey through the Australian Outback food web by choosing a **carnivore**, or meat eater. These tertiary consumers are at the top of the food chain. That means that, for the most part, they don't have any enemies in the Outback (except for humans).

When it's time for the tertiary consumer to eat, pick its meal and flip to that page. As you go through the book, don't be surprised if you backtrack and end up where you never expected to be. That's how food webs work—they're complicated. And watch out for those dead ends! When you hit one of those, you have to go back to page 7 and start over with another tertiary consumer.

The main role an animal plays in the Australian Outback food web is identified by a color-coded shape. Here is the key to that code:

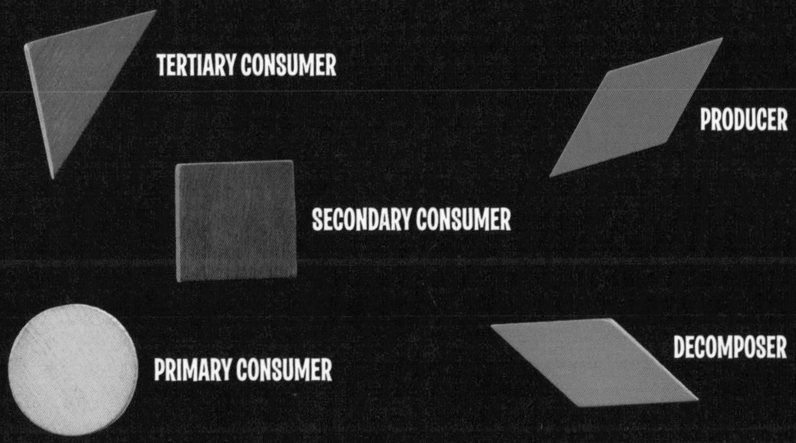

To choose . . .

. . . a dingo, TURN TO PAGE 8.
. . . a saltwater crocodile, TURN TO PAGE 20.
. . . a wedge-tailed eagle, TURN TO PAGE 36.
. . . a Gould's monitor, TURN TO PAGE 49.

To learn more about an Australian Outback food web, GO TO PAGE 34.

DINGO *(Canis dingo)*

With a yip and a growl, the mother dingo sends her five pups scurrying back to the den. She's dug a hole under a log to keep the pups safe. But they're getting bigger now. They've grown bolder about straying from home.

This mother dingo and her family may look like a friendly dog with cuddly puppies. An adult dingo is about the size of a Labrador retriever, and they belong to the same family as dogs. But don't be fooled into thinking they're pets. These are definitely wild animals. You'll sometimes hear them howl at night, as wolves do. Wolves are dingoes' close relatives.

The mother dingo coughs up a fluid. She's not sick. It's water, and her puppies eagerly lick it up. It'll be the only liquid they drink on this hot day in the Outback.

Toward evening, the mother dingo gives her pups a nuzzle as they settle down. Then she leaves the den to look for supper. Outside, she's joined in the gathering darkness by two other dingoes.

Most dingoes are tan with white patches on their feet and tails. But these two are red and black. More and more often, dingoes are interbreeding, or mixing, with domestic dogs (tame dogs, such as house pets). This interbreeding means that purebred dingoes are becoming scarcer. Wildlife experts think wild purebred dingoes are in danger of becoming **extinct**.

The mother dingo sniffs at a dead animal carcass left along the road. Dingoes will eat **carrion** if they have to. She's just about to dig in when a jeep roars over a nearby hill. Its bright lights blind her. She panics.

The dingoes scatter. It turns out that they're lucky they were scared away from their meal. That carcass wasn't road kill. It was dingo bait—poisoned meat people leave out for dingoes to eat. Lots of sheep farmers hate dingoes. Dingoes will hunt and kill slow-moving sheep. So farmers often shoot or poison dingoes.

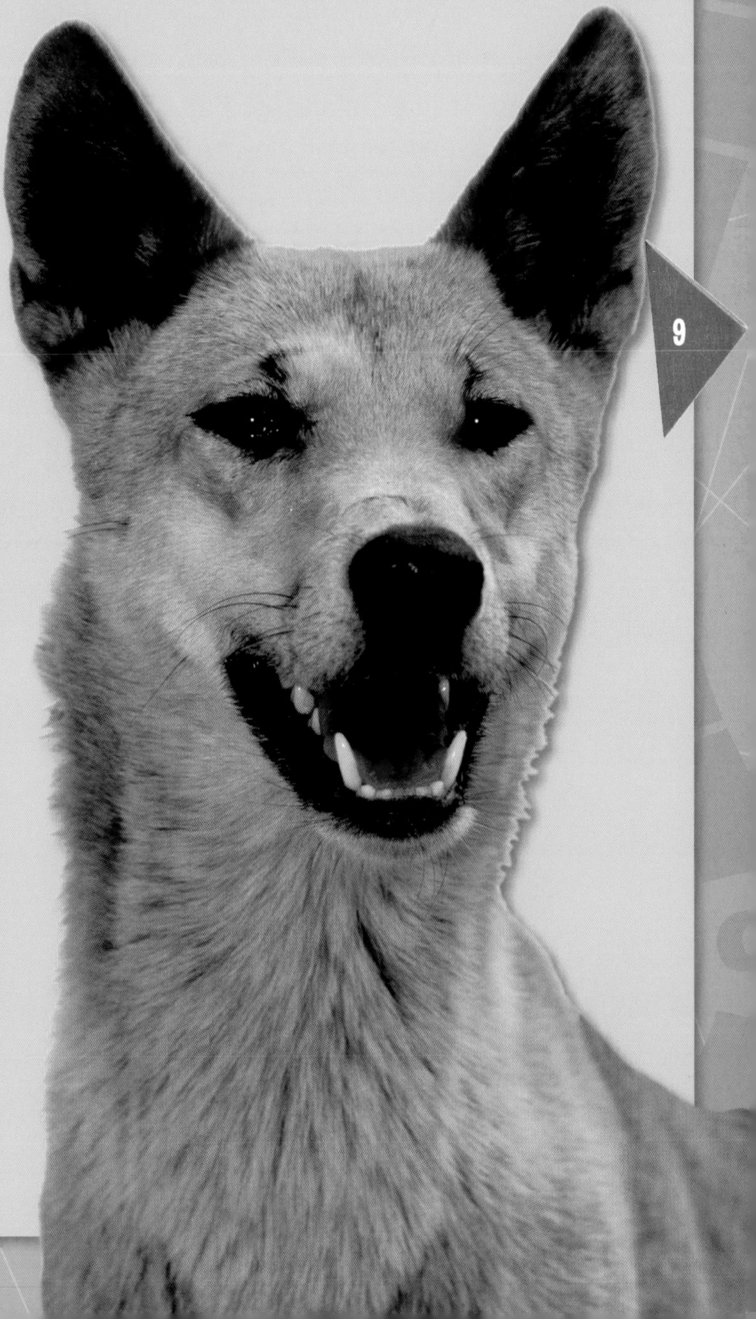

The small pack keeps moving. They'll roam just a small area tonight, but every few days, they'll shift to a new territory. They'll rotate through 32 square miles (83 square kilometers) before starting over again.

The Dingo Fence

Dingo bait isn't the only way that Australians have tried to keep dingoes off their sheep farms. In the 1880's, Australians built the world's longest fence to keep dingoes out of the southeastern part of the continent. That area is home to many of Australia's large sheep farms. The wire fence is more than 3,000 miles (5,000 km) long. It was only partly successful. Fewer dingoes are found south of the fence. But without dingoes around as predators, kangaroos and rabbits thrive. They eat a lot of the grass the sheep need to survive.

Soon they spot a young red kangaroo. It leaps mightily. But, working together, the dingoes surround it and bring it down. They take turns pulling off chunks of meat. The mother dingo gulps it down quickly.

Now, with a full tummy, she's ready to head back to the den. When she gets there, she'll throw up the meat for her pups—just as she did with the water. In the meantime, her stomach starts to digest the food. That makes it easier for her pups to eat later.

Last night for dinner, she was lucky in her hunt too. She gulped . . .

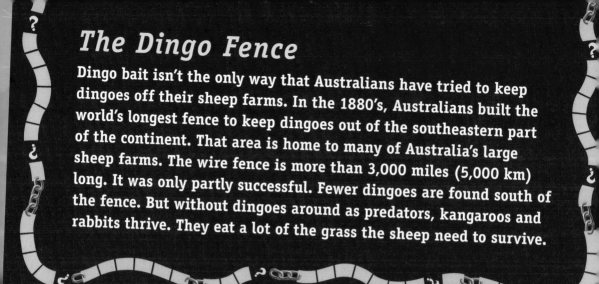

Dingoes chase a kangaroo.

. . . a western barred bandicoot hidden in the brush. To see what another western barred bandicoot is up to, TURN TO PAGE 56.

. . . another red kangaroo. To see what another red kangaroo is up to, TURN TO PAGE 40.

. . . a northern quoll. To see what another northern quoll is up to, TURN TO PAGE 44.

. . . a greater bilby that poked his head out of his burrow at the wrong time. To see what another greater bilby is up to, TURN TO PAGE 48.

. . . emu eggs stolen from their nest. To see what another emu is up to, TURN TO PAGE 16.

. . . a Queensland koala, moving to a new tree. To see what another Queensland koala is up to, TURN TO PAGE 27.

. . . a nest of European wild rabbit babies. To see what another European wild rabbit is up to, TURN TO PAGE 46.

. . . a dead short-beaked echidna, hit by a car. To see what another short-beaked echidna is up to, TURN TO PAGE 58.

FRILLED LIZARD *(Chlamydosaurus kingii)*

The young frilled lizard basks in the sun on the rocky outcrop. He's not full-grown yet, but he's been on his own since the day he hatched from his egg. And as a **reptile**, he's **cold-blooded.** The more rays he soaks up, the warmer his blood is inside him—and the faster he can move.

Other reptiles also look for the sun's warmth. A huge carpet python slithers across the rock. She came to bask. But this frilled lizard is just the right size for a meal—and she hasn't eaten in weeks. She slips closer.

Without warning, the frilled lizard opens his mouth. A collar of skin pops up like an umbrella around his face. The skin is called a frill, or a ruff. The frill makes the lizard look larger and fiercer. He hisses and rushes the python. She scoots back in alarm. But she doesn't retreat far enough. So the lizard thrashes his tail and bares his sharp teeth. He looks just like a tiny ferocious dinosaur. It's enough to scare off most animals.

This snake, however, is too hungry to be easily discouraged. She slides forward again.

The lizard spins around, raises up on his two hind legs, and races for the nearest tree. He scampers up and crouches flat on a branch. He'll have to wait out the python. But at least there's plenty to eat up here.

Last night for dinner, the lizard ate...

. . . crickets just hatching from their eggs. To see what other crickets are up to, **TURN TO PAGE 57.**

. . . bush flies hovering over a dead kangaroo. To see what other bush flies are up to, **TURN TO PAGE 45.**

. . . a just-hatched budgerigar. To see what another budgerigar is up to, **TURN TO PAGE 32.**

TAWNY FROGMOUTH

(Podargus strigoides)

A tawny frogmouth closes its eyes and stretches out to blend in among the tree branches.

That's not a broken tree limb up at the top of the tree. It's a tawny frogmouth. This large bird is snoozing, standing upright. His yellow gold eyes are closed. With his silvery gray feathers, he looks just like part of the tree. Most creatures passing by never even know he's there.

The frogmouth only stirs when his mate arrives. She'll sit on their nest of twigs while he hunts tonight. He lets out a booming cry, "Oom-oom-oom." Then he flutters to a different branch. And waits. His hunting doesn't really look all that different from his sleeping.

Frogmouths look like owls, but they aren't related. Frogmouths have short legs with weak feet. No owl-like talons for them. Frogmouths use their wide mouths and sharp beaks to catch their prey.

Below, a kangaroo mouse wanders by. It's just what the frogmouth was waiting for. He flaps down and pounces. Snap! The mouse is pinned in the frogmouth's beak. And with a quick shake and a toss against the tree, the mouse is killed. Dinnertime.

Last night for dinner, the frogmouth ate...

The frogmouth's wide mouth earned the bird its name. Its mouth reminded people of a frog's mouth.

. . . a western barred bandicoot scooting from one bush to another. To see what another western barred bandicoot is up to, TURN TO PAGE 56.

. . . a baby ghost bat chasing a centipede. To see what another ghost bat is up to, TURN TO PAGE 54.

. . . a young carpet python just hatched from her egg. To see what another carpet python is up to, TURN TO PAGE 18.

. . . a frilled lizard looking for a place to stay warm at the end of the day. To see what another frilled lizard is up to, TURN TO PAGE 12.

. . . a small spectacled hare-wallaby scratching out a place to take a nap. To see what another spectacled hare-wallaby is up to, TURN TO PAGE 30.

. . . crickets munching on dead leaves. To see what other crickets are up to, TURN TO PAGE 57.

. . . a marsupial mole chomping on some grubs. To see what another marsupial mole is up to, TURN TO PAGE 35.

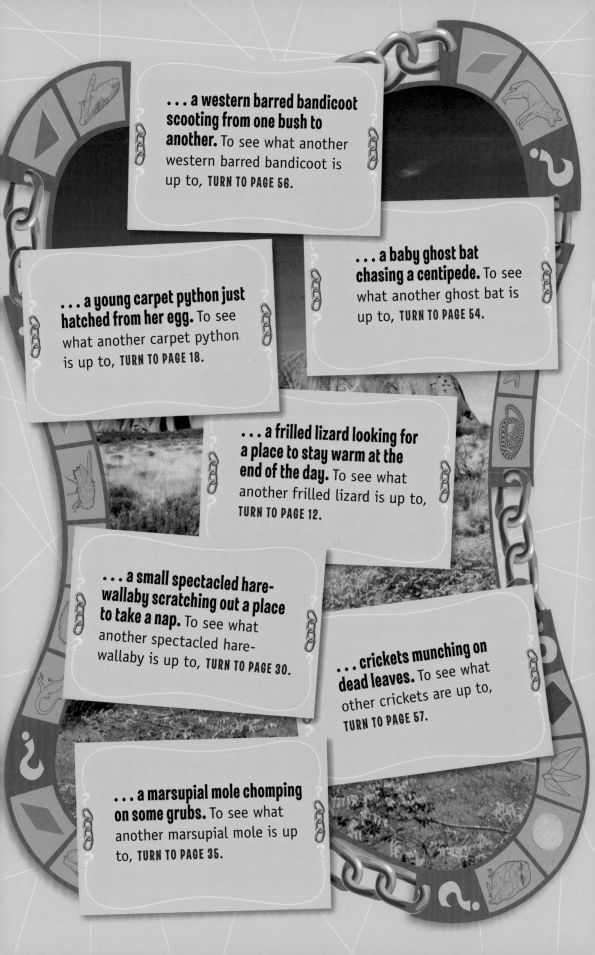

EMU *(Dromaius novaehollandiae)*

The emu settles on his nest. For fifty-five days, he won't budge. No eating. No drinking. No bathroom breaks. Just sitting. But he will be rewarded. The eggs under him will change from a dark bluish green to a light grey. And then they'll be ready to hatch.

The emu shades them from the hot Outback sun with his wings. Emus don't fly, so their wings have become small and weak. But the droopy feathers that hang from the emu father's wings provide good shade.

Suddenly, a Gould's monitor appears through the brush. He's looking for an easy treat—an egg, maybe. The emu father quickly reacts. He stretches his neck out and trumpets out a booming call. His long neck makes the sound louder. Other animals can hear it almost 2 miles (3 kilometers) away.

The emu's blast scares the monitor off. He's lucky the emu father didn't get up. The emu has a mean kick and could easily kill the monitor. He goes back to tending his nest. In the commotion, an egg has rolled out. He nudges it back to the center of the nest. Just fifty-four more days to go.

When the emu is ready to eat again, he'll dine on . . .

Adult emus can grow to be 5 to 6 feet (1.5 to 1.8 meters) tall. They weigh from 65 to 120 pounds (30 to 54 kilograms).

. . . the scrubby brush and grass of the Outback. To see what the plants of the Outback are like, **TURN TO PAGE 24.**

CARPET PYTHON *(Morelia spilota)*

Thirty-five. Thirty-six. Thirty-seven. Thirty-seven carpet python eggs lie inside a hollow log. They are about the size of golf balls.

The mother python snuggles her 6-foot (2-meter) body around the eggs. Her black and brown coloring looks just like the dead leaves around her. Her coiled body will keep the eggs warm and their temperature even until the snakes are born.

Like all snakes, the python is **cold-blooded**. Warm-blooded animals make their own body heat and keep their insides at a steady temperature. Cold-blooded animals draw their body heat from outside sources such as the sun. But nights are cold in the Outback. So as the sun sets, the python begins twitching her muscles. Those little movements will help raise her body temperature.

Keeping her body temperature steady helps the python to survive. It also determines whether her eggs will hatch male or female babies. The warmer she keeps the eggs, the more boy pythons she'll have.

As she rests, a dingo sniffs around outside the log. He is looking for a snack. He paws at the log and then noses the leaves in the hole. Like a whip, the python lashes out and sinks her teeth into the dingo's nose. With a yelp, the dingo retreats. The python settles back around her eggs.

Pythons are not poisonous snakes. A python hunts by sneaking up on prey and wrapping her body around it. The python squeezes the prey tight enough to kill it. Then she swallows the meal whole and lets it digest slowly.

While a python is guarding a nestful of eggs, she doesn't eat much. She uses her energy to keep the eggs warm. ***But last night for dinner, this carpet python hunted and swallowed...***

. . . a young Gould's monitor resting on a termite mound. To see what another Gould's monitor is up to, TURN TO PAGE 49.

. . . a spectacled hare-wallaby caught in a midmorning snooze. To see what another spectacled hare-wallaby is up to, TURN TO PAGE 30.

. . . a budgerigar at the edge of her flock. To see what another budgerigar is up to, TURN TO PAGE 32.

. . . a marsupial mole that poked his head out at the wrong time. To see what another marsupial mole is up to, TURN TO PAGE 35.

. . . an emu chick that strayed too far from the nest. To see what another emu is up to, TURN TO PAGE 16.

. . . a western barred bandicoot startled out of the brush. To see what another western barred bandicoot is up to, TURN TO PAGE 56.

. . . a tawny frogmouth pouncing on a mouse. To see what another tawny frogmouth is up to, TURN TO PAGE 14.

. . . a frilled lizard sunning on a rock. To see what another frilled lizard is up to, TURN TO PAGE 12.

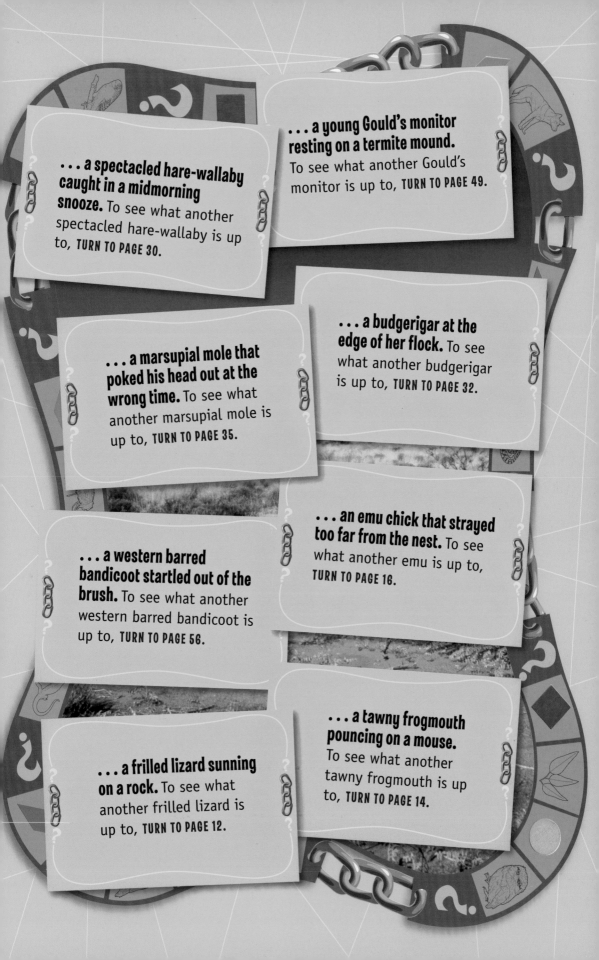

SALTWATER CROCODILE *(Crocodylus porosus)*

In the blistering heat of the day, the saltwater crocodile has found a cool spot. He lies submerged in the muddy water of a **billabong**. But this water hole is slowly disappearing. It's evaporating, or drying up, in the heat. In the next few weeks, the croc will have to go in search of more water.

In the meantime, he stretches out his 20-foot (6-meter) length and waits for another animal to come by for a drink. He'll kill most prey with a single snap of his jaws. The rest he'll drag into the water and drown.

The crocodile sees a movement on the side of the billabong. He pushes off with his feet on the muddy bottom to investigate. It's not food, it's another croc. This is a small one, searching out a new water hole after his dried up. With a flick of his tail, the big croc shoots across the small pond. With a roar, he explodes out of the water at the junior crocodile. This is *his* billabong. The smaller croc thinks about staying and fighting for only a moment. Then he retreats. The larger one chases after him for a few yards, just to be sure.

Smart Crocs

Saltwater crocodiles are among the world's smartest reptiles. They talk to one another using four different calls. Baby crocs chirp inside their eggs to tell the mother croc it's time to unbury them. Young hatchlings emit a distress call when they are in danger. Older adult crocs growl long and low when they're looking for a mate. They hiss and cough to announce that they want to be left alone.

Saltwater crocs, or salties as they're called in Australia, are the world's biggest and most dangerous crocodiles. They can kill large prey, including humans. In fact, people were once so scared of salties that they shot them on sight. It wasn't until the crocs were in danger of becoming **extinct** that people stopped killing them. Luckily, salties have made a strong comeback and are doing well in the wild.

Last night for dinner, this croc snapped up . . .

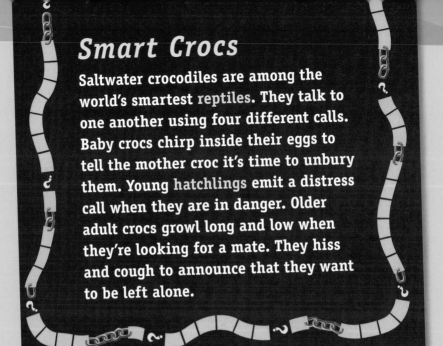

A saltwater crocodile snaps up a fish.

. . . a dingo sniffing near the water's edge. To see what another dingo is up to, TURN TO PAGE 8.

. . . a water-holding frog just burrowing up from the mud. To see what another water-holding frog is up to, TURN TO PAGE 52.

. . . a short-beaked echidna rolled into a ball. To see what another short-beaked echidna is up to, TURN TO PAGE 58.

. . . a northern quoll scampering across the sand. To see what another northern quoll is up to, TURN TO PAGE 44.

. . . a Gould's monitor skulking around for some eggs. To see what another Gould's monitor is up to, TURN TO PAGE 49.

. . . a red kangaroo stopping by for a sip of water. To see what another red kangaroo is up to, TURN TO PAGE 40.

. . . a greater bilby scratching for seeds. To see what another greater bilby is up to, TURN TO PAGE 48.

. . . a spectacled hare-wallaby emerging from his bush. To see what another spectacled hare-wallaby is up to, TURN TO PAGE 30.

PLANTS OF THE OUTBACK

Spiky, spiny, thorny. The plants of the Outback have to be able to withstand blistering sunlight, cold nights, and months—sometimes even years—without rain. They've got to be tough to survive. That means saving every last drop of water and fighting off any animals who want to snack on them.

a baobab tree

Because of their size, trees need more water than other plants. So there just aren't many trees in the Outback. The ones that are there have survived by adapting—changing to make the most of their environment.

Low wattles, or acacia trees, are sprinkled throughout the Outback. Their thorns keep away many animals that want to eat their blooms and leaves. Baobab trees have very thick trunks. They store water deep in the trunks. Sometimes Aborigines, Australia's native people, tap baobabs for a drink when they need water. Eucalyptus trees need more water to grow than other Outback trees do. But some eucalyptus types grow in dry areas. Their leaves are small and waxy to conserve, or save, water. And their smelly leaves are poisonous—to everyone but koalas.

eucalyptus leaves

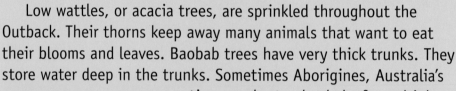

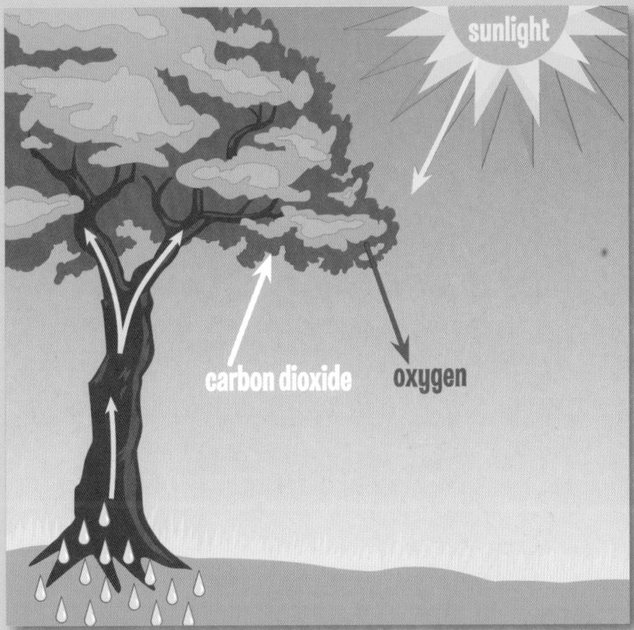

Plants make food and oxygen through photosynthesis. Plants draw in carbon dioxide (a gas found in air) and water. Then they use the energy from sunlight to turn the carbon dioxide and water into their food.

Grass is thick and tall in some parts of the Outback. In other places, it is short and patchy. Either way, it provides food and moisture for all sorts of animals. And when it does finally rain, a rainbow of flowers erupts across the floor of the Outback.

Plants can't survive without sunlight, water, and food. Plant leaves draw carbon dioxide, a gas, from the air. Their roots draw water and **nutrients** from the soil. The plants use energy from the sun to turn the carbon dioxide and water into food.

Some of the plants' food also comes from the bodies of dead animals. As the animals **decompose**, bacteria breaks the carcasses down into nutrients.

Flowers color the landscape after a rain.

Last night for dinner, the plants' nutrients in the soil came from . . .

. . . dead plants and leaves.

. . . the carcass of a dingo. To see what another dingo is up to, TURN TO PAGE 8.

. . . the carcass of a saltwater crocodile. To see what another saltwater crocodile is up to, TURN TO PAGE 20.

. . . bush flies that spread animal dung. To see what other bush flies are up to, TURN TO PAGE 45.

. . . the carcass of a wedge-tailed eagle. To see what another wedge-tailed eagle is up to, TURN TO PAGE 36.

. . . the carcass of a red kangaroo. To see what another red kangaroo is up to, TURN TO PAGE 40.

. . . the carcass of a ghost bat. To see what another ghost bat is up to, TURN TO PAGE 54.

. . . the carcass of a Queensland koala. To see what another Queensland koala is up to, TURN TO PAGE 27.

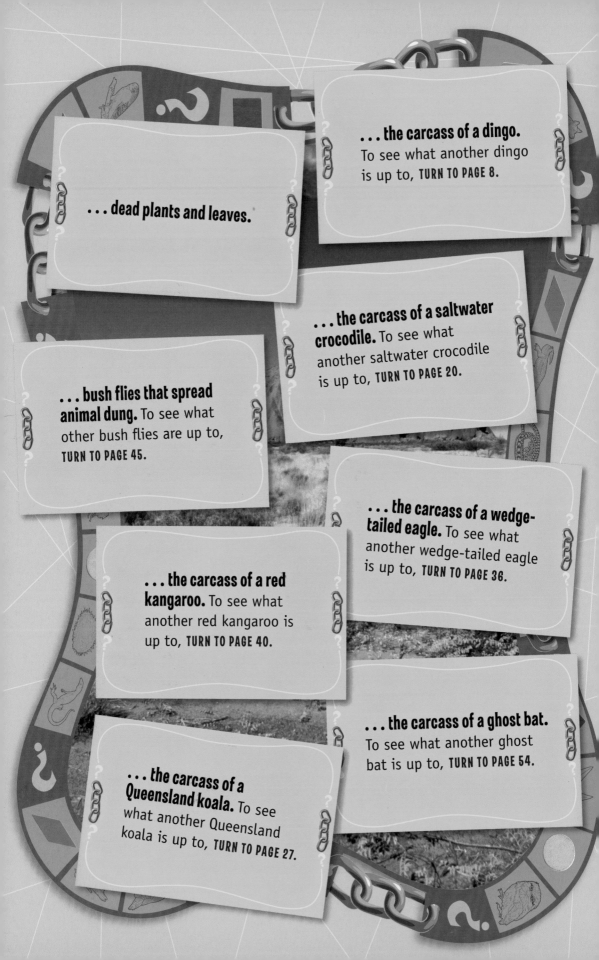

QUEENSLAND KOALA *(Phascolarctos cinereus adustus)*

The Queensland koala clamps down on a branch of a eucalyptus tree. The branch is high above a **billabong**. With those long claws and extra thumb, the koala is secure in her perch. She can—and does—sleep without falling out of the tree. Not much will convince her to come down. Koalas are slow moving and like to sleep—sometimes up to eighteen hours a day.

When the koala gets hungry, she leans forward to sniff a leaf with her big, extra-sensitive nose. She's a picky eater and smells each and every leaf she puts in her mouth. This leaf meets her approval. She munches it down.

Koalas are **herbivores**, or plant eaters. An adult can eat 2.5 pounds (1 kilogram) of eucalyptus leaves a day. Australia has more than six hundred kinds of eucalyptus trees.

Not *a Teddy* Bear

This koala may look cuddly cute with her big fluffy ears, teddy bear nose, and sleepy movements. But watch out! Her personality definitely isn't cuddly. Koalas will scratch or bite if other animals—including people—get too close. First, they make a ticking sound as a warning. Then they swipe out with those long black claws.

Maybe koalas are just frustrated that people think they're some kind of bear. Bears and koalas are not related.

A koala with her baby munches on a eucalyptus leaf.

After eating, the koala shifts her weight. Hugging tight to her back is her baby—a miniature version of herself.

Koalas are **marsupials**—they have pouches in which their young grow. A dime-sized newborn wiggles his way to the pouch. Once inside, he guzzles her milk until he's big enough to be introduced to the world. And when he is, he'll ride with his mom for a while until he learns all he needs to know about being a koala.

Last night for dinner, the koala sniffed and swallowed . . .

. . . only the just-right eucalyptus tree leaves.
To see what the plants of the Outback are like, TURN TO PAGE 24.

SPECTACLED HARE-WALLABY

(Lagorchestes conspicillatus)

The sun scorches today. But the spectacled hare-wallaby rests comfortably in his shallow burrow under a clump of tall grass. The wallaby could hardly be better suited for the Outback's extreme climate. His two-toned fur can keep him either cool or warm. Today, the light-colored fur reflects the strong sun rays, keeping him cool.

And if there's no rain and no water to drink? No problem. He can get all the fluid he needs from the morning dew and the leaves he eats. He has the most efficient kidneys of any **mammal**. Kidneys help get rid of a body's wastes by flushing them out as urine. The spectacled hare-wallaby's kidneys get rid of his waste using only a tiny bit of his body's water.

Threats

Like other wallabies species, spectacled hare-wallabies are getting scarcer. Animals that are new to the Outback threaten the wallabies' safety and food. Humans have brought animals such as foxes and house cats to the Outback. These animals hunt and kill wallabies. Other nonnative animals, such as cattle and rabbits, don't eat wallabies. But they eat the grass that the wallabies eat and shelter under. Humans also change the wallaby's habitat. As humans build more houses and roads, wallabies have less shrubby space to live on.

He stretches out, panting. Panting helps the wallaby keep his temperature steady. But it also provides moisture. The air animals exhale contains water, and even that bit of moisture is reused by the wallaby. It is recycled to his stomach.

The spectacled hare-wallaby doesn't waste his energy in the heat of the day. But at dusk, he'll perk up and get his food. ***Last night for dinner, the spectacled hare-wallaby chewed . . .***

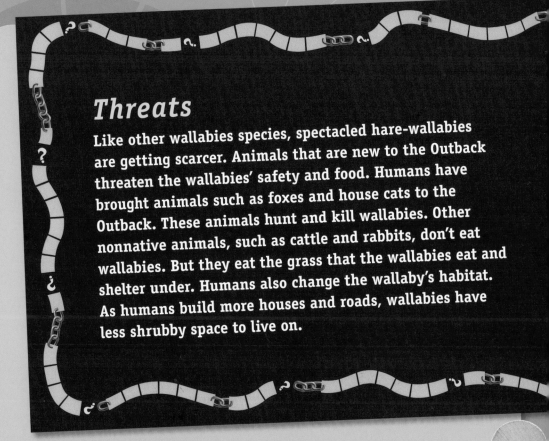

. . . grass and leaves. He needs lots of leaves to get enough **nutrients**. To see what the plants of the Outback are like, **TURN TO PAGE 24.**

BUDGERIGARS *(Melopsittacus undulatus)*

The budgerigar pecks at the ground. No, he's not swallowing tiny bugs or even small seeds. He's swallowing the dirt itself. The soil contains **minerals** that his body needs.

After a quick sip of water from the **billabong**, he flits to the top of a eucalyptus tree. There, hidden in its branches, is his lifelong mate. He's a more common green and yellow budgie. She's a rarer blue. Together they've gnawed branches and shaped a nest in the tree.

She's busy these days. Now that there's been a little rain, she's been laying an egg in their nest every two days. She'll lay six to eight eggs. The eggs will hatch just as they were laid—one every two days. He's got a big job ahead of him. Once the eggs hatch, he'll take over tending them.

Around them the tree trembles with other budgerigars. They chatter and preen (groom their feathers) as they watch out for one another. When the night grows dark, they quiet down and draw close together for warmth and safety.

Last night for dinner, the budgerigar swallowed . . .

Flocks of Budgies

Budgerigars live in flocks of twenty to sixty birds. A budgie's whole life revolves around the flock. Within the flock, the birds have a strong sense of order. If one budgie flies off on his own, others will fly after him and force him to return to the group. This sense of group behavior helps budgies perform amazing feats in flight. A thousand budgies can fly in one direction in search of water. Then, without any obvious signal, all one thousand will turn and fly in another direction—without bumping into one another.

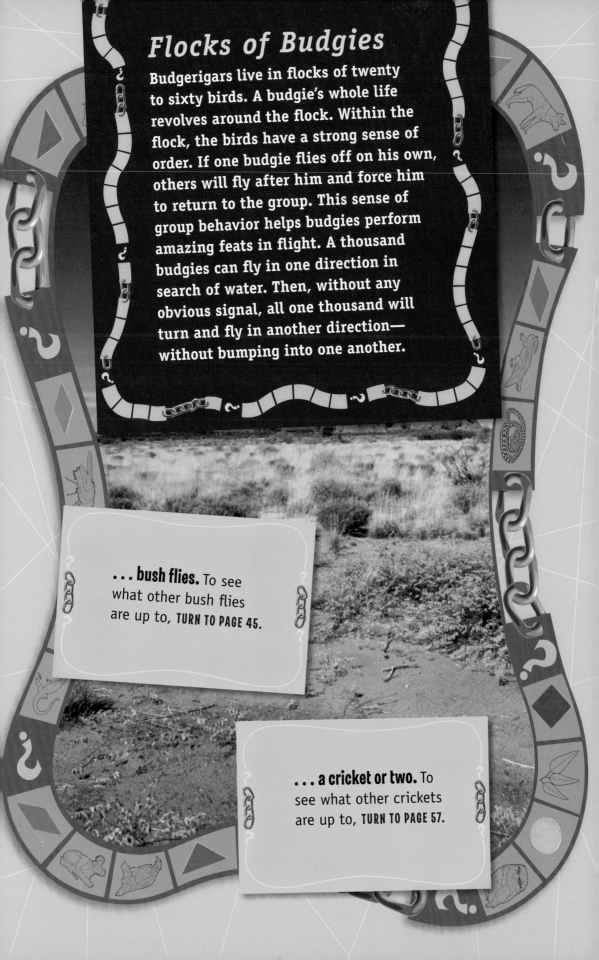

. . . bush flies. To see what other bush flies are up to, **TURN TO PAGE 45.**

. . . a cricket or two. To see what other crickets are up to, **TURN TO PAGE 57.**

AN OUTBACK FOOD WEB

In the Outback, energy moves around the food chain from the sun to plants, from plants to plant eaters, and from animals to the creatures that eat them. Energy also moves from dead animals to the plants and animals that draw nutrients from them.

MARSUPIAL MOLE *(Notoryctes typhlops)*

You may think you saw the head of a southern **marsupial** mole pop up through the sandy soil. But chances are slim that it really was one. The moles are in danger of becoming **extinct**, and this is a ***DEAD END***.

Marsupial moles are scarce for many reasons. Humans once trapped them for their yellowish fur. Dingoes, wild cats, and foxes hunt them for food. And the big trucks used for transportation and mining pack down the soil so the moles can't dig.

Digging is what marsupial moles are made to do. Their whole body is built to "swim" through the sand. They use their hard noses and front paws to burrow. Their backbones are rigid to make them stronger diggers. And they are blind, so the dirt doesn't bother their eyes. Once underground, the moles hunt for their favorite food—young insects.

WEDGE-TAILED EAGLE *(Aquila audax)*

Stretching out both of her huge wings, the wedge-tailed eagle soars over the Outback. She's easy to recognize. For one thing, she's the largest bird of prey in Australia. And second, her tail has a point, or a "wedge."

The eagle makes flying look easy, but she's always adjusting her wing muscles to catch the wind better. With a few flaps, she climbs higher. She can soar up here for hours without having to flap her wings once. Now she's at 6,000 feet (1,800 meters)—that's more than 1 mile (1.6 kilometers) high! She tips her wings to turn. These few miles she's circling are her home territory. She patrols it often.

She's also scanning for prey. And there! A rabbit hops lazily along in the open. It's having a midmorning snack. The eagle angles her wings down and circles lower. Then, swooping low over the ground, she snatches the rabbit up.

That rabbit was simple stuff. She could have spotted it from 2 miles (3 km) away. Picking it up was no big deal either—she can lift half her body weight. Sometimes she gangs up with other eagles. Together, they can hunt down and dine on a full-sized kangaroo!

Wedge-tailed eagles have big wingspans—the measurement from the tip of one outstretched wing to the tip of the other. An adult female's wingspan may reach 7.5 feet (2.3 m). This eagle has used her wings to zoom down and capture a rabbit.

The Nest

Wedge-tailed eagles usually build huge nests in the tallest trees. But some live in parts of the Outback where there are few trees. In those cases, eagles build nests from enormous piles of sticks on the sides of rocky cliffs. An eagle pair will often add a fresh layer of sticks to the nest floor. But they're not too neat about it. Down at the bottom of the cliff you may find another big pile of sticks—pieces that they dropped while working on the nest.

Clutching the rabbit in her sharp talons, the eagle carries her prey back to her nest. Here her mate rests, keeping their two eggs warm. They'll take turns hunting until the eggs hatch in about forty-five days. Then she'll stay with them for the first thirty days while he hunts. ***Last night for dinner, she shared with her mate . . .***

. . . a northern quoll caught out in the open. To see what another northern quoll is up to, TURN TO PAGE 44.

. . . a dead short-beaked echidna, hit by a car. To see what another short-beaked echidna is up to, TURN TO PAGE 58.

. . . a European wild rabbit crossing a clearing. To see what another European wild rabbit is up to, TURN TO PAGE 46.

. . . a carpet python sunning on a stone. To see what another carpet python is up to, TURN TO PAGE 18.

. . . a budgerigar in midflight. To see what another budgerigar is up to, TURN TO PAGE 32.

. . . a dingo pup playing with a lizard. To see what another dingo is up to, TURN TO PAGE 8.

. . . a young red kangaroo that bounded too far from his mother. To see what another red kangaroo is up to, TURN TO PAGE 40.

. . . a marsupial mole digging for insects. To see what another marsupial mole is up to, TURN TO PAGE 35.

RED KANGAROO *(Macropus rufus)*

Sproing. Sproing! The red kangaroo cruises by. Her huge back legs pump together. Her tiny front legs are curled against her chest. With each bounce, she pushes her enormous feet against the hard red earth. The tendons (strong, fiberlike tissue) in her heels act like rubber bands. The tendons stretch and snap back together. That snapping is what gives the kangaroo her spring. She has enough power to sail more than 20 feet (6 meters) with each leap. When kangaroos move, they spend most of their time in midair.

And they are made to move! When kangaroos are traveling, they don't even have to breathe. The impact of each landing squeezes the air in and out of their lungs for them.

Kangaroos can travel almost 30 miles (48 kilometers) an hour. But today, this kangaroo isn't moving at top speed. One of her babies, called a joey, hops along beside her. She moves more slowly so he can keep up.

The mother kangaroo's head suddenly bobs up. The shadow of a wedge-tailed eagle has fallen across the ground. Danger! The joey tries to somersault himself into the pouch on his mother's stomach. But she keeps the muscles around the pouch relaxed, and he tumbles back out. He looks at her, confused. Surely she won't let the eagle get him?

The mother kangaroo huddles the joey next to her for protection. But the pouch is off limits. The truth is, he's just gotten too big. And she's got a new joey in her pouch.

The red kangaroo is the world's largest marsupial. Adult males, called boomers, can stand 6 feet (2 m) tall and weigh up to 198 pounds (90 kilograms).

Kangaroos are **marsupials.** These special animals grow their babies in their stomach pouches. A few days earlier, a thumbnail-sized joey was born. Pink and hairless, the newborn joey still needs a safe place to grow. The newborn climbed up the mother's fur and into her pouch. The newborn joey will stay safe there until the joey is stronger and bigger.

Female kangaroos, called fliers, are almost always pregnant. A flier takes care of her joeys until they're about one year old. So she often has more than one baby with her. She has a baby in the womb, a young joey in the pouch, and an older joey by her side.

It's time for the older joey to learn to fend for himself. As they wait out the eagle, she licks his face. This passes on her bacteria to him. Bacteria are tiny living things that animals carry

Amazing Legs

Kangaroo legs are built for speed. Scientists have put kangaroos on treadmills and found something unusual. Unlike most other animals, kangaroos aren't strained by going top speed. They tire at top speed at the same rate they tire going more slowly. In fact, kangaroos are awkward at slow speeds. One reason is that they can't move their hind legs separately. That makes walking difficult for them. While grazing, they hobble along, using their front paws and tail for balance.

But in water, it's another story. Kangaroos suddenly can move their legs independently. And—as you might imagine with their huge feet—they are excellent swimmers.

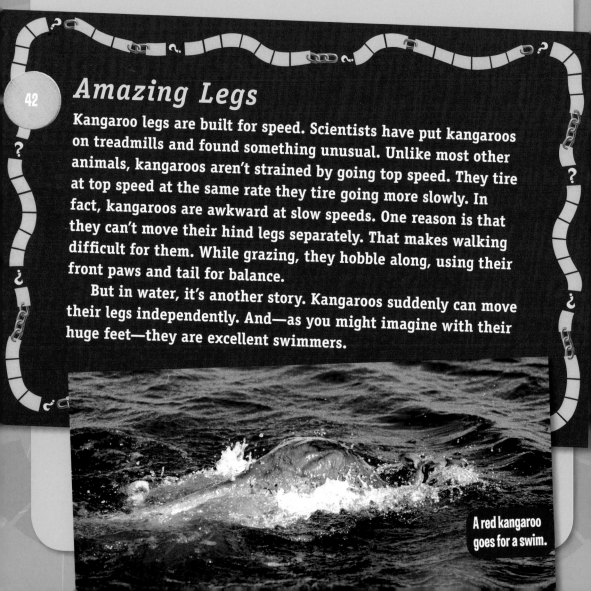

A red kangaroo goes for a swim.

in their stomachs and mouths. The bacteria will help the joey digest the grass he eats. Kangaroos are **herbivores**—they eat only plants. This kangaroo and her joey will munch on grass all day long. The grass does not have much nutrition. So they have to eat a lot of it to survive.

The joey rips the tough grass leaves up. Kangaroos' jaws come in two parts, with a stretchy band between them. With each mouthful, the sides of the joey's lower jaw come apart. This allows him to get a bigger mouthful.

A young kangaroo licks its front paws.

Inside his mouth, he grinds the grass against ridged molars, or back teeth. When the molars wear down, they fall out and the teeth behind them move into place. At some point, the kangaroo runs out of new teeth. He can't eat anymore and will die. But most kangaroos don't live long enough to run out of teeth.

Next to him, his mother pants. The sun and the temperature are rising. Soon it'll be time for a snooze. They'll eat again when the sun goes down. With her back paws, she scratches out a hollow in the dirt. It'll be cooler here. The joey joins her. They start licking again. This time they concentrate on their front legs. It's not just that they want to keep clean. Their front paws have extra blood vessels. Keeping that skin moist actually cools their whole bodies. And they can use all the help they can get. It'll reach 110°F (43°C) today in the Outback.

Last night for dinner, the mother kangaroo and her joey ground up . . .

. . . more leaves and grass. To see what the plants of the Outback are like, **TURN TO PAGE 24.**

NORTHERN QUOLL *(Dasyurus hallucatus)*

The northern quoll pounces on a toad. It's just the right size for dinner for this **marsupial**. Frogs and toads are the quoll's favorite meal. But this toad is bad news. This is a cane toad, and it is very poisonous. The northern quoll doesn't know it as he chews on the toad, but he's doomed. This is a ***DEAD END***.

People brought cane toads to Australia in 1935. Beetles (a type of bug) were damaging Australia's sugarcane fields. People released the toads into the fields to eat the beetles. But the toads soon overran the regions they were released in. Unlike Australia's native frogs and toads, cane toads kill most animals that eat them. They endanger not just northern quolls but many other animals too.

BUSH FLIES *(Musca vetustissima)*

A female bush fly buzzes straight up a resting dingo's nose. The dingo sneezes, and the fly is shot back out. She buzzes back to land on his eye. He shakes her off. She flits to a scrape on his paw. The dingo gives up and lets her land.

If there were just a few bush flies, this one wouldn't seem so annoying. But there are millions just like her. Everywhere you go in the Outback, swarms of flies follow. Bush flies are a way of life in Australia.

That female fly is pesky and determined for a reason. She needs to get protein, a chemical substance used by the body. Without protein, she can't lay her eggs. And the only way for her to get protein is from animals' tears, spit, nose, blood, sweat, urine, or poop. If she weren't so persistent, her species wouldn't survive.

After getting her protein, she's off again. She's looking for a place to lay her eggs. Lucky for her, there's dingo dung, or poop, nearby. It's the perfect home for her eggs. Within just a few hours, they'll hatch into dung-eating **maggots**. Then it'll be time for them to burrow underground. They'll continue to grow underground until they emerge as the next generation of bush flies.

Bush flies are decomposers. They eat dead plants and help break the plants down into **nutrients**. The flies leave those nutrients in the soil for other plants and animals to use.

Last night for dinner, the bush fly maggots ate . . .

. . . the leftover bits of plants and grass in the dung. To see what the plants of the Outback are like, **TURN TO PAGE 24.**

EUROPEAN WILD RABBIT *(Oryctolagus cuniculus)*

With his long incisor teeth, the European wild rabbit crunches down on a tuft of grass. When it's gone, he scratches at the dirt. Ah, more of the tasty plant. He nibbles the roots. By the time he hops away, he's eaten the whole plant. There's nothing left for new grass to grow back from.

Rabbits aren't native to Australia. In the 1700s and 1800s, European settlers brought rabbits to southeastern Australia. Rabbits breed quickly, and the population swelled. Within years, millions of rabbits swarmed across the southern and central parts of the continent.

The huge rabbit population is very destructive to the environment. The rabbits destroy grass and native plants, leaving little behind for other animals. Rabbits are to blame for several mammal species becoming **extinct**. Other species of animals and plants are **endangered** by the rabbit.

The Rabbit-Proof Fence

In 1901 Australians began building a 2,023-mile (3,256-kilometer) rabbit-proof fence across Western Australia. The fence was built to be high enough so rabbits couldn't jump over it. And it was sunk deep enough in the ground that rabbits couldn't dig under it. But like other rabbit-controlling ideas, it wasn't very successful. Rabbits slipped by to the other side before it was finished in 1907.

The rabbit's destruction of plants also causes soil erosion. With no plant roots to hold the soil in place, it blows away. This erosion has damaged Australian farming practices.

To try to control the wild rabbit population, Australians have hunted the animals and poisoned their warrens, or dens. People have also purposely introduced diseases into the rabbit population.

These methods have killed large numbers of rabbits. But a female rabbit can have five litters of four to five rabbits a year. And those rabbits can start having their own babies when they are just four months old. It's hard to control an animal population that grows that fast. Australians continue to look for solutions to their rabbit problem.

Baby rabbits play just outside their warren.

In the meantime, this rabbit continues to eat. ***Last night for dinner, he devoured . . .***

. . . grass, brush, and the leaves on bushes and trees. To see what the plants of the Outback are like, TURN TO PAGE 24.

GREATER BILBY *(Macrotis lagotis)*

Sorry, this is a ***DEAD END***! The greater bilby is **endangered** in parts of Australia and threatened in others. Just one hundred years ago, this cat-sized **marsupial** was found across the Outback. It slept in sandy burrows by day and foraged for seeds and insects at night. In the 2000s, there were fewer than one thousand greater bilbies left.

Lesser Bilby

Wildlife experts hope the greater bilby won't go the way of its close relative, the lesser bilby. The lesser bilby has been extinct since the 1950s. The last trace of the rabbit-eared mini-kangaroo lookalike was a skull found under a wedge-tailed eagle's nest in 1967. The skull was less than fifteen years old. But there's been no trace of lesser bilbies since then.

It's been difficult trying to save the bilbies. Cattle and other livestock push them out of their habitats. But one of the worst problems is feral cats. Feral cats are pet house cats that have turned wild. The feral cats breed and multiply. Now there are seventeen million feral cats in Australia. And they often love to hunt bilbies.

GOULD'S MONITOR *(Varanus gouldii)*

With a flick of his strong claws, the Gould's monitor slashes open a termite mound. This large lizard is looking for an easy place to rest. And someplace hidden is the safest spot for him. As he digs out a space in the termite mound, a dingo approaches. The dingo just ate and isn't looking for prey. And this monitor is almost 4 feet (1.2 meter) long—a little too big for a meal anyway. The dingo is just curious.

But the monitor doesn't know that. He sees the curious dingo as a danger. The monitor raises his long neck. He flicks his forked tongue in and out. He hisses a warning. The dingo retreats a little, but not far enough for the monitor. Balancing with his tail, the monitor rears up on his hind legs. He's mad and scared. He charges the dingo.

Goannas

Monitor lizards thrive in the Outback. Everywhere you look is a different kind sunning on a rock. Australians also call the lizards goannas. It's thought that the word *goanna* comes from *iguana*. The first European settlers saw the monitors and thought they looked like iguanas—another kind of lizard.

The dingo jogs away, looking over his shoulder. Whew! The monitor relaxes and drops back down on all fours. But then the dingo comes back, this time closer than ever! The monitor tries another lunge. The dingo doesn't run away. He sniffs a little closer.

The monitor does the next best thing. He runs. He scampers up a tree and presses himself flat on a branch. The dingo eyes him from below and then leaves—finally. That was close.

The Gould's monitor may be frightened by large animals such as the dingo. But he's quite the predator himself. He has sharp teeth and claws. And as some snakes do, he can swallow his prey whole. ***Last night for dinner, the monitor ate . . .***

. . . a young carpet python slithering across the sand. To see what another carpet python is up to, TURN TO PAGE 18.

. . . a marsupial mole found under a rock. To see what another marsupial mole is up to, TURN TO PAGE 35.

. . . a water-holding frog just waking up. To see what another water-holding frog is up to, TURN TO PAGE 52.

. . . a western barred bandicoot scratching in the dirt. To see what another western barred bandicoot is up to, TURN TO PAGE 56.

. . . a European wild rabbit digging a new burrow. To see what another European wild rabbit is up to, TURN TO PAGE 46.

. . . a red kangaroo, after it was hit by a car. To see what another red kangaroo is up to, TURN TO PAGE 40.

. . . a tawny frogmouth with a hurt wing. To see what another tawny frogmouth is up to, TURN TO PAGE 14.

. . . a dead short-beaked echidna. To see what another short-beaked echidna is up to, TURN TO PAGE 58.

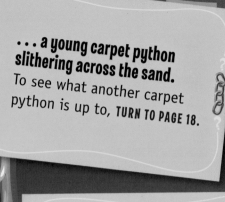

WATER-HOLDING FROG *(Cyclorana platycephala)*

A burst of rain sprinkles down on the hard dry earth of the Outback. It hasn't rained here in almost six months. The water starts to collect and soak into the ground. Two feet (0.6 meters) down, it dampens a grayish green blob. The blob stirs. No, it's not a pocket of mud. It's a water-holding frog, and she's just coming out of a deep resting stage.

First, she starts to breath deeper and her heart beats faster. Then she starts munching her cocoon, or covering of skin. Before she went underground, she sucked up as much water as possible into her plump body. Then, deep underground, she built a cocoon around herself from her own skin. It helped her to keep the water inside her body. Who knew how long she'd be underground? In the Outback, it can go for years without raining. But since it's finally rained, the frog wakes again. The cocoon is her first meal in six months.

With her huge back legs, she digs her way back to the Outback surface. The rain has cleared, but there are still puddles around. And the **billabong** is filled again. With a snoringlike noise, she calls for a male water-holding frog. She needs a mate and has to work fast. In the heat of the Outback, those puddles will soon disappear.

After mating, she will lay her eggs in a pocket of water near the billabong. Her tadpoles will be in a race to survive—they'll need to develop into fully formed frogs by the time the water disappears.

Now, it's on to finding a real meal. ***The water-holding frog chomps down . . .***

Frog Water

Australia's native people are known as the Aborigines. Aborigines have lived in the Outback for tens of thousands of years. They know many ways to survive in the Outback. Aborigines know that the water-holding frog can be used as a source of emergency water. They will find and dig up frogs. The frog has stored its water in its bladder. So an Aborigine will simply put the back of the frog in his mouth and squeeze the water out for a drink. Ah, refreshing.

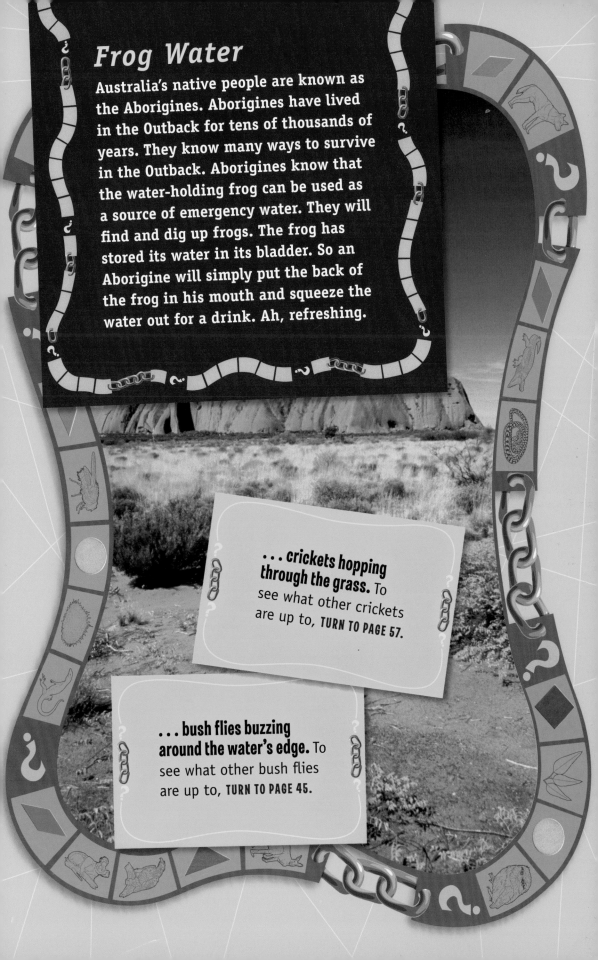

. . . crickets hopping through the grass. To see what other crickets are up to, **TURN TO PAGE 57.**

. . . bush flies buzzing around the water's edge. To see what other bush flies are up to, **TURN TO PAGE 45.**

GHOST BAT *(Macroderma gigas)*

As dusk falls, the ghost bat emerges from a crevice in the rock. Behind her, a stream of other female bats follows. This is a girls-only colony. The boys have their own roost.

She flaps to a familiar tree. In the growing darkness, pale fur on her back and front give her a ghostly look. That's where the ghost bat gets its name. She finds her usual perch and promptly hangs upside down, folding her wings around her carefully.

She may look at rest, but really she's hunting. Her excellent hearing and vision are just the tools she'll need when the opportunity arises. And here it comes!

At the base of the tree, a mouse scurries around a tuft of grass. He thinks he's safe in the dark, but up above, the bat is alert. Silently, she drops down. The mouse never even sees her coming. His world suddenly goes dark as the ghost bat wraps her wings tightly around him. Then she finishes him off—by biting him in the neck. It's no wonder that ghost bats are sometimes called Australian giant false vampire bats!

The bat carries her dead prey up to the top of the tree to eat it. She's a sloppy eater. In fact, you can tell where ghost bats roost by the mess of bones below on the ground.

Last night for dinner, the ghost bat swooped down to attack . . .

. . . a water-holding frog that just laid her eggs. To see what another water-holding frog is up to, **TURN TO PAGE 52.**

. . . a frilled lizard crawling across a rock. To see what another frilled lizard is up to, **TURN TO PAGE 12.**

. . . lots of bush flies. To see what other bush flies are up to, **TURN TO PAGE 45.**

. . . a baby Gould's monitor hunting for the first time. To see what another Gould's monitor is up to, **TURN TO PAGE 49.**

. . . a couple of crickets. To see what other crickets are up to, **TURN TO PAGE 57.**

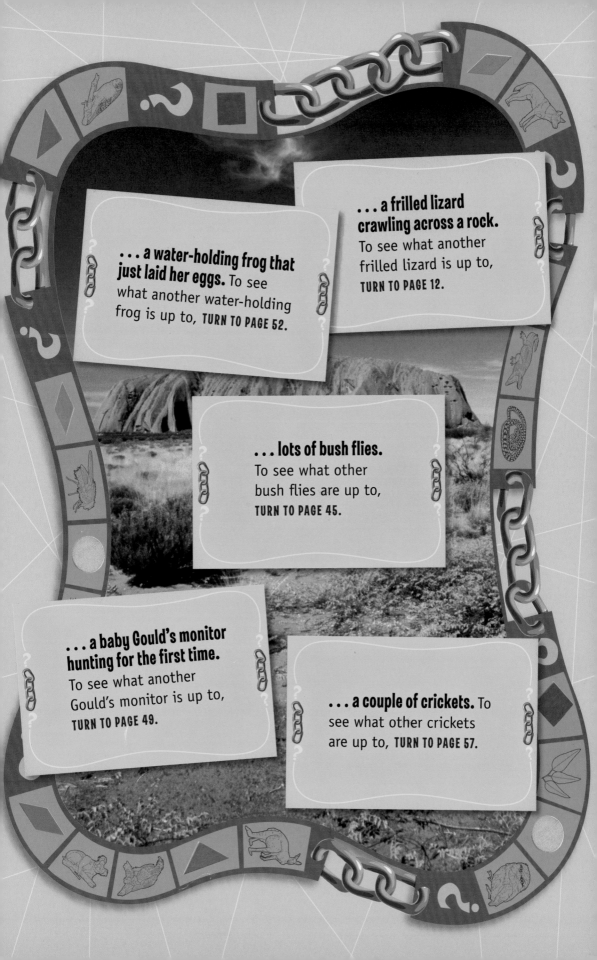

WESTERN BARRED BANDICOOT

(Perameles bougainville)

The hidden grass nest under that bush is empty. It used to be the home of a western barred bandicoot, but the animal has been gone for a while. Foxes and cats, which are not native to the Outback, have found the western barred bandicoot a little too easy to catch. And now these tiny, furry **mammals** are almost impossible to find. That's why this is a ***DEAD END***.

Western barred bandicoots are threatened by the increased clearing of the Outback. Clearing occurs when humans cut down trees and uproot plants. Humans clear land to make room for farms and buildings. But without plant life, bandicoots are in trouble. They make their nests under shrubs, and they eat berries, seeds, and plant roots. They also eat the earthworms and insects found near plants.

CRICKETS

(Orthoptera gryllidae)

Darkness falls and the day cools. The cricket rouses in his burrow under dead wattle leaves. First, his long antennae emerge. Then his four small front legs and four wings unfold. Once his giant back legs are out, he pushes off and springs through the air. He lands 3 feet (0.9 meters)away. That's quite a jump for something his size. Imagine if you could jump 80 feet (24 m) from a standstill!

Once out in the open, he starts his singing. But he doesn't sing with his mouth. The edge of his hind legs are lined with a row of little barbs. He drags the barbs against his front wings to make a rhythmic sound. Chirp. Chirp. Chirp. He calls for a female.

Scientists have studied the chirps of crickets. They learned that the warmer the weather, the faster crickets chirp. Scientists have figured mathematical formulas that use cricket sounds to tell the temperature.

If a female is out there listening, she'll hear his call through her knees. That's where cricket ears are—in the knees of their front legs.

But no one answers tonight. So he's off to do his next job of the evening—eat some food. ***Last night for dinner, the cricket nibbled on . . .***

. . . dead leaves and grass.
To see what the plants of the Outback are like, **TURN TO PAGE 24.**

SHORT-BEAKED ECHIDNA *(Tachyglossus aculeatus)*

The short-beaked echidna shuffles along the ground. Her spiny body sways with each step. At a large stone, she pauses. She shoves her beak under the edge of the stone and flips it. Her beak is covered in skin. She needs that beak to get at food. If it gets damaged, she'll die.

The echidna has a 7-inch-long (18-centimeter) wormlike tongue. Imagine having a tongue half as long as your body! With her tongue, she slurps up the insects hiding under the stone. She crushes the insects against the spikes in the top of her mouth. Then she can swallow them. She doesn't have teeth to chew the bugs nor any stomach juices to dissolve them. When the food gets to her stomach, a hairy rough lining grinds up the food for digestion.

An echidna uses its tongue to grab termites.

But she's not done eating. With her strong front claws, she rakes at the ground. Soon dirt is flying. She sticks her beak in—and gets a noseful of dirt. No matter. She clears it with a couple of puffs of air (and a snot bubble) and keeps after those hidden bugs. You can hear her from yards away. And a Gould's monitor has just turned her way. . . .

Even though the echidna has no outer ears, she has excellent hearing. She hears the monitor approach. She tucks her head in and rolls up. He nudges her, but there's nothing he can do with that ball of spikes. He soon lumbers away.

She stretches out again. Her spikes, or spines, are not like those of a porcupine or a hedgehog. Each of her spines is attached to muscles. She can move them like fingers. She uses them to climb or to roll herself over. Imagine being able to move each hair on your head whenever you want!

Right now she uses her spines to get herself into a sitting position. She lays a marble-sized egg and then rolls it up her soft tummy to tuck it into her pouch. The echidna is a **marsupial**, meaning that her baby will finish growing inside a pouch on her body.

The echidna is also a **mammal**—an animal that feeds her young with milk from her body. But she is a very unusual mammal. Most mammals give birth to a live baby. But the echidna lays eggs. Egg-laying mammals are called **monotremes.** The echidna is one of only two monotremes in the world. (The other is a platypus, an Australian water animal.) Her baby will hatch from the egg and remain in her pouch until it grows spines and can survive on its own.

In the meantime, she's got to feed herself. ***Last night for dinner, she dug up more worms and bugs such as . . .***

Echidna Spines

Echidna spines are very strong. They've been known to puncture car tires when the cars have accidentally hit echidnas. The spines protect the echidnas from nearly all predators. But some dingoes have figured out a way around those spines. When the echidna balls up, the dingo will urinate on its face. This makes the echidna unroll, and the dingo attacks its soft belly.

. . . crickets. To see what other crickets are up to, **TURN TO PAGE 57.**

GLOSSARY

bacteria: tiny living things made up of only one cell

billabong: in the Outback, a pool of water similar to a large pond

carnivore: an animal that eats other animals

carrion: the bodies of animals that have died or were killed by predators that are eaten by other animals as food

cold-blooded: a term for animals that use outside energy, such as heat from the sun, to warm their body temperature

decompose: to decay, or break down, after dying

decomposers: living things, such as insects or bacteria, that feed on dead plants and animals

endangered: at risk of becoming extinct

extinct: no longer existing

food chain: a system in which energy is transferred from the sun to plants and to animals as each eats and is eaten

food web: many food chains linked together

habitats: areas where a plant or animal naturally lives and grows

hatchlings: young animals newly hatched from eggs

herbivores: animals that eat plants

maggots: the larvas of certain insects, such as flies

mammals: animals that have hair and feed their babies milk from their bodies

marsupial: a mammal that gives birth to a live baby very early in the baby's development. A marsupial baby finishes growing in a pouch on the outside of its mother's body.

minerals: substances found in nature that animals need to survive

monotremes: egg-laying mammals

nutrients: substances, especially in food, that help a plant or animal survive

predators: animals that hunt and kill other animals for food

primary consumers: animals that eat plants

producers: living things that make their own food

reptiles: cold-blooded, egg-laying animals with backbones

secondary consumers: animals and insects that eat other animals and insects

tertiary consumers: animals that eat other animals and that have few natural enemies

FURTHER READING AND WEBSITES

Australian (and Nearby Islands) Animal Printouts
http://www.enchantedlearning.com/coloring/Australia.shtml
Enchanted Learning's website is full of simple information, puzzles, quizzes, and coloring sheets of your favorite Outback animals.

Australia's Endangered Animals
http://www.kidcyber.com.au/topics/Austendangered.htm
Learn about some of Australia's endangered animals and what is threatening them.

Burt, Denise. *Kangaroos*. Minneapolis: Lerner Publications Company, 2000. As part of the Nature Watch series, Burt's book looks at the Outback's most famous marsupial.

Lewin, Ted, and Betsy Lewin. *Top to Bottom*. New York: HarperCollins, 2005. This husband and wife children's author-illustrator team chronicle their travels through Australia with cartoons as well as realistic watercolor illustrations.

Markle, Sandra. *Tasmanian Devils*. Minneapolis: Lerner Publications Company, 2005. This book in the Animal Scavenger series looks at the life cycle and habits of Tasmania's unique marsupials.

Parish, Steve. *Australia Rare and Endangered Wildlife*. Broomall, PA: Mason Crest Publishers, 2003. This book features one-page profiles on many of the animals of Australia that are fighting to survive.

Perth Zoo: Australian Bushwalk
http://www.perthzoo.wa.gov.au/Animals--Plants/Australia/Australian-Bushwalk/
Australia's Perth Zoo features the Australian Bushwalk—a tour of the country's many habitats. Visitors to the zoo website can take a virtual bushwalk and find photographs and profiles of many Outback animals.

Wild Kids: Arid Zone
http://www.amonline.net.au/wild_kids/arid_zone.cfm
The Australia Museum's website looks at the different physical features of the Outback and the animals who dwell there.

SELECTED BIBLIOGRAPHY

AustralianFauna.com. 2006. http://www.australianfauna.com/ (July 3, 2008).

Australian Government. "Threatened Species and Ecological Communities." *Department of the Environment, Water, Heritage, and the Arts. Resources.* 2008. http://www.environment.gov.au/biodiversity/threatened/ (August 8, 2008).

Australian Wildlife Conservancy. N.d. http://www.australianwildlife.org/ (July 3, 2008).

Burnie, David. *Animal: The Definitive Visual Guide to the World's Wildlife*. New York: DK, 2005.

Franklin, Adrian. *Animal Nation: The True Story of Animals and Australia*. Sydney: University of New South Wales Press, 2006.

Mattison, Chris. *Lizards of the World.* New York: Facts on File, 2004.

———. *Frogs and Toads of the World.* New York: Facts on File, 1992.

New South Wales Government, Department of Environment and Climate Change. "Native Plants and Animals." *National Parks and Wildlife Service*. 2008. http://www.nationalparks.nsw.gov.au/npws.nsf/Content/Native+plants+and+animals (July 2, 2008).

Smith, Roff. *Australia: Journey through a Timeless Land*. Washington, DC: National Geographic Books, 1999.

Tasmania. "Native Plants and Animals." *Department of Primary Industries and Water.* 2008. http://www.dpiw.tas.gov.au/inter.nsf/ThemeNodes/SSKA-4X33SG (July 3, 2008).

INDEX

Photo Acknowledgments

The images in this book are used with the permission of: © Doug Armand/Stone/Getty Images, pp. 1, 11, 13, 15, 19, 23, 26, 33, 39, 51, 53, 55; © John W Banagan/Iconica/G[illegible] Inc., p. 8; © Martin Ha[illegible]/Photo[illegible] pp. 9[illegible] AUSCAPE, pp. 10, 16, 42; © [illegible]nda Wright/Nation[illegible] Images, pp. 12, 22; © A.N.T. Photo Library/NHPA/Photoshot, pp. 14 (top), 20, 25 (bottom), 35, 45, 49; © Gerry Ellis/Minden Pictures/Getty Images, pp. 14 (bottom), 24 (top); © Konrad Wothe/Minden Pictures/Getty Images, pp. 17, 41; © Jerry Dupree/Dreamstime.com, p. 18; © Daniel Zupanc/NHPA/Photoshot, p. 21; © Howard Rice/Gap Photo/Visuals Unlimited, p. 24 (bottom); © Thorsten Milse/Robert Harding World Imagery/Getty Images, p. 27 (top); © Ann & Steve Toon/NHPA/Photoshot , p. 27 (bottom); © ZSSD/Minden Pictures/Getty Images, p. 28; © Theo Allofs/Visuals Unlimited, p. 29; © Frank Woerle/AUSCAPE, p. 30; © Dave Watts/NHPA/Photoshot, pp. 31, 59; © Stephen Dalton/NHPA/Photoshot, p. 32 (top); © D. Parer & E. Parer-Cook/AUSCAPE, pp. 32 (bottom), 52; © Nicholas Birks/AUSCAPE, pp. 36, 38; © Jean-Jacques Alcalay-BIOSPHOTO/AUSCAPE, p. 37; © Mitsuaki Iwago/Minden Pictures/Getty Images, p. 40; © Ted Mead/The Image Bank/Getty Images, p. 43; © Jason Edwards/National Geographic/Getty Images, p. 44; © R. Usher/WILDLIFE/Peter Arnold, Inc., p. 46; © S. Muller/WILDLIFE/Peter Arnold, Inc., p. 47; © NHPA/Photoshot, pp. 50, 54; © Babs Wells/Oxford Scientific/Photolibrary, p. 56; © Roland Seitre/Peter Arnold, Inc., p. 57; © iStockphoto.com/Phil Morley, p. 58 (top); © Kathie Atkinson/AUSCAPE, p. 58 (bottom). Illustrations and map: © Bill Hauser/Independent Picture Service.

Front cover: © Doug Armand/Stone/Getty Images (landscape); © A.N.T. Photo Library/NHPA/Photoshot (crocodile); © Mitsuaki Iwago/Minden Pictures/Getty Images (kangaroos); © James Hager/Robert Harding World Imagery/Getty Images (emu); © iStockphoto.com/Jeremy Edwards (koala).

About the Authors

Don Wojahn and Becky Wojahn are school library media specialists by day and writers by night. Their natural habitat is the temperate forests of northwestern Wisconsin, where they share their den with two animal-loving sons and two big black dogs. The Wojahns' other Follow That Food Chain books include *A Temperate Forest Food Chain, A Desert Food Chain, A Rain Forest Food Chain, A Savanna Food Chain*, and *A Tundra Food Chain*.